The Crimean War

Queen Victoria's War
with the Russian Tsars

HUGH SMALL

TEMPUS

ABOUT THE AUTHOR

Hugh Small is the author of *Florence Nightingale, Avenging Angel*. He is an acknowledged expert on the war in the Crimea and has appeared on Channel 4 News, BBC2, Sky News and contributed to History Today on the subject. He lives in Central London.

Additional Crimean War material can be found on the author's website. *www.hugh-small.co.uk*

Front cover illustration: Officers and a sergeant of the 89th Regiment in camp above Sebastopol in 1865. Colourised by Tempus Publishing. (Library of Congress)

WORCESTERSHIRE COUNTY COUNCIL	
927	
Bertrams	15.12.07
947.0738	£17.99
BV	

First published 2007

Tempus Publishing
Cirencester Road, Chalford
Stroud, Gloucestershire, GL6 8PE
www.tempus-publishing.com

Tempus Publishing is an imprint of NPI Media Group

British Library Cataloguing in Publication Data.
A catalogue record for this book is available from the British Library.

ISBN 978 0 7524 4388 1

Typesetting and origination by NPI Media Group
Printed and bound in Great Britain

Contents

Acknowledgments

I would like to thank the editor of the *Journal of the Society for Army Historical Research* for permission to use material from my article in the autumn 2005 issue on *The 1855 Allied Campaign Plan*. I acknowledge the permission of the Director of the National Army Museum to quote from Lord Raglan's papers, and am grateful to the staff there and at the Newcastle Collection at Nottingham University, the National Archives of Scotland, the Queen's Lancashire Regiment Museum at Preston, the British Library, the National Archives and many provincial record offices. In the context of the last I would also like to thank those who have worked behind the scenes to make it possible to consult an ever increasing number of archive catalogues online.

I have benefited from the research of members of the Crimean War Research Society, and from discussions with many of them, including Keith Smith who kindly allowed me to include some of his photographs. The quotation from Mark Adkin's *The Charge* is by permission of the publisher, Pen & Sword Books Ltd. I would also like to acknowledge the important role played in my research by the London Library.

Truth: The First Casualty of War

The truth about sensible Victorian Britain's invasion of Russia in the winter of 1854 has never been published. This is because a deliberate deception was mounted during and after the Crimean War to disguise Britain's failures, and historians have been deceived ever since. The original purpose of the deception was to downplay the importance of the war by blaming its outbreak on mistakes by discredited politicians and to reassure Victorian public opinion that Britain had not suffered from the indecisive outcome. Historians today still rely on versions of official documents which were altered to disguise the reasons why Britain invaded the Crimea, and retell a 'fairy tale' (in the phrase of William Howard Russell, who was present) pretending to describe events on the battlefield. The British Government suppressed inconvenient official studies of what went wrong in Florence Nightingale's hospital. Both French and British Governments kept secret a mutiny of the British generals, which caused their joint siege of Sebastopol to continue after its futility became obvious and then made Britain's exasperated ally withdraw from the struggle. Official documents containing the truth on all this and more have lain unexamined since they were released fifty years after the war. There has been little interest in the Crimean War from academic historians; they may have been put off by the early portrayal of the war as a historically irrelevant mistake.

It is understandable that British historians close to the events should misrepresent a war in which their side did badly. It is also understandable that their government should cooperate by withholding documents that would have revealed the truth. At the end of the war the popular mood was ugly, and there was strong feeling that heads should roll (at least figuratively) among the aristocrats who had at first mismanaged the conflict and then allowed it to end prematurely. The truth would have been inflammatory.

The British Government had tried to create a symbolic victory by ending the stalemated war with a ceremonial bang in late 1855. Using explosives, their demolition teams reduced to rubble the Russian naval dockyards and military arsenal at Sebastopol, on the shore of one of the world's finest natural harbours. After a bloody sixteen-month siege of Russia's most prized military installation, British statesmen claimed that the Russian invasion of Turkey three years earlier had been avenged and that the forthcoming Treaty of Paris would prevent Russia from ever again deploying warships in the Black Sea or from fortifying Sebastopol or any other port on its shore. They declared victory.

The peace was unpopular in Britain, where there was no victory parade as there was in France. The government tried to drum up enthusiasm for a ceremony of rejoicing, involving fireworks and illumination of public buildings, by combining it with the Queen's birthday. The popular feeling remained that there was unfinished business, that 'we have driven the robber from the gates of Turkey but have refused to take him into custody' in the words of one London newspaper. It was a peace 'which France insisted upon, and which the British people somewhat sulkily acquiesced in'.[1] The nation's anger was heightened by the way the arsenal and dockyards of Sebastopol had finally fallen after simultaneous assaults by French and British troops. The French easily captured their objective, the key fortress of the Malakoff, but the British were driven back from their objective at the Redan fortress and contributed nothing to the victory. A British diplomat articulated the resentment that this caused, 'We were all sick and angry when the news came. The general should have sent every man he had in that army to take the Redan or to die in it before he allowed the French to claim, as they had a right to do, that they took the Malakoff ... and to let them see the backs of our soldiers in retreat.'[2]

Unsurprisingly, the British troops idling in the Crimea in the summer of 1856, waiting for their transports home or to colonial garrisons, began to look on their French comrades with animosity. Traditional rivalry, in suspense as long as the Russians were the common enemy, now reappeared. A British officer wrote, 'I heard lots of our fellows say yesterday, "how I wish those bloody French would just come out with their sixty thousand men and fight us".'[3]

The bitterness in Britain had a human dimension: more than 20,000 British soldiers had died in the war. One example of these individual tragedies may illustrate the loss to the country. William Poole, a twenty-year-old infantry captain from Shropshire who was shot during the final pointless attack on the Redan, was one of 400 army officers to die. Poole was the son of an artillery officer who fought at Waterloo; he was educated at Rugby and joined the 23rd Regiment – the Royal Welch Fusiliers – as an ensign (second lieutenant) at the age of eighteen. One year later he landed in the Crimea with his regiment and fought at the Alma and at Inkerman. During the long siege of Sebastopol he made himself unpopular with some of his comrades by complaining about the way the war was going. He moonlighted as a trader – buying whole sheep and slaughtering them and selling the parts retail. This entrepreneurship was useful when the commissariat food distribution system broke down, but was also frowned on by his fellow officers. By the summer of 1855 he had tired so much of the war that he 'sent in his papers' officially requesting to resign his commission and go home. This was his privilege, but was considered unpatriotic. On September 8th the French and British launched what proved to be their final infantry assault on Sebastopol, and carnage ensued particularly among the officers of the 23rd who tried bravely and unsuccessfully to lead their unwilling raw recruits into the Redan fortress through a hail of short-range grapeshot. Poole was out in front despite having resigned his commission and was shot through the body, the missile nearly severing his spine. He was in severe pain for several weeks – a 'miserable existence' according to his commanding officer. In the third week of September the Official Gazette arrived showing that Poole had been 'gazetted out' of the army on 7 September – the day before the battle in which he had been wounded. On 24 September Poole died, conscious and talking until the last few hours and aware that he had not needed to lead the assault because he was already a civilian.[4]

William Poole's conflicting sense of duty and independence of spirit seem typical of a certain type of Englishman of that time. It was a mixture that had contributed to the unique industrial strength and social stability of the nation. It was in theory a time of searching parliamentary debate and open government, and Poole's family would have been confident that the truth about this unsatisfactory war and the final doomed assault would become known. After 150 years, now that reputations are no longer a subject of personal or party pride, it is easier to meet their expectations. We can cast a cold eye on those times, do without the fictions, and learn the lessons of the war at last.

The fictions tend to appear at crucial turning points in the war's history, and it is 'an easy inference', as the lawyers say, that they were designed to mislead. The analysis which follows identifies the lies and the facts that they conceal, and highlights the new facts in a revisionist account of the Crimean episode. It should be more entertaining than previous accounts if only because what you are not supposed to know is always more interesting. It is a psychological as well as a military and political history, recording how a historical delusion is created, sustained and even reinforced over the years.

One thing that emerges is that the distortions, by giving undue credit to greater men, have concealed the qualities of the common soldiers of Victorian Britain. Until now the other ranks in the Crimean campaign have been admired mostly as victims, for their passive qualities of bravery and stoicism under inhuman treatment. We have been kept in ignorance of their tactical genius and initiative, which convinced politicians at home to overrule the generals and let the men fight the way they wanted to. In those days before battlefield signalling equipment was available, military personnel at all levels were expected to disobey orders when they knew them to be wrong. The common soldier, well-armed, informed, and extensively trained, was not the blindly obedient automaton of the First World War but an important decision-maker. This new insight holds the key to understanding one of the few truly glorious military victories in history: the Charge of the Light Brigade.

2

Britain's Anti-Crusade Against Russia

Many accounts of the Crimean War set the scene by emphasising that Britain had not fought a major land war since defeating Napoleon in 1815 and by 1855 was committed to peaceful coexistence with other nations in the interests of free trade. London's Great Exhibition of 1851 is often invoked to describe a climate of peace and prosperity in the Britain of the 1850s which was supposedly incompatible with war. Such scene-setting is appropriate for a conclusion that Britain drifted into hostilities in 1854 without good reason, manipulated by Turks and Frenchmen, and this is the interpretation favoured by the earliest historians still smarting from the war's disappointments. An alternative conclusion, that British statesmen were following an intelligent geopolitical strategy in going to war, was not put forward until well over a century later. In 1991 Professor Andrew Lambert analysed admiralty correspondence to show that a desire to counter a Russian challenge to the Royal Navy was instrumental in Britain's decision to fight. This new view has since become widely accepted among experts, although it leaves much unexplained. Professor Lambert's example helps to answer the question, always directed at revisionists, 'why has no other historian said so before?' by showing that a long time can pass before dispassionate historians get around to examining the available documents. If we now accept that Britain didn't enter the war simply because its statesmen were asleep at the wheel we can set the scene differently.

In 1854, Britain was in charge. The Napoleonic Wars of the generation before had added enormous strength to British foreign policy in two ways. First, the naval victories culminating in Trafalgar established Britain's mastery of the seas. Second, Britain's unique steadfastness in opposing Napoleon's mission of conquest, by fighting and by subsidising the armies of its Allies in the struggle, gave the country a reputation as an honest broker and peacemaker in international affairs. Partly this reputation also rested on Britain's preference for expansion through international trade rather than through conquest. Britain was the only country committed to free trade, and most of its foreign policy was geared to opening up markets. Markets for its own manufactured goods: Britain produced half of the world's total of smelted iron. Markets for other countries' goods too: Britain owned 40 per cent of the world's merchant shipping. On its small islands it possessed one half of all the railway lines of Europe and Asia, with most of the remainder being built and often run by British operators or financiers. Since the late 1840s Britain had experienced unparalleled prosperity which was being felt by all classes. At the out-break of the Crimean War, Britain was the world's only superpower, its pre-eminence far exceeding that of the US today.

The free trade idea to which Britain owed its power and prosperity was a liberal one; traditional Tory landowners had opposed it because the free import of grain reduced the value of their land. The liberal way to expand world trade was to liberate nations from the old empires which bound them into trade monopolies, and give them constitutional governments in which the self-interest of the people would favour the competitive free trade at which Britain excelled. Britain encouraged the liberation of the new South American states which seized inde-pendence from Spain in the 1820s, and fought for the independence of Greece from the Ottoman Empire later in the decade. In 1836 the British Government authorised the recruitment of 10,000 British vol-unteers to fight in Spain on the liberal constitutionalist side in the civil war, which was in fact a proxy war between liberal European govern-ments and authoritarian ones including Russia. The Duke of Wellington and other Tories strongly objected to the role of British troops in Spain. Nevertheless the British Auxiliary Legion was a major contributor to the liberal victory and many of its officers and men later fought in the Crimea.

Britain therefore regularly favoured force to pursue its imperial aims, while avoiding direct rule of overseas territories unless they were inca-pable of organising their own trading links. Throughout the whole of the nineteenth century, British trade with countries coloured red on the map never much exceeded one third of all Britain's trade.[1] Not all trade was good: in 1807 Britain banned the transatlantic slave trade. By 1840, the dangerous West African station occupied twenty-five Royal Navy vessels and 3,000 men chasing illegal slave ships. Replacing its once-profitable slave trade with trade in manufactured goods allowed Britain to occupy the moral high ground while still enriching itself. The liberal ideals of independent constitutional government and free trade were noble enough to justify threats or actual use of force, and went hand-in-hand to promise a new world order under British leadership. Free trade and warfare were therefore not incompatible – the second was necessary to protect the first in a world where autocratic empires were opposed to the whole idea of open markets.

In the 1850s most of the continent of Europe was under the control of three empires – the Russian, the Austrian (Austro-Hungarian, with strong ties to other Germanic states), and the Turkish (Ottoman). The last tolerated a degree of self-rule to its outlying provinces, but the others maintained rigidly centralised authoritarian regimes devoted to suppressing the revolutionary and nationalist forces that had burst out most recently in 1848.

The Russian Empire had been constantly expanding by conquest since the fourteenth-century princedom of Muscovy had extended its rule over other ethnic Russians. The geography of the Eurasian land mass encouraged Russia's absorption of provinces on its border by a process well described by Tolstoy in *Hadji Murad*: local chiefs invited their Russian neighbour to help in their own rebellions, and then found them harder to get rid of than their former oppressors. In the 150 years following the accession of Peter the Great in the late 1600s Russia had acquired a great European empire, pushing its frontiers 700 miles towards Paris, 600 miles nearer to Stockholm, 500 miles nearer to Constantinople, and 1,000 miles closer to Teheran. It had built a new European seaport in its captured Baltic domains: St. Petersburg, which replaced Moscow as capital until Lenin reversed the change in 1918. By seizing control of Poland, Russia had abrogated the terms of the 1815 Congress of Vienna, at which the victorious Allies, including Russia and Britain, had redrawn the map of Europe after the defeat of Napoleon.

Russia, and continuing Russian expansion, was a great obstacle to world trade. The Russian grain trade was of great interest to Britain

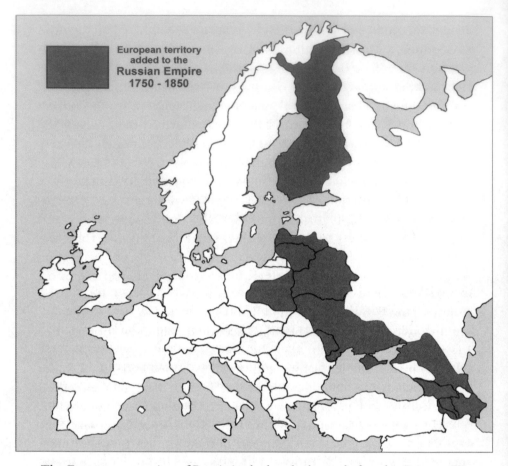

The European expansion of Russia in the hundred years before the Crimean War (Source: McNeill, *Position of Russia in the East*).

but the Russians' refusal to hear of free trade forced Britain to develop the grain trade of the Ottoman Empire instead. The treaties existing between Britain and Turkey had permitted Britain to bully the weaker Ottoman Empire into a free trade policy.[2] The opening of the Danube delta (controlled by Russia and the gateway for east European grain) to international traders was one of the stated British diplomatic objectives of the Crimean War. This is not emphasised by those historians who portray the war as an unsuitable adventure for a trading nation.

Free trade and Russian expansion were not the only areas of dispute between Britain and Russia. The 1832 Reform Act had given Britain exceptional political freedom, and dissidents from all over Europe enjoyed safe refuge there to the resentment of Austria and Russia who believed that escaped revolutionaries should be handed back to them for punishment. This was also a bone of contention between the Turkish Empire and Russia because the Turks, encouraged by their friends the British, refused to act against political refugees fleeing through their territory on their way to asylum in Britain or France.

After Britain, France was the most powerful independent state in Europe. The revolution of 1848 had overthrown the restored Orléans monarchy and as a result that country was also considered by Austria and Russia to be a danger to the established order. France's new ruler, the forty-five-year-old Napoleon III, was the nephew of the first Napoleon, being the son of Louis Bonaparte, King of Holland. He had begun his political career by taking part in revolutionary attempts against the restored monarchy in France, and had been elected to the largely ceremonial role of President when the Second Republic was formed after the revolution of 1848. In 1851 the French Army mounted a bloody coup, dismissed the legislature, and installed Napolean III as absolute ruler of France. His domestic support was not very solid, and he courted the powerful French Roman Catholic hierarchy by sending gunboats to Constantinople to demand more privileges for Roman Catholic clergy in the Holy Land, which was then part of the Ottoman Empire. Turkey accepted these demands, provoking Russia which supported the rival Orthodox Church clergy and saw the French success as threatening its own territorial ambitions in Turkey.

France under Napoleon III was eager to pick a fight with Russia, which had destroyed the half million-strong army the first Napoleon had invaded with in 1812; the defeat had hastened the collapse of the first French Empire. Napoleon III himself also saw Russia as an obstacle to his personal vision of a Europe of independent states like France and Britain (he was an Anglophile, having been exiled there like so many other continental revolutionaries). The French Army after its recent bloody intervention in domestic politics sought an opportunity to act respectably on the world stage. It therefore suited France to court trouble with Russia in the Ottoman Empire.

The Ottoman Empire, in contrast to that of Russia, had been gradually shrinking since the high tide of its expansion had brought it to the gates of Vienna in 1683. In 1783 Russia had captured the Crimean peninsula from the Turks, and in 1829 some additional territory in the Caucasus on the east coast of the Black Sea. Although the 1815 Congress of Vienna at the close of the Napoleonic War had pledged the Great Powers to maintain the territorial *status quo* in Europe – by force of arms if necessary – this pledge did not extend to European Turkey. Many European powers saw Turkey's Balkan states as an area in which they could still play territorial monopoly. Russia was particularly ambitious in this area and as Turkey's hold over its semi-autonomous Balkan provinces diminished, Russia aggressively asserted the rights that it had obtained from Turkey's Muslim rulers to be the guarantor of the safety of Christians in these provinces.

Tsar Nicholas I of Russia was known as the Iron Tsar for his blind faith in his three principles of government: autocracy, religious orthodoxy, and the 'russification' of his conquered dominions. He maintained personal control of a police state that dictated every aspect of its subjects' lives, even maintaining spies in school classrooms and forbidding teachers to travel abroad in case they absorbed liberal ideas. His belief in the rightness of his absolute rule made him unwilling to listen to advice and his ministers unwilling to give it. He believed that the collapse of the weak Turkish Empire was both imminent and desirable, and that unless he moved quickly other European powers might install their own puppet governments in the orphaned Turkish provinces.

In the spring of 1853, after the French had extracted their concessions from the Sultan, Tsar Nicholas sent his envoy to Constantinople to demand favours for Russia's rival Orthodox Church. Secretly, Russia's envoy was also instructed to demand that the Turks sign a new treaty formalising Russia's protectorate over all the Christian subjects of Turkey, a treaty which would strengthen Russia's right to occupy Turkish territory almost at will. The Tsar's envoy to Constantinople was not a diplomat but an old soldier, Prince Menshikov, who had fought against Turkey in past wars. This choice deliberately emphasised an iron fist approach to diplomacy without the camouflage of a velvet glove. There was not much room for diplomacy in Menchikov's instructions: he was to take the draft treaty with him and if the Turks refused to sign it he was to threaten war and to say that Russian troops were massing on the Turkish border ready for an invasion.

The Tsar was not bluffing. It is probable that he really believed his own claim that the new treaty he demanded was no more than a clarification of treaties that already existed, which he claimed Turkey had violated by its favourable treatment of the rival church. It seems that his ministers did not dare to tell him that he might be wrong in law. Western diplomats in St Petersburg and Constantinople, when they found out what Menshikov was demanding, did not hesitate to point out to the Tsar and the Sultan that it went beyond previous treaties. Tsar Nicholas did not take their opinion seriously, but the Sultan and his advisers did and they were further encouraged to resist Menshikov by the action of the French in ordering their Mediterranean fleet to sail from Toulon to Turkish waters as a gesture of support.

The Turks refused to accept the new treaty and on 21 May 1853 Menshikov stormed out of Constantinople, figuratively slamming the door behind him. He reported to the Tsar that the failure of his mission to Constantinople had been due to the machinations of Lord Stratford de Redcliffe, the highly experienced British Ambassador to Turkey. This was guaranteed to enrage Tsar Nicholas, who detested Stratford and his power. Formerly Sir Stratford Canning, the Ambassador was a cousin of the late Foreign Secretary and Prime Minister George Canning and had been a diplomat since the Napoleonic Wars. In 1832 he had been posted to St. Petersburg but the Tsar had refused to allow him into Russia, fearing his reputation for getting his own way with foreign rulers. Lord Palmerston, Foreign Secretary at the time, then flouted the custom that Ambassadors must be approved by their hosts in advance and refused to appoint anyone in his place, insultingly leaving a junior *chargé d'affaires* in charge of the St Petersburg Embassy. In 1852 Stratford had again irritated the Tsar by supporting Turkey against him in another quarrel. When Menshikov came to Constantinople in 1853 to demand a new treaty behind a smokescreen of complaints relating to the rights of Orthodox clergy in the Holy Land, Stratford persuaded the Sultan to bend over backwards to put right all the specific ills that Menshikov complained of. This weakened Russia's case for revising the treaty. Stratford's advice therefore did contribute to the mission's failure, but Menshikov's behaviour in blaming Stratford's anti-Russian views and personal resentment of the Tsar demonstrated his lack of diplomatic skill. It personalised and trivialised the issues, and disguised from the Tsar that the Sultan had also been strongly influenced by the prompt despatch of the French Mediterranean fleet to support Turkey.

On 31 May the Tsar sent an ultimatum to Constantinople saying that he would invade and occupy Turkey's semi-autonomous territories of Moldavia and Wallachia (now Romania)[3] unless Turkey accepted the new treaty within eight days. The Tsar did not think that other countries would react violently to this threat, and he was right. He knew that Britain would object, but he had little to fear because he was convinced that Britain could not possibly find common cause against him with its ancient enemy France.

Britain at this time was under a shaky coalition government consisting of liberals and some conservatives (including the Prime Minister Lord Aberdeen) who had deserted their party because they believed in free trade. The Court – Queen Victoria and Prince Albert – did not stay neutral in disputes between ministers as they were supposed to do but instead used their power of patronage on the conservative side.[4] The coalition was uneasy enough in normal times, but Russia's threats to Turkey produced a pronounced split between pacifist conservatives and bellicose liberals. The Court and the conservative ministers were unperturbed at the prospect of the Christian Russians liberating the Balkan provinces and even Constantinople from the 'Mohammedan' Turks, whom they regarded as barbarians incapable of progress. Conservatives thought of Russia as a friend: Britain's ally against Bonaparte and later against the Turks in the war of Greek liberation. Lord Aberdeen when Foreign Secretary in 1844 had listened without objection to Tsar Nicholas's plans to take over parts of the Turkish Empire.[5] Aberdeen had since stated publicly that the Turks had no business in Europe, and the Court agreed with him; at the time of the Russian ultimatum to Turkey Prince Albert proposed that Turkey should be compelled to withdraw from Europe – including Constantinople – entirely. Furthermore, neither the Court nor the conservatives liked Napoleon III, who was pressing the British Government to support the Turks. They thought him a dangerous *parvenu* whose recent adoption of the title Emperor Napoleon III within weeks of the death of the Duke of Wellington was an insult. They saw it as a calculated gesture of defiance against the prohibition on re-establishment of the Bonaparte dynasty imposed by the victors of Waterloo. The more conservative ministers and their supporters at Court believed that the French and the Turks were deliberately provoking the Russians in an attempt to make Britain go to war against her old ally.[6]

The popular press disagreed, and mocked the government for its pacifism. The official Conservative opposition were keen to discredit their disloyal former colleagues who were now in government, and cynically supported more liberal voices calling for strong action against Russia. The liberals in the coalition government included the Home Secretary Lord Palmerston, whose assertive track record on Russia contrasted strongly with the appeasing line of Lord Aberdeen. When he had been Foreign Secretary in 1848 Palmerston had obliged Russia to withdraw from Turkey's European provinces even though the Turks themselves had requested their presence to quell disorder. The following year, when Russia helped Austria in brutally suppressing an uprising in Hungary, the Tsar had demanded that Turkey hand over Hungarian patriots who had escaped to the Balkan provinces. Palmerston sent a British fleet to Constantinople to bolster the Turkish refusal and the Tsar backed down.[7] In the British public's eyes these recent incidents counted for more than the Greek War of Independence or the Waterloo campaign, in which Russia had been on Britain's side. Palmerston's anti-Russian record made him the natural champion of those who urged a tough stand against Russia now. For the liberals the ever-expanding and autocratic Russian Empire was a threat to the future of constitutional government in Europe, and France's willingness to combine with Britain against the Tsar now presented a unique opportunity to resolve this long-standing problem.

The liberals argued that Turkey had shown itself capable of reforming itself, for example in reducing religious discrimination and adopting free trade. They did not share with their conservative colleagues the Russian Tsar's belief that Turkey, the 'Sick Man of Europe', must be encouraged to expire.[8] In their attitude to the French, also, Palmerston and the conservative faction in the coalition were at loggerheads. Liberals favoured Napoleon III as the product of anti-monarchical revolution, although he was less popular with the extreme-left Radicals because of his repressive domestic policy. Palmerston had actually lost his long tenure of the Foreign Office over his support for Napoleon III. According to reports in the press, Palmerston had tried to dismiss the Ambassador in Paris who was helping Victoria and Albert to undermine the new French Emperor, and the royal couple persuaded the Prime Minister to dismiss Palmerston instead. Palmerston's policy was vindicated, because Napoleon III sent the misbehaving Ambassador home anyway and later used his personal charm at Windsor to win the admiration of Queen Victoria and her husband.

At the time of the Russian ultimatum to Turkey the public remembered that it was Victoria and Albert's fault that Palmerston was not Foreign Secretary and that they had to put up instead with the appeaser Lord Aberdeen who had taken over much of the foreign affairs portfolio from the nominal Foreign Secretary Lord Clarendon. Public feeling against Prince Albert became hostile on account of his supposed sympathy for Russia and the Court's earlier treatment of Lord Palmerston.

When Palmerston learned that the Russians had backed their demands for a new treaty by an ultimatum to the Turks he urged the Prime Minster to respond by sending a British ultimatum telling the Tsar that Britain would go to war if Russia carried out its threat to invade Turkish territory. Aberdeen refused[9], but he did belatedly summon the Royal Navy to join the French fleet at the Dardanelles as a gesture of solidarity with Turkey. The Turks, emboldened by this, rejected the Tsar's demands and in July 1853 Tsar Nicholas sent his armies to occupy the Balkan territories of Turkey.

The Russian occupation did not immediately provoke war, and the other 'Great Powers' – Austria, Prussia, France, and Britain – now tried to make Turkey appease Russia to secure withdrawal. The Powers drafted an agreement, the Vienna Note, under which Turkey would recognise that Russia was the protector of Christians in the Turkish Empire. This fell short of the treaty that the Tsar had wanted, but would have been a concession by Turkey because until then Russia only had the right to petition Turkey if it believed that Christians were being victimised. The Turkish Government was accustomed to doing as it was told by the Great Powers but on this occasion it dug its heels in and refused to sign this Vienna Note. On 4 October 1853 the Turks issued an ultimatum to the Russians saying that if the occupying troops were not withdrawn in fourteen days Turkey would declare war. At this moment, apparently unaware that the Turks had issued the ultimatum[10], the Cabinet in London ordered the fleet to pass through the Dardanelles and anchor at Constantinople which further emboldened the Turks. The Turks declared war on Russia, without notifying Britain in advance, on 18 October 1854 and went on the offensive against the occupying Russian troops in what is now Romania.

Six weeks later a dramatic event converted a regional conflict into a European war. The Russians caught most of the Turkish fleet, laden with troops, in harbour at Sinope in the Black Sea and sank it with a loss of several thousand Turkish lives, using explosive shells for the first time in naval warfare. The British newspapers called Sinope a 'massacre' and pilloried the government for having sent the fleet to Constantinople without instructions to intervene. The conservative ministers who dominated the Cabinet at first stood firm in their desire to avoid going to the help of Turkey, believing that Turkey had brought the disaster of Sinope upon itself by sending its inadequate fleet to provoke Russia. They rejected the advice of their liberal colleagues and the French Emperor to send the Royal Navy into the Black Sea to clear it of Russian warships. But within a few days they changed their minds, probably because Lord Palmerston resigned from the Cabinet in protest.

The old diplomat crafted his protest with great skill. His letter of resignation to the Prime Minister complained about the Cabinet's failure to order the Royal Navy into the Black Sea but at the same time criticised the unrelated Cabinet decision to bring forward a bill to reform the electoral system. Palmerston had previously indicated that although he disagreed with the reform plans, it was not a resigning issue; now he seemed to go back on that and left the Prime Minister free to decide which of the two reasons to use as an explanation for his resignation. Lord Aberdeen and Queen Victoria were both glad to be rid of Palmerston and agreed that it would be best to say that he had resigned out of opposition to reform. This would decrease Palmerston's popularity with Radicals and would make it impossible for other Cabinet members, similarly opposed to appeasement of Russia but unlike him in favour of reform, to resign in sympathy with him and bring down the government. Most people now expected Palmerston to join the mainstream Conservative opposition party, but he simply sat on the sidelines for a few days. The British press and public were not taken in by the official story that Palmerston, a known hawk and liberal, had resigned over reform. His popularity increased because he had made it appear that he was the only one prepared to resign over the failure to confront Russia. Queen and Prime Minister had both been pleased to see Palmerston isolated and the government saved; however, they were soon to realise that his very isolation was the key to his power.

After a few days of reflection, the conservatives in the Cabinet came round to the view that they could no longer avoid following Palmerston's advice to send the fleet into the Black Sea to clear it of

Russian ships. The Russian action at Sinope, regardless of whether it was an atrocity or whether it was the Turks' fault, had been an insult to the all-powerful Royal Navy which was Britain's most important asset on the world stage. It was humiliating that the Royal Navy had stood by almost within earshot while the Russian fleet destroyed that of their Allies. Even those who had no wish to see Turkey remain in Europe now decided that Russia's actions were beyond the pale. Prominent among Cabinet conservatives and appeasers who changed their minds at this point was Sir James Graham, First Lord of the Admiralty. Eight days after news of Sinope reached London, he wrote to the Prime Minister, 'I have been one of the most strenuous advocates of peace with Russia until the last moment, but the Sinope attack and recent events have changed entirely the aspect of affairs. I am afraid that a rupture with Russia is inevitable.' The other 'recent events' that he was referring to would have to include Palmerston's intervening resignation and the public outcry that followed.

The Cabinet now agreed to the French Emperor's proposal to proclaim that any Russian warship found in the Black Sea would be sunk, and sent the Royal Navy through the Bosphorus to enforce the proclamation. A few days later Palmerston asked for his job back, claiming to have discovered that the Cabinet was not so determined on electoral reform as he had believed but also remarking that he was pleased that the fleet was in the Black Sea. Queen Victoria querulously complained that she had already offered Palmerston's job of Home Secretary to somebody else, but the new candidate hastily withdrew when Palmerston asked to be reinstated. A short ten days after he had left, Palmerston was back and one of the most careful and effective tactical resignations in British politics was over.[11]

Sinope was the result of a miscalculation by Tsar Nicholas. It was no heat-of-the-moment attack: the Tsar himself had authorised the action, and Prince Menshikov had commanded some of the Russian ships involved. The Tsar had correctly anticipated that the general distaste felt in the west towards the Turkish lifestyle would encourage appeasement in the face of his bloodless occupation of the Principalities. However, he failed to foresee the effect that Sinope would produce. In particular he misunderstood the Austrians, whom he thought to be his Allies because of their shared belief in autocracy and empire, and he underestimated his hereditary enemies the French, whom he thought to be militarily weak and anyway incapable of cooperating with the British.

Perhaps the Tsar was ignorant of the Austrian Prime Minister's response when he was asked whether Austria was grateful to Russia for helping Austria to brutally suppress the uprising in its Hungarian dominion in 1848: 'Austria will astonish the world with the magnitude of her ingratitude.' Austria now kept its promise; concerned that war on their borders would further destabilise their fragile empire, they rapidly distanced themselves diplomatically from Russia for fear that Russia's enemies would seek to aggravate Austria's domestic problems.

In the face of threatened action from the Royal Navy, the Russian fleet withdrew to its Black Sea fortress of Sebastopol but Russian troops did not immediately withdraw from Turkish territory. In February 1854 Britain and France sent the Tsar an ultimatum to leave the occupied provinces, and when he failed to respond both countries declared war on Russia at the end of March. Thus it was that Christian Britain found itself fighting to defend the Muslim occupation of the ancient seat of the Christian Church at Constantinople against a crusading Russia bent on its liberation.

The British coalition government was split along party lines as far as its objective in declaring war. For the liberals (as for most of the country) the objective was to roll back Russian expansion, to liberate the peripheral states incarcerated in what Karl Marx was already calling the Russian Empire's 'prison of nations', and to give those states constitutional governments which would naturally lead them to adopt free trade. In contrast, the objective that persuaded the conservatives in the government to lift their veto on war was the destruction of Russian naval power. This latter, limited, view of the war's objectives would soon disappear when the conservatives were ejected from the government during the war, as discussed in a later chapter. Any analysis which concludes that Britain fought only to constrain Russian naval power is therefore incomplete.

The idea that Britain and France might invade Russia may seem strange to us, given the lack of success of Napoleon and Hitler with apparently similar projects. This perception adds credence to the view that Britain's declaration of war was a mistake. Unlike Napoleon, though, the European powers planned to nibble at the disaffected edges of the Russian Empire, not march on Moscow.

And unlike Hitler's opponent, the Russia of 1854 was completely un-industrialised and had no friends. As we will see, the liberal vision of a peaceful and reduced Russia was not an unrealistic dream and is one which is being belatedly realised in our time.

3

From Phoney War to Invasion

EUROPE UNITES

The governments in London and Paris first sent their troops to Varna, in what is now Bulgaria, after the Tsar in April 1854 besieged the Turkish fortress of Silistria, on the south bank of the Danube. The Tsar found that his regional support was not as strong as he had expected. The inhabitants of the Balkans, oppressed by Turkish rule though they were, did not seem to relish being occupied by Russia. Their neighbours, the Austrians, had also become very hostile to the Russians and were mobilising a large army against them. The Austrians never declared war, but they ordered Russia to leave the territory they had occupied and signed an agreement with Turkey under which Austrian troops could drive the Russians out if necessary.

The first hostilities between Britain and Russia occurred in April, when the Royal Navy bombarded Odessa, but it was to be five months before the land armies would get to grips with each other. On 13 June the first Franco-British troops to reach the Balkans disembarked at Varna in Bulgaria only seventy miles from Silistria, close enough to hear the Russian siege guns. By mid-July there were 50,000 French, 60,000 Turkish and 20,000 British troops encamped among the lakes spreading inland from Varna. Also in attendance were the British and French fleets – the Royal Navy alone counting 25,000 sailors and 3,000 guns and affording a formidable protection and supply train for the army as long as the latter stayed near the coast. Further north there were 104,000 Turkish troops including the 20,000 besieged at Silistria.[1]

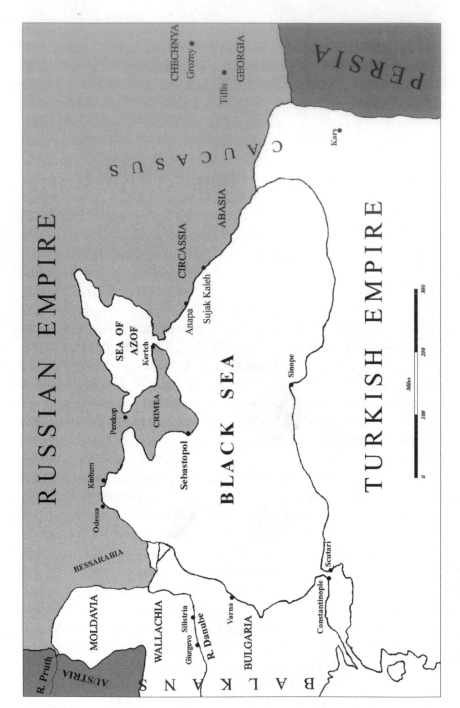

The Crimean Theatre of war.

The French and British armies were very different. The French Army included conscripts, initially enlisted for three years and then placed in reserve and called up when required. The initial three year enlistment was sufficient to give training in weapons and drill to every Frenchman who could not afford to pay a substitute, and the civilian reserve of former conscripts was the backbone of the French Army. In addition, some middle class men joined the ranks voluntarily as the only way to progress to officer status in what was a respected profession. Pay was not high, opportunities for pillage were expected, and families sent money to their sons in the ranks rather than *vice versa* as in England. Britain prided itself in being nearly the only European state not to need conscription because it could afford to pay well. As a colonial power with far-flung manpower needs, a three-year enlistment would not have allowed enough time for transport and acclimatisation as well as a useful period in the colonies. Also, the reserve was not an idea in favour in Britain, where civilians with military training were seen as a threat to political order. In 1847 a Limited Enlistment Act allowed men to sign up for ten or twelve years, so the ranks were made up partly of the hard-core unemployed (among whom many were Irish) who had signed up for at least 22 years and partly of younger men who had signed up because of temporary hardship or a desire to see the world. Unlike the French, the British Army almost excluded the middle class and neither officers nor men had much experience of management or commerce.[2]

The French officers were much more professional than their British equivalents, but the caricature of the rich young English swell in a loud check suit making jokes in Latin and mad on hunting is misleading. Many such officers existed, particularly at the start of the war, but it would be a mistake to think that when a man purchased a commission he acquired the power and responsibility that goes with that rank today. In the day-to-day business of the regiment nearly all the work was done by the non-commissioned officers, who were much more powerful than they are nowadays, assisted by the adjutant who was usually a commissioned former NCO. To a certain extent, junior officers were there for political, ornamental, and social reasons; that was the privilege that they purchased. Many officers joined up for a few years hoping their regiment would be sent to the Cape Colony, where the climate and the hunting were marvellous, and if a posting to the disease-ridden Indies fell to the regiment's lot they made themselves scarce. As the

Crimean War progressed, there was a high turnover of British officers. As conditions worsened, professional soldiers who were attracted by allowances that increased in proportion, and by the promotion lottery that accompanied a high mortality, tended to replace more affluent dilettantes who exercised their right to send in their papers and go home.

Another significant difference between the French and British was in supply strategy. The French Army traditionally lived off the land, while the British liked to supply their army by sea, from Britain if necessary. This difference had helped Wellington to defeat the French at Torres Vedras in the Peninsular War. Wellington had persuaded the friendly locals to burn their crops for miles around so that the French invaders starved while the Royal Navy fed Wellington's army on biscuit baked in Woolwich. This difference, in the Crimea, was aggravated by the difference in pay levels. The British complained that the French stole everything available, or at best did not pay market rates but at a price they set themselves. The French would have been justified in complaining that the British, with their exorbitant pay, could force up prices or buy up everything and leave nothing for their impecunious Allies.

Such differences encouraged the two governments to keep the armies separate, under separate commanders, which did not help coordination on the battlefield. But at Varna in the summer of 1854 the armies shared a common problem – they could not get to the front because of a lack of baggage transport.

The plan had been that the British would engage local drivers with their carts at generous rates to carry the armies' baggage the seventy miles or so inland to Silistria where they could help the besieged Turks. The problem was the local drivers, Bulgarians who disappeared as soon as they had received their first day's pay. The Bulgarians did not like their Turkish masters, and were not fired by a patriotic desire to help their masters' Allies. In fact rather than finding themselves on friendly territory as they expected, the Allies admitted that they were more like an 'army of occupation' helping Turkey to maintain a precarious presence in its disaffected provinces. The Commissariat couldn't even get enough carts to deliver the beer ration to the disgruntled men camped eighteen miles from Varna.[3] When the continued lack of baggage transport forced the army to remain idle, the cynics in it began to refer to themselves as 'the army of *no* occupation'.

The weather was hot and oppressively humid. It sapped the officers' enthusiasm for conducting repetitive drills and the men soon lost interest in the sports that were organised as an alternative. The powerful local *raki* had to take the place of Messrs. Barclay and Perkins' porter and the sight of soldiers lying dead drunk beside the roads to the camp became commonplace. Flogging (which had recently been reduced in severity to avoid permanent disablement) was incapable of keeping the vice in check. Only activity and a sense of purpose could restore morale.

After a few weeks there was a new plan: the army would advance to relieve Silistria using pack horses for baggage transport, thus dispensing with the unreliable Bulgarian human element. It was estimated that 14,000 animals were needed, and buyers scoured the countryside for them. They had only acquired 5,000[1] when the distant rumble of the heavy guns ceased: on 24 June the Russians abandoned their siege of Silistria in the face of strong Turkish resistance. The Turks then went on the offensive and attacked the Russians at Giurgevo in early July. On 25 June a British cavalry detachment was sent to the Danube to look for Russians but returned on 11 July without finding any. Two weeks later the Tsar ordered his generals to withdraw from all the occupied territories. Simultaneously, the French commander, Marshal St Arnaud, sent a sizeable force northwards to find and attack the Russians remaining in the Dobrudja, a region just south of the mouth of the Danube. This expedition was motivated partly by a desire to disperse the troops in the face of a cholera epidemic that had broken out in the allied camps. However, the French took the sickness with them to the Dobrudja, and thousands died. They did not encounter the Russians, and their survivors returned to Varna in mid-August.

At this point, in August 1854, despite the failure of the expeditionary force to engage the Russians the politicians could justly claim a victory because the arrival of a multinational force in Turkey's Balkan provinces had caused Russia to end the occupation. In the same month Austrian troops, with Turkey's consent, began peacefully occupying the provinces from which Russia had withdrawn. They stayed there throughout the war as an international peacekeeping force, withdrawing soon after the war ended. British and French politicians could rightly claim that the Austrians would not have been so assertive if they had not sent the multinational force to the Balkans. It was an impressive trial and demonstration of Britain's and France's ability to forge an international coalition and to transport 70,000 men and their equipment to any coast in Europe.

It is hard to see how this deployment of British and French troops could have been avoided. It is true that Tsar Nicholas did back down when faced with actual force so it is possible that an early ultimatum, as proposed by Palmerston, might have stopped him invading. But an ultimatum from the British alone would probably not have been enough; the Tsar underestimated France's and Austria's readiness to oppose him, not Britain's.[5] It would have been very hard to negotiate a joint ultimatum in the time available, and it might not have convinced the Tsar because of his belief that France could not even find 20,000 men and his failure to understand that Austria was serious about helping the Allies. After the Tsar had invaded, the joint French-British ultimatums to him demanding withdrawal, supported by an Austrian note blaming him for the war that would follow if he rejected these ultimatums, produced no effect.[6] Other evidence has also recently emerged showing that Tsar Nicholas planned to 'liberate'all the Balkan provinces of Turkey immediately unless Turkey signed a treaty granting him new powers in those provinces[7] – powers that would have allowed him to annexe them at a later date.

For the first century and a half after the war historians dwelt at length on the diplomatic blunders after Russia invaded and the alleged machinations of the French, the Turks, and Lord Stratford to bring Britain into the war. The emphasis was on excusing the outbreak of what was seen as an unnecessary war, but any blunders and deceptions seem less important if one accepts that an armed response by European powers at this time was necessary and sufficient to halt Russian aggression. Those who thought at the time that war could still be avoided after the Russian invasion were those who thought that the invasion was not an act of war and that Turkey should sign the Vienna Note or even – like Prince Albert and the conservative wing of the Cabinet – should abandon their European provinces including Constantinople. Those who thought otherwise believed that requiring Turkey to sign a piece of paper – any piece of paper – to get her own territory back was a bad precedent for world peace. Nowadays we would probably take the latter, liberal, view.

Britain was also criticised for joining France in declaring war on Russia before Austria and Prussia had been a given chance to join in the declaration, thus allegedly rupturing the 'Concert of Europe'.[8] A post-modern alternative view might suggest that a declaration of war is not always the most appropriate way to support armed intervention. If

Austria and Prussia had declared war it would have been an invitation to Russia to open a new front along their 1,000-mile common border and fan the still-glowing embers of revolution within. The Anglo-French declarations of war allowed them, as maritime powers, to harass Russia in the Pacific and the Baltic, but Austria and Prussia were in no position to do so. The lack of a declaration of war did not stop Austria from giving formal approval to the actions of Britain and France or from deploying its troops on Turkish territory as a defence against the Russians.

While the phoney war was proceeding in the Balkans, an Allied amphibious force was sent to the Baltic to try to engage the Russian navy there. Except for the destruction of one uncompleted Russian fortress, little was achieved, the Russian navy staying in the shelter of its forts outside St Petersburg. France and Britain, disappointed at not meeting the Russian Army or navy in battle, might then have reluctantly declared victory and brought their armies home from the Balkans had not Austria now taken the momentous step of joining with them in approving additional steps to reduce Russia's power and prevent a recurrence of the aggression against Turkey. This approval formalised itself in agreements signed in August between Britain, France, and Austria, who made up all the non-Russian 'Great Powers' of Europe, with the exception of Prussia which usually followed Austria but in this case nervously hung back. The independent part of Italy, then known as Piedmont-Sardinia, and Turkey fought alongside Britain and France, and Sweden and Spain also volunteered to fight on the Allied side. The principle of collective security established in the 1814–15 Congress of Vienna made the three agreeing Great Powers plus Russia and Prussia something like a European 'Security Council'. The vote was therefore three to one in favour of escalating the war against Russia, with one abstention (if Prussia, which withdrew from the conference, is counted as abstaining and Russia as dissenting). The signatories, plus other countries supporting their agreed war aims, constituted well over 80 per cent of Europe outside Russia. This gave Britain and France a high degree of the international support that would be prized today as a justification for continuing the war. This European dimension to the war has until now not been emphasised in history, which has been keen to portray the war as a British political blunder.

The Great Powers agreed on four war aims over and above Russia's withdrawal from Turkey's Balkan provinces. The Four Points all required

Russia to give up privileges that it had acquired over the years in the Black Sea and the Turkish Empire. The most difficult point, for Russia, was that it should agree to revise the 1841 Straits Convention which had granted it a dominant military and naval strength in the Black Sea. The exact terms of a treaty to replace the Straits Convention were to be fixed by the negotiations in Vienna between all the Great Powers. Meanwhile, Britain had temporarily achieved this point by repudiating the Convention, bombarding Odessa, and blockading the Russian fleet and its huge naval base and arsenal at Sebastopol which were the instruments of Russia's domination of the countries around the Black Sea.

The strategy for continuing the war was left to those who were expected to do the fighting – Britain, France, and Turkey. They and not the broader coalition were responsible for deciding where to attack Russia. It was an arrangement that would be seen as suitable today – the more distant states with the best resources, plus the victim of aggression, combining to do the fighting while other states give formal approval and participate in continuing efforts to bring about a diplomatic solution.

THE CRIMEAN OPTION

In September 1854 French, British, and Turkish troops sailed from Bulgaria to the Crimea with the aim of capturing the Russian stronghold of Sebastopol, where the dockyards and arsenal were the source of the Russian threat to Turkey. The main proponent of this strategy in the war councils in Bulgaria was Lord Raglan, Commander-in-Chief of the British Army. The French commander, Marshal St Arnaud, had been instructed by his home government to follow Lord Raglan wherever the latter chose to go; nonetheless, St Arnaud told Raglan of his opposition to the plan.

One of the most flagrant untruths told about the Crimean War is that Lord Raglan invaded the Crimea peninsula because orders from the British Government left him no choice. The written orders that show otherwise have been available for many years, but historians continue to rely on a spurious version that was published in 1863 to disguise the real objectives of the war.

Lord Raglan, born Fitzroy Somerset and the younger son of a Duke, was aged sixty-six. He had been the late Duke of Wellington's favourite staff officer ever since he had accompanied the future Duke to the peninsula in 1808. He was the Duke's military secretary in Portugal and secretary to the Paris Embassy when Wellington was Ambassador there after Napoleon Bonaparte's abdication. Raglan was wounded at Busaco in the peninsula and lost an arm at Waterloo. He married Wellington's niece, and when Wellington became Commander-in-Chief, Raglan became his military secretary for twenty-five years until the Duke's death in 1852. Raglan was then raised to the peerage and selected to lead the expedition against Russia in 1854. He had never led troops in the field, but was considered diplomatic and personable enough to ensure cooperation between armies and navies of different nationalities. He was a tall handsome man with a kindly face and smile who seldom wore uniform, but instead dressed like a typical English country gentleman in a soft felt hat and a jacket and outdoor trousers. People found it very difficult to argue with him, possibly because his courtly amiability always made his opponents feel they were in the wrong.

On 16 July 1854, in Varna, Lord Raglan received an official secret despatch from the Minister of War which had been sent on 29 June. He expected it to contain an order from the home government to leave Bulgaria and capture the Russian naval base at Sebastopol in the Crimea. He had already received a private unofficial letter telling him that the minister would submit an official despatch to this effect to the Cabinet for approval before sending it to Raglan. But when he opened the promised official despatch, Lord Raglan found the Cabinet's instructions not quite as clear-cut as the minister had led him to expect. The Cabinet placed specific conditions on the Sebastopol plan, and presented him with other options if these conditions were not met.

The Cabinet orders ruled out one obvious option: marching north against the Russian Army that was retreating from Turkish territory. The Cabinet did not know that Raglan couldn't do that anyway, because he had found it impossible to obtain sufficient baggage animals. The Cabinet favoured an attack on Sebastopol, according to the Duke of Newcastle, 'I have ... to instruct your Lordship to concert measures for the siege of Sebastopol, unless, with the information in your possession, but at present unknown in this country you should be decidedly of opinion that it could not be undertaken with a reasonable prospect of success.' But the minister's despatch then laid down further conditions and included alternatives for Raglan's guidance if he thought an attack on Sebastopol was not reasonable. It is a curious fact that these important conditions and alternatives (printed in italics in the extract below) have never once been discussed in print by British historians. When the despatch was published in 1863 these italicised passages were omitted, making it appear that Cabinet and military were solidly united behind a 'Sebastopol or nothing' strategy and that they gave Lord Raglan orders which left him no choice:[9]

It is probable [continued the official despatch] that a large part of the Russian army now retreating from the Turkish territory may be poured into the Crimea to reinforce Sebastopol. If orders to this effect have not already been given, it is further probable that such a measure would be adopted as soon as it is known that the Allied armies are in motion to commence active hostilities. As all communications by sea are now in the hands of the Allied Powers, it becomes of importance to endeavour to cut off all communication by land between the Crimea and the other parts of the Russian dominions. *This would be effectually done by the occupation of the Isthmus of Perekop; and I would suggest to you that, if a sufficient number of the Turkish army can now be spared for this purpose, it would be highly important that measures should be taken without delay for sending an adequate force to that point, and associating with the troops of the Sultan such English and French officers as would assist, by their advice, in holding permanently the position. With the same object, important assistance might be rendered by Admiral Dundas, if he has yet been able to obtain any vessels of a light draught which would prevent the passage of Russian troops to the Crimea through the Sea of Azov.*

It is unnecessary to express any opinion, at this distance from the scene, as to the mode in which these operations should be conducted, or the place at which a disembarkation should be effected; and as the latter will, of course, be decided with the advice and assistance of the French and English Admirals, it is equally unnecessary to impress upon your Lordship the importance of selecting favourable weather for the purpose, and avoiding all risks of being obliged by storms to withdraw from the shore the vessels of war and transports when only a partial landing of the troops has been effected.

I will not, in this despatch, enter into any consideration of the operations which it would be desirable to undertake in Circassia or the coast of Abasia. The reduction of the two remaining fortresses of Anapa and Sujak Kaleh would be, next to the taking of Sebastopol, of the greatest importance, as bearing upon the fortunes of the war; but not only is their fall of far less moment than that of Sebastopol, but the capture of the latter might possibly secure the surrender of the Circassian fortresses.

In the event, however, of delay in undertaking these operations being inevitable, and the transports being in consequence available for any other service, I wish you to consider, with his Highness Omar Pasha and Marshal St Arnaud, whether some part of the Turkish army might not be conveyed by steam from Varna, and, by a combined movement with the forces of General Guyon and Schamyl, so entrap the Russian army in and around Tiflis as to compel its surrender to superior numbers .

From the complete text of the minister's official despatch it is clear that the Cabinet's preferences were:

1   That the French, British, and Turkish forces should invade and seal off the Crimea and besiege Sebastopol, subject to certain conditions.

2   That if Raglan considered that the conditions were not met, the same forces should attack the Russians in the Caucasus, first by destroying the Russian fortresses of Anapa and Sujak Kaleh in Circassia and then by undertaking further unspecified operations in Circassia and Abasia.

3   That if neither of those were possible immediately, Raglan should allow the Royal Navy to transport the Turkish Army to the Caucasus, where they were to join the English-born General Richard Guyon serving with the Turks and the legendary Murid leader Schamyl to attack the Russian Army at Tiflis in Georgia. In this case, the minister did not specify the destination of the British and French armies so it may be assumed that he thought they would winter where they were in Bulgaria.

The war's most biased British chronicler, Kinglake, published the misleading abridgement of these orders in 1863. At the time, only he and the government had access to the original secret despatch. Kinglake silently inserted rows of asterisks where he had suppressed the text italicised above, but this did not seem to alert other historians to the need to check sources. Fortescue, the 1920s historian of the British Army who detested Kinglake's writings, knew that a prominent general had proposed an attack on Circassia as an alternative to Sebastopol but said that it was typical of politicians that they should not mention this possibility in their orders to Raglan. He was obviously relying on Kinglake's first edition, as everyone has done since. The latest scholarly history of the war says, quoting Kinglake, that the government offered Raglan only two options

– to attack Sebastopol immediately or to delay if he thought fit.[10]

It may be harsh to assume that Kinglake's omission was a lie rather than an attempt to save paper, but one of his embellishments which is definitely a deliberate untruth has also been repeated by most historians since. This is his statement that Raglan showed the secret despatch to George Brown, one of his Divisional Commanders and his main confidant, and asked his advice on whether to attack Sebastopol. This is obviously untrue, and Kinglake must have known it. Raglan only asked Brown's opinion on the private letter from Newcastle which mentioned no alternative to Sebastopol. Brown's account of the meeting makes this clear because he refers to the date of the correspondence. The opinion that Brown gave to Raglan does not even make sense if he was looking at a document with alternatives in it. Kinglake says, and Brown confirms, that Brown told Raglan that if Raglan didn't attack Sebastopol the government would send out a new commander who would.[11] But sending out somebody else to attack Sebastopol would only work if Raglan did nothing, which the official despatch did not allow him to do. The government would hardly be able to send someone out to recall the British from Anapa, or the Turks from Tiflis, for an attack on Sebastopol.

Kinglake's enduring lie seems compatible with his admitted purpose of defending Lord Raglan's reputation. It tries to exonerate Raglan against the charge that he attacked Sebastopol unwisely, and corroborates Raglan's later false statement that there had been no disagreement on the wisdom of the attack. Raglan shared the official instructions with five people: Admirals Dundas and Lyons, the commander and second-in-command of the Mediterranean Fleet, Marshal St Arnaud, the French Commander-in-Chief, and two French Admirals.[12] The reactions of the five have never been published but according to Sir George Brown's unpublished memoir both Dundas and St Arnaud, Raglan's most senior colleagues, strongly objected to Raglan's Sebastopol expedition. Brown was critical of their objections and reports that Dundas did everything to obstruct the expedition while St Arnaud proposed what Brown thought was the strange idea of attacking Anapa in Circassia instead. This idea of St Arnaud's was, it should be noted, based on Raglan's official instructions which St Arnaud had seen and Brown's reaction is further evidence that Brown had not seen them. An attack on Anapa was much more in tune with French strategic objectives. An attack on Sebastopol would leave the French open to charges that they were merely helping the Royal Navy to eliminate a maritime competitor rather than fighting Russian expansionism. The French Minister of War, Vaillant, had given St Arnaud explicit instructions to attack Anapa.[13]

The official despatch laid out for Raglan the excuses he could use for not invading the Crimea. These included insufficient strength; the lowest estimate of Russian strength in the Crimea was 45,000[14], but most estimates put the total at between 70,000–80,000, which was more accurate. The ships available could only carry 61,000 of the 90,000 Allied troops available[15], at the most optimistic guess less than half the textbook three-to-one superiority required to mount a siege, and then only by leaving behind ambulance wagons, transport animals, medicines, and other essentials. Raglan could have cited the very recent death from disease of 10,000 men in the French and British camps, which was unknown to the Cabinet. The minister himself pointed out that the Russian Army retreating from the Danube would surely pour into the Crimea and instructed Raglan to send Turkish troops to close the peninsula at its top end, at Perekop, before attacking Sebastopol. Raglan produced two reasons for not occupying Perekop: first, the climate there would be fatal to the troops; and second, that he thought that Omar Pasha would not want to send Turkish troops there because he would want them to stay in the Balkans to keep an eye on their Austrian Allies.[16] If either of these excuses was true (and the second appears to be proved insincere by Raglan at the same time persuading Omar to send 6,000 troops to Sebastopol) he could have used it as a reason for not invading the Crimea. He could also have blamed Commissariat difficulties and inadequate land transport arrangements in the army which had become apparent in Bulgaria. He could have used all of these as 'information in your possession, unknown in this country', in the Cabinet's words, justifying postponement of the Crimean campaign. These last two problems – lack of land transport and Russian troops and supplies evading the naval blockade and entering the Crimea across the land bridge – were the two most important causes of the Allies' later sufferings.

There were good reasons why many Cabinet members would have reservations that would have prevented them from approving the 'Sebastopol or nothing' orders that Kinglake invented. First, on the political level, the more liberal members of the coalition Cabinet did not see Sebastopol as an end in itself; they (as well as more radical thinkers like Karl Marx) wanted to liberate the Crimea and Russia's other recent conquests. It is true that conservatives like Sir James Graham temporarily dominated the coalition, and they did not share the liberals' desire to spread the benefits of constitutional government across Europe. These conservatives had only reluctantly been dragged into the war as a result of Sinope and would be satisfied by limited war aims that would prevent further challenges to the Royal Navy.[17] Sebastopol, the main Russian naval base, therefore only satisfied the conservative element in a very polarised Cabinet; Graham later did everything he could to prevent Raglan from choosing one of the alternatives permitted by his Cabinet instructions.[18]

Second, on the military level the attack on Sebastopol was seen as very risky. Expert military opinion, often supported by prescient arguments, was almost unanimously *against* attacking Sebastopol.[19] General Sir John Burgoyne, the army's Inspector of Fortifications, had told the government that Sebastopol could not be captured unless the whole of the Crimean peninsula was occupied first. He correctly forecast that the Royal Navy's wooden capital ships would be powerless against Sebastopol's stone forts – an opinion that must have annoyed the admiralty judging by their disastrous attempt to prove him wrong. Other military experts pointed out that the main threat to Turkey was not Sebastopol at all. The reference in Raglan's instructions to the Caucasus as an alternative to the Crimea was in line with advice received among others from General James Shaw Kennedy, a Waterloo veteran who commanded the forces in the north of Britain. Shaw Kennedy ridiculed any suggestion of attacking Sebastopol, and said that it was much more important to secure the southern part of the Caucasus against Russian attacks on Turkey[20] and then drive the Russians northwards. Omar Pasha, the Turkish commander, thought so too, and was reluctant to allow his troops to accompany Raglan to the Crimea. Their fears were well-founded, because a Russian attack southwards through the Caucasus later resulted in the only serious Russian success of the war. This was the capture of an enormous swathe of Turkey and the important fortress town of Kars together with its garrison of 18,000 troops including ten generals. This victory immensely strengthened Russia's hand in negotiations to end the war.

Kinglake's universally-believed spurious version of the order to attack Sebastopol has done far more than simply protect Raglan's reputation. The condition that the Crimea be sealed off by land as well as by sea, and the alternative of attacking in the Caucasus, show that the military objective most acceptable to the whole Cabinet was the liberation of recently-conquered Russian territory, preferably including Sebastopol. Making Sebastopol appear to be the only goal gives the war a purpose that reflects a narrow conservative and admiralty view, ignores the European dimension, and is irrelevant to subsequent history.

Uncovering the lie about Raglan's orders reveals much about the objects of the war but it does not tell us why Raglan chose to attack Russia at its strongest point. There are several possibilities, one of which was that Raglan (a high Tory like his mentor the Duke of Wellington) may not have wanted to get involved in a war of liberation on the side of constitutionalist forces. There were only two places that Raglan could attack, if he were to follow the orders. He could go to the Caucasus and help in a war of liberation or he could go to the Crimea and capture Sebastopol. It is significant that he did not discuss this alternative with his immediate subordinates. General de Lacy Evans, the commander of one of the army's five infantry divisions, said later, 'I did not have the honour of being consulted' on the decision to invade the Crimea. A good reason for Raglan not to discuss the minister's letter with Evans was the reference in it to the Caucasian alternatives. Evans would have argued in favour of them. He would have argued that after reducing the two Russian enclaves in Circassia British and French forces should cooperate with the forces of General Guyon, Omar Pasha, and Schamyl in the wider Caucasian theatre.

Evans, like Raglan, had served under the Duke of Wellington in the Peninsula and at Waterloo. He was now a Radical member of parliament as well as a general, and like most Radicals he was a long-standing enemy of the Russian Tsar. Evans strongly believed that Britain should help the people of Russia's subject countries, such as those in the Caucasus, to fight for their independence. He had extensive experience of using British forces in conjunction with those of a foreign power. In 1835 he had accepted the command of the British Auxiliary Legion in Spain in the Carlist War, a unit of 8,000 men who were recruited in Britain by the Spanish Government to fight for the cause of constitutional government against the Carlists (reactionary rebels who were supported by Europe's absolutist powers including Russia). The Auxiliary Legion in Spain had been promoted by Lord Palmerston, against resistance from reactionary critics in Britain including Wellington and, presumably, his *protégé* Lord Raglan. Palmerston's official approval of the Legion was controversial because Britain itself had not been at war in Spain. Also controversial was the fact that Evans had operated in an equal or subordinate role with Spanish generals.

Britain was now at war with Russia, so the official presence of British troops alongside Caucasian rebels would be justified. But regardless of any political and military justification for fighting with Schamyl, Lord Raglan would not have felt comfortable accompanying such an expedition because he had an absolute horror of working with irregular troops. It has been suggested[21] that an Anglo-French Caucasian expedition at this time would have liberated the entire Caucasus as well as preventing the disaster at Kars. The idea of a Chechnya permanently freed from Russian control by European troops in 1855 certainly has its allure today.

Another influence that may have determined Raglan to attack Sebastopol was that of Sir James Graham, First Lord of the Admiralty, the conservative politician who had argued most strongly against going to war until he was persuaded by the Russian navy's 'massacre' at Sinope. Graham saw the war not as a defence of Turkey or a liberation of Russia's captive nations but as a struggle for sea power, and the naval base of Sebastopol was the most important element of Russia's naval power in the east. The Duke of Newcastle was Graham's opposite number at the War Office; his post had only just been created in an attempt to organise the army along the efficient lines of the navy, and Newcastle as its first occupant was probably under the influence of Graham when he first gave Lord Raglan his opinion that Sebastopol would be the only target. Graham's priorities eventually prevailed in Cabinet, but only subject to strong conditions and with mention of the alternatives. The second in command of the Mediterranean fleet, Sir Edmund Lyons, knew from Sir James Graham of the admiralty's preference for Sebastopol and argued in favour of it with Raglan, unlike his superior Admiral Dundas (who would soon retire and leave his place to Lyons).

Raglan could have kept the British Army in Bulgaria, or taken it to Constantinople, if he did not agree with the Caucasian proposal, sending the Turkish Army to Tiflis in line with the Cabinet's third alternative. It might have been hard for him to maintain morale in this case, and to prevent many troops from volunteering to go with the Turks. This would have become especially difficult once cholera broke out in the army. Although we cannot know for sure what made Raglan decide to invade the Crimea, the cholera epidemic (which was already well established among the French troops when he made his decision) seems the most likely cause. One thing is certain: he did not go to the Crimea because of 'peremptory' orders from his government, as he and others have always claimed.

In reality Raglan had it within his means to beat the cholera. There was widespread belief that stagnant water and piles of ordure provided a breeding-ground for the disease, although the specific role of microbes in the first and the flies on the second was not yet recognised. Raglan's medical staff had already pointed out the need to construct latrines in the right place and to filter the drinking water.[22] Observers had pointed out that de Lacy Evans' Second Division was sensibly encamped in small units close to faster-running streams and suffered less from disease.[23] Prevention of disease was a highly politicised topic; at home, at this very time, the General Board of Health was being disbanded due to right-wing politicians' pressure on what they saw as a huge waste of tax money. In Britain cleansing the towns by separating sewage from drinking water was a very expensive business requiring higher taxation of the wealthy voters, hence the political controversy and Tory opposition to the idea that epidemics could be prevented. For an army in the field the hygiene measures would have been much simpler, but they were not taken.

The cholera struck early in July when the weather broke. The rains came and the earth, baked hard by a month of drought, shrugged off the water and sent it running through the camps where 90,000 soldiers sat idle. The rain cleansed the ground, and the ordure that accumulated on the edge of the camps was tidily swept into the lakes and rivers that provided drinking water. Where before, in the baking heat, there had been a few fatal cases a week of what was euphemistically called 'English cholera', hundreds were now dying in camp from what was admitted to be a full-blown epidemic of the Asiatic form of the disease. The Royal Navy's ships hurriedly put to sea from Varna, but the drinking water had been infected and hundreds of bodies were thrown overboard in a few days.

The disease killed five hundred British soldiers in July, a thousand in August. In the French Army, which had brought the disease with it from France, it was worse. In three months the epidemic killed 8,000 French soldiers.[24] When the French Army marched north to the Dobrudja in July, the cholera epidemic travelled with him and it seemed that the whole of Bulgaria was unsafe. And news arrived that there was now epidemic cholera at Constantinople and Gallipoli too. There were no safe shores on the Black Sea any more, except the Caucasus and the Crimea.

An attack on Sebastopol at this unsuitable time of year could have been the only way acceptable to Raglan of dealing with the cholera epidemic and its effect on the morale of the troops. A British cavalry officer noted on 13 August, 'the men and officers are getting daily more disgusted with their fate. They do nothing but bury their comrades. They say loudly that they have not been brought out to fight, but to waste away and die in this country of cholera and fever.' A week later, 'We hear that there is a mutiny in the French encampment, the soldiers swearing that they will no longer remain here to die like dogs; they will go anywhere and do anything, but remain here to die they will not.'[25]

Three days after this rumour of mutiny in the French camp, Marshal St Arnaud published an inspirational proclamation to his army apparently throwing secrecy to the winds and announcing that the Allies were to attack Sebastopol and emphasising that the Crimea was 'a country as healthy as our own'. Six days later, on 31 August, Lord Raglan published a businesslike and detailed set of instructions to officers for landing on the enemy coast, which began 'The invasion of the Crimea having been decided upon'. In a letter home Captain Sterling, brigade-major in the Highland Brigade, railed against a 'most unnecessary publication, which in all probability was despatched forthwith by boat to Odessa and to Sebastopol by Russian spies'.[26] Three weeks were to elapse between the French publication and the disembarkation in the Crimea. The reason for the abandonment of secrecy may have been to forestall further disorder among the troops, particularly the French. Commanders and ministers were less in control of their armies than they would like historians to believe.

4

From Success to Stagnation

A fleet of 350 ships left Varna on 7 September 1854, with each steamship towing a line of sailing vessels carrying a single regiment with its stores, ammunition and artillery. There had never been such a spectacle on the planet, and the troops were awed at the sight. At night, the fleet anchored in the middle of the Black Sea like a floating town, with lights at the masthead and band music floating over the waves. They cruised along the coast of the Crimea until they found one of the previously-reconnoitred beaches that was bare of Russian troops, and began disembarking unopposed at a place they called Old Fort near Eupatoria, thirty miles north of Sebastopol, on 14 September. The cholera epidemic abated somewhat while they were at sea, where drinking water and sewage were temporarily separated, but as soon as they were back on land the disease returned in force.

On 19 September after a nearly flawless landing on a hostile shore they began their march south towards Sebastopol, a compact mass of men four miles wide and three miles long. The French were on the right, nearest the sea, their subdued blue uniforms contrasting with the bright red of the British. The fleet moved alongside them as they advanced and in the case of the British carried all the men's packs and tents, the lack of which was causing and would continue to cause great hardship. The expedition reminded at least one participant of the English buccaneering expeditions of two centuries before, when marauding bands protected by their privateer ships attacked settlements on the Spanish Main and held them to ransom.[1]

Between the landing-place near Eupatoria and the fortress of Sebastopol the ground was relatively flat and deserted, and there were four rivers that the Allied armies had to cross: the Bulganak, the Alma, the Katscha and the Belbek. The weather was very hot and the troops were exhausted and parched when they arrived at the Bulganak in the early afternoon. The Light Brigade of the British cavalry, on the left wing of the army (the landward side) discovered a detachment of Cossacks 2,000 strong on the other bank of the river and prepared to charge them even though outnumbered two to one. These odds were more than acceptable to the British cavalry, which was one of the wonders of the military world and not to be compared to the primitive and ill-equipped Cossack horsemen. Skirmishers had already begun to exchange carbine fire at long range when Lord Raglan discovered that there was a Russian infantry division behind the Cossacks, hidden from the view of his cavalry commanders. Judging the situation unfavourable for an infantry engagement, Raglan ordered the British cavalry to retire. As they did so, the Cossacks jeered them derisively. To add injury to insult, a Russian field gun lobbed a few round shot into the retreating cavalry squadrons and wounded four men. Being jeered at by the ragged Cossacks under the eyes of their own infantry was a degrading experience for the proud British cavalry. The infantry took malicious pleasure in the humiliation of their elaborately dressed and comfortably mounted cavalry comrades. 'Serve them bloody right, silly peacock bastards' wrote a private in the 41st Regiment in a letter home.[2]

The Russian defenders did not give battle here in the morning, as expected, but fell back to the next line of defence: the River Alma. The south bank of this river seemed to the Russians to be a good position from which to hold back an army advancing from the north. The north bank sloped gently to the river but the defenders' south bank rose in a series of hills which were highest near the sea, forming steep cliffs for the couple of miles nearest the mouth. The road to Sebastopol crossed the river about three miles inland, running through a pass in the southern hills, and the Russians placed powerful batteries of field guns astride this road about 600 yards south of the river crossing. A mile further upstream they had built a low parapet of earth on a hillside overlooking the river which formed a natural killing-slope or *glacis* in front of it, and had armed this earthwork with more guns. All these guns had the river in their sights and well within range; they could reach up to 600 yards or more north of the river and were practicing at targets in that area as the Allied Army appoached. Allied guns, firing uphill, would have a shorter range.

For five miles upstream from the sea, the south bank was well defended and the Allies would have to march well away from their ships if they wanted to outflank the Russians. The Russians were outnumbered – they had about 40,000 men and 108 guns against 61,000 men and 128 guns for the Allies. Their plans were to use this small force to delay the Allies' advance for a few weeks while more troops could be assembled behind them. Prince Menshikov, the Tsar's truculent envoy to Constantinople and one of the victors of Sinope, commanded the Russian Army. He was relying on the strength of the Russian position, but its strength was illusory.

The winner of the battle of the Alma has received relatively little attention in the history books, the only book dedicated to the battle even claiming it was not available to the British.[3] It was the new Minié rifle, and its role has been downplayed not least because it was wielded most effectively by regiments that refused to advance on the enemy.

The staple firearm of the infantry in armies until then was the percussion smoothbore musket, firing a round lead ball. This ball was made slightly smaller than the bore, so that it could be loaded from the muzzle easily even after the bore became encrusted with the residue left by burnt gunpowder. The loose fit limited the velocity of the ball and gave it a random spin, which as golfers know causes poor accuracy. The musket was dangerous only up to about 300 yards and accurate only to about 100. Even a thick greatcoat offered considerable protection from it. The main function of the musket was to act as a support for the bayonet, which was supposed to do most of the work: 'The bullet is foolish, the bayonet is wise'.

A rifle was not smooth-bored but instead used an elongated bullet that fitted tightly into spiral grooves ('rifling') inside the barrel so that it sealed the bore and emerged spinning uniformly around the direction of travel. Until the 1850s a rifle was slow to reload because the tight-fitting bullet had to be rammed down the dirty bore from the muzzle. Rifles were given to specialised regiments that were often deployed sparingly alongside the infantry and used, for example, to pick off enemy officers in battle.

In 1843 a French officer, Claude Minié, invented a new bullet and rifle. The bullet was of similar diameter to a musket ball but it had a pointed nose and a flat back end that was hollowed out. It was used in a rifle that had shallow rifling inside a bore which was larger than the bullet so that it could be loaded easily, despite gunpowder fouling, like a smoothbore. The hollow back end of the bullet made a sort of lead skirt that billowed out when the gunpowder exploded behind it, enlarging the diameter of the bullet so that it gripped the rifling and sealed the bore. When the Russians got sight of these bullets they christened them, for obvious reasons, 'thimbles' – a deceptively homely term for something that they later learned to dread.[4] The bullet weighed significantly more than a musket ball, and the powder charge had to be heavy to expand the lead skirt. The increased velocity and bullet weight gave the rifle a fierce kick and many soldiers dumped part of the powder charge when loading, but if they could stand the recoil the rifle could easily kill a man at 600 yards or more. It was also accurate at that range and had a folding adjustable sight graduated to 900 yards. At closer ranges one Minié bullet could kill several men standing one behind the other, which was unfortunate for the Russian infantry who were trained to fight in densely packed columns. However it was not the close range penetration of the Minié that was to win at the Alma, but its long range capability.

Just before the war the British seized on the French invention and, taking advantage of the mass production facilities of the Birmingham gun trade, contracted for 34,000 Minié rifles for issue to the infantry. Four out of five of the British infantry divisions which landed in the Crimea already had the rifle, many of them issued since they left England. Many senior officers were openly hostile towards this new-fangled device, and most of the rest were very slow to see its merits. Captain Sterling, the crusty brigade-major of the Highland Brigade wrote, 'We are changing our firelocks for Minié rifles, which is an untried arm for large bodies of men. The prudence of the change at this moment may be doubted; our advantage has been and always will be, in closing rapidly with the enemy; when you are near enough, the old gun is as good as the new one.' This erroneous view was shared by his close friend and Brigade Commander Sir Colin Campbell. The opposite view had prevailed at the War Office when the weapon was ordered and issued in such a hurry.

At midday on 20 September the Allied armies came in sight of the Alma and the two leading British divisions each rearranged itself from a group of regimental phalanxes into a single two-deep line. Each division had two brigades each comprising three regiments of about 800 men per regiment, and became over a mile wide when formed into double line. The spreading out into line was criticised at the time because the two leading divisions ended up overlapping each other by a few hundred yards, but we would consider it a miraculous manoeuvre today even if the men weren't under fire. The Second Division under General de Lacy Evans was astride the main road and facing the Russian guns defending it. Beside Evans and to his left the Light Division under Sir George Brown faced the Russian earthwork, and on Evans' right the French faced the cliffs on the lower reaches of the Alma. Each British division faced a strong group of field guns that, because of the difference in height, could hit them before they were close enough to reply with their own artillery. Behind the Light Division was the First Division, comprising three regiments of Guards and three of Highlanders. The plan was that this First Division under Prince George the Duke of Cambridge, Queen Victoria's 35-year old cousin, would follow up the Light Division as a second attacking wave.

First, though, the French attacked the heights near the mouth of the river. This was not part of a well worked-out strategy, in fact St Arnaud thought he had persuaded Raglan to advance simultaneously on a broad front and try to turn the enemy's flank on the other (inland) side. But Raglan now decided to delay his own advance until the French had succeeded, and simply made his troops lie down on the ground within range of the Russian guns, in a position from which they could quickly reach the river when the time was ready. They lay there for nearly an hour and a half, from 1:15 to 2:45 p.m., suffering occasional casualties as the Russian gunners tried to get the exact range. This was just one of the great advantages of fighting in line, as only the British did. Unlike the columns favoured by the French and Russians, the line could be safely halted if things were not going according to schedule. The line did not present such an easy target to artillery as a fat column or square when stationary, and if it lay down it was not vulnerable to sharpshooters.

Bosquet's division, on the right near the sea, arrived at the river first and found the opposite bank undefended apparently because the Russians believed that the cliffs were too steep there for attackers to climb. Further upstream, where the divisions of Canrobert and Prince Napoleon (another nephew of Napoleon Bonaparte) were to cross, the

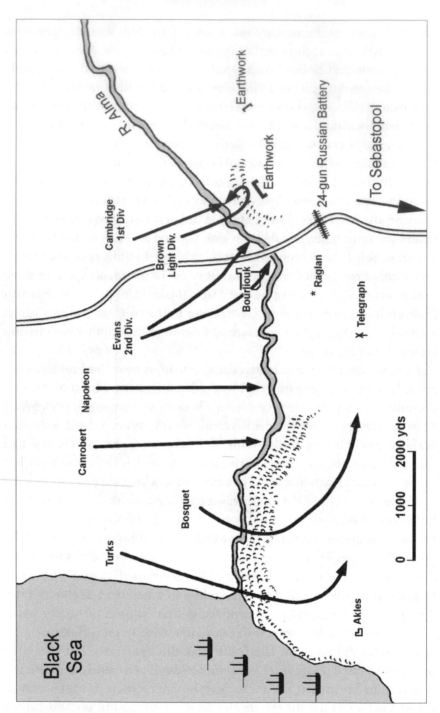

The Battle of the River Alma.

narrow space between the opposite bank and the hills was crowded with Russian troops, and nine steamers of the Allied fleets opened fire on these positions. The Russians sustained heavy casualties from this enfilading fire despite being over a mile from the ships which could not enter the river mouth, and soon began to withdraw further inland and onto the heights behind them where an unfinished signalling tower known as the Telegraph became the focus of their defence.

At the head of Bosquet's division down by the river mouth was a regiment of Zouaves who rushed across the river, climbed the 150-foot cliffs, and opened fire with their rifles on the only Russian troops they found there. Menshikov had stationed only one isolated regiment next to the sea at the village of Akles which was too far back to see the danger from the French until the latter were on the plateau. Seeing the Zouaves' success, Bosquet sent the rest of his division across the river to join them, and they found a ravine up which they hauled the French artillery to the top of the cliffs. Hearing of the unexpected success of the Zouaves, Prince Menshikov overreacted to the danger and, riding several miles himself to see how the French had turned his left wing, ordered up his reserves of seven regiments of infantry and four batteries of artillery to the cliffs. This deprived the Russian centre of both its commander and its reserves at a very critical moment. When the first Russian artillery battery arrived, it found their infantry in retreat under a withering rifle fire from the Zouaves who were in advance of Bosquet's division. The Zouaves' officers now directed their men to turn their fire on the Russian gunners rather than the infantry, and within a short time forty-eight of the 100 artillerymen in the 10-gun Russian battery were dead or wounded as were most of their horses. The Zouaves were firing at a range of 700 yards, too far for the Russian gunners to reach them with grapeshot.[5] Grapeshot is the cannon equivalent of a shotgun cartridge, scattering many projectiles from each discharge, and is more lethal against infantry but only effective at a very few hundred yards compared to a thousand or more for solid cannon balls.

Most of the French infantry did not have the Minié rifle, even though it was a French innovation. Like other innovators, the French had converted to an 'intermediate' technology – they had replaced their smoothbores with a rifle that had a spike inside the bottom of the barrel against which the soldier had to ram the bullet to expand it. This 'Thouvenin system' had certain disadvantages as far as accuracy and speed of loading compared to the Minié, but it had the advantage of already having been used in the field in Algeria so that French officers understood better than the British how to exploit their infantry's weapon.

Up until this moment, field artillery had needed little protection against massed infantry because grapeshot from cannon had a longer range than the old smoothbore infantry muskets. Apart from two small earthworks opposite the British divisions, the Russians had dug no trenches or fortifications and therefore had nowhere to hide from the new infantry rifle's long and deadly reach.

By the time the rest of Menshikov's urgently-summoned artillery arrived on his left flank, the whole of Bosquet's division had reached the plateau. Bosquet now only had twelve guns against the Russians' twenty-eight, but the French guns were of larger calibre and longer range and Bosquet's infantry with their rifles kept the Russian artillery at a distance where only the heavier French guns could take effect. When Menshikov's reserves of infantry reached the scene, they tried to mount a bayonet charge against Bosquet's division and the Turks, who had now joined Bosquet, to drive them back to the river. But Bosquet's men refused to engage in hand-to-hand fighting and kept the Russian infantry at bay with their rifles so that the Russians returned to the defensive.[6] Something of a stalemate ensued as Canrobert's and Prince Napleon's divisions were still on the other side of the Alma, hesitating to cross in the face of the Russian troops now massed around the high point of the Telegraph directly opposite them. At this moment Prince Napoleon sent word to Evans, on his left, that it was time for the British to advance and take some pressure off the French.

Raglan was still waiting for the French attack to succeed before committing himself. He had told Evans (commanding the division nearest the French) not to take orders from the French on his right, and when the French pressed Evans to advance he sent to Raglan to ask permission to obey.[7] This prompted Raglan to attack the centre even though he was not yet satisfied with the French advance. It was a fortunate decision, which profited from Menshikov's depletion of his centre.

At about 2.45p.m. Lord Raglan ordered the Light, First, and Second Divisions forward, with the First behind the Light. He did not give them any guidance apart from this, and expected their divisional commanders to give further orders. As soon as the men rose from their prone positions and moved forward the Russian skirmishers set fire to the village of Bourliouk, in front of Evans's division, in which they had previously placed piles of hay. The hay burned quickly and created a cloud of fine smoke over the village which stayed for the rest of the battle and masked much of the action there from Russian observers to their great disadvantage. The advancing British line had to break up to pass through and around the smouldering houses. They forded the river under heavy fire from fourteen Russian guns in the earthwork and twenty-four astride the road. If they went beyond the river, they would be within range of grapeshot.

There were two literary personages advancing in this first wave. One was the man who was later to become the war's best-known historian: Alexander Kinglake. Kinglake was an old Etonian and the son of a banker. He trained as a barrister but preferred writing, travelling, and observing military operations. On the morning of the Alma he met Lord Raglan who invited him to accompany him during the battle and to dine with him in the evening. The other literary camp-follower could not have been more different from Kinglake: he was a convivial *Times* reporter named William Howard Russell, known as Billy to the troops. Russell was Irish, the son of an unsuccessful Protestant businessman and a Roman Catholic farmer's daughter. He had been raised in Dublin, first as a Catholic and then as a Protestant. Russell tried to attach himself to Lord Raglan's retinue at the Alma to observe the battle, as Kinglake had done, but was rudely ejected; one imagines that he would have been a fish out of water at his Lordship's dining table. The friendless Russell trailed along behind the Second Division and seems to have spent most of the battle sheltering in the smoking ruins of Bourliouk village trying unsuccessfully to see what was going on. Kinglake, on the other hand, followed Raglan and his staff when they crossed the river at about the same time as the leading divisions and rode up a small and conveniently deserted hill on the British right flank from which they could watch the battle unfold. Lord Raglan encouraged a couple of field guns to be brought up to this position, which fired a number of round shot from here towards the Russians during the battle.

A mile and a half upriver from Raglan, opposite the Russian earthwork, the Light Division climbed the river bank and found that they were sheltered by a second bank that rose sharply before levelling out into the gentle slope commanded by the Russian guns in the earthwork directly in front of them. The river crossing had scrambled the men's line

formation, and as they were coaxed out of their shelter by their officers they emerged on the killing-slope in even looser formation. Once
out, most of them charged the Russian gun emplacement rather than
advancing in a mile-wide line against it and the Russian infantry columns on either side of it. Seeing the British converging in disorder on
the earthwork, the Russian gunners limbered up and pulled their guns a
quarter-mile back from where they could pitch shells into a disorganised
mob of at least 2,000 infantry milling about the abandoned 300-yard
long parapet. Russian muskets also found easy targets in this crowd,
the survivors of which were soon running back towards the river in
confusion.

The Duke of Cambridge had stopped his First Division, the second wave, for lack of further orders from Raglan. General Evans on
his right got the Duke started again by giving him an order to advance
that he pretended came from Raglan, who was nowhere to be found.
The Duke crossed the river too late to reinforce the Light Division in
the Russian earthwork they had occupied and were now abandoning.
His division consisted of three regiments of Guards, on the right, and
Sir Colin Campbell's three regiments of Highlanders on the left. The
Guards, in particular, were extremely fussy in their drill and were making extraordinary efforts to keep step in a parade-ground line formation
when marching under fire through vineyards and even the river itself.
The recent rout of the disorganised Light Division showed that their
fussiness was not without merit. The smart First Division now set out
to improve on the Light Division's undisciplined advance, and climbed
out of the dead ground and began to dress themselves into line under
fire. Irritated by the dawdling of his chief the Duke of Cambridge, the
Guards' brigadier ordered his half of the division forward without delay[8]
and unfortunately the Scots Fusilier Guards, the middle one of his three
regiments, obeyed him and charged up the hill unformed in a repeat
of the mistake of their predecessors of the Light Division. The Light
Division fleeing back to the river pursued by Russian artillery fire ran
straight into these Scots Fusilier Guards and sent many of them sprawling.
Some of the Scots Guards, bruised and apparently infected by the panic,
returned to the shelter of the bank and remained there for the rest of the
battle, ignoring repeated orders to advance.[9] Others, and nobody can
agree how many, gradually reformed in the 500-yard gap that their regiment had left in the otherwise impeccable Guards line. The two Guards

regiments on either side of the gap (Coldstreams and Grenadiers) would not budge forward until the gap was filled and these regiments while waiting, joined according to some by the disobedient Scots Guards hiding in the river, fired volleys into the Russian columns opposing them.[10] Some fourteen volleys (at least 20,000 rounds) of Minié fire poured into the unprotected Russian infantry from beyond the range of the Russian smoothbore muskets and artillery. These fourteen volleys would have lasted for about ten to fifteen minutes, and at that range would have had an intensity and accuracy equivalent to four or five twentieth-century machine guns. Without advancing, 2,000 Guards were able to rout in this way 15,000 Russian infantry on their own killing-slope.[11]

The Guards' officers made excuses for even the well-disciplined Coldstreams' and Grenadiers' hesitation in obeying the orders to advance: the officers claimed that the orders were inaudible because the men were cheering so loudly, and/or the men had not been trained in reloading their rifles while advancing.[12] Probably the men simply knew better and recognised, in one of many documented incidents during the war which demonstrated that the British rank and file had better tactical sense than their officers, that the bayonet's supremacy was at an end. They had been hurriedly trained by specialist staff officers from the Hythe School of Musketry in the use of the new rifle, including the science of judging range up to 1,000 yards by noting how much detail was visible on the enemy's uniform and setting the new adjustable sights accordingly. Infantry officers were not issued with the rifle and were often unfamiliar with its use. Wolseley reports that early in 1854 only one officer from each regiment was sent to Hythe for instruction in the rifle; it was not a popular assignment and his regiment sent an officer who only had one arm.[13] After the war William Howard Russell mentioned 'officers who declaim against the Hythe school for its supposed tendency to make the soldier too independent of his officer.'[14] Over and over again in the records of the war we find the British other ranks making inspired use of the Minié without any apparent orders from above, and often in defiance of orders to the contrary. After the battle a British officer who had not been engaged passed through the Russian lines and reported in amazement, 'I passed numbers of dead and wounded men, most of them killed by musketry more than half a mile from the line of fire.'[15]

On the right of the Light and First Divisions, General de Lacy Evans's Second Division had not left the shelter of the river bank. They were under a heavy cannonade from the twenty-four guns astride the road, which had the British within grapeshot range and had caused many casualties. Evans, unlike the commanders of the Light and First Divisions on his left, did not order his regiments to advance beyond the river and the Guards later claimed that Evans's men shirked the battle.[16] Evans's forte was the effective use of artillery to support infantry, and he was busying himself assembling artillery to oppose the Russian batteries blocking his infantry advance.[17] The men of his 30th Regiment, sheltered behind an extremely steep part of the river bank, could see the Russian gunners clearly 600 yards away. When presented with a similar battery at a similar distance, the four regiments of the Light and First Divisions had obeyed their officers' commands to charge the artillery position at the bayonet with catastrophic results. The 30th Regiment of Evans's Second Division, left without orders[18], tried a different approach to the Russian gunners, similar to that of Bosquet's Zouaves. They shot them.

There were three Russian batteries: the 1st and 2nd Light Batteries of the 16th Artillery Brigade and the 3rd Heavy Battery of the Cossack Artillery Brigade. This made a total of twenty-four guns[19], a quarter of the Russian guns at the Alma, attended by at least 200 gunners and as many horses packed into a compact target area undefended by earthworks. The British 30th Regiment alone, sheltered behind the river bank, could maintain for a full thirty minutes a rate of fire against this exposed target equivalent to two modern light machine guns.[20]

The Russian gunners knew they were under fire, but they probably did not know that their assailants were down at the river. They would have been looking for them at half the distance, at a range where their grapeshot could have wiped out any attackers. Even if they looked towards the river, they may not have seen the rifle flashes because of the smoke and flames from the burning village. Their horses, tethered behind the guns, were soon nearly all wounded and floundering on the ground. Gunners were dropping too, and then the colonel commanding the artillery emplacement received a bullet in the chest.[21] Soon after he was carried to the rear, the general in overall command of the Russian artillery and two of his staff galloped up. Seeing that horses and men were in dwindling supply and that the guns would soon be immobilised, he ordered them to the rear. The surviving gunners had to manhandle the guns up the slope for lack of horses, and left four guns behind. The pass to Sebastopol was now open to the British.

On the left the Guards and Highlanders of the First Division, the second wave, were now marching up the slope in the middle of which was the Russian earthwork where much of the Light Division had been routed. The Highlanders' commander Sir Colin Campbell didn't believe in the long range of the new rifles, and ordered his men 'Don't pull a trigger till you're within a yard of the Russians!'[22] The remaining Russians departed for Sebastopol before he got that close. His second-in-command Captain Sterling, who had earlier criticised the issue of rifles to the infantry, wrote on the day after the battle that the mere sight of the highland regiments advancing 'without firing a shot' drove the Russians off, and that if the Guards had advanced at a similar pace without firing it would have saved many 'innocent Russian lives' – showing that his moral sense was more acute than his tactical insight. On further reflection, the lessons of the battle became clearer to him; two weeks later in another letter home he claimed that his Highlanders had shot many Russians after all and grudgingly admitted that 'their Miniés seem to shoot very strong'. It is clear from this that the common soldier was teaching at least some of his officers how to fight.

British troops fired ninety thousand Minié cartridges at the Alma – the quantity normally carried into battle by only two regiments. It is now a truism that a huge number of cartridges is fired for every soldier hit, but that is because the troops have learned to shelter from rifle fire. At the Alma the Russians were totally unprepared to face massed infantry equipped with this weapon; about 1,800 Russian soldiers lost their lives in the battle, and the rifle must have accounted for most. British dead numbered 381, and French only 140.[23]

Billy Russell, the *Times* journalist who was ejected from the group surrounding Lord Raglan, seems to have used details supplied by members of Raglan's party (probably Kinglake) for use in his newspaper report written that day and published in the Times on 9 and 10 October. For example, Russell reported that Lord Raglan ordered two guns to be bought up to his isolated position in front of the right flank, and that just a few shots from these two guns routed the Russian infantry facing the Guards. These shots were solid cannon balls of only four inches diameter fired at or beyond their maximum range of 900 yards.[24] It is understandable that Raglan's group should attribute distant effects to actions taken by their own party; an officer on Raglan's staff even claimed that the two guns in their group drove away the twenty-four Russian guns blocking the main road with their first two shots. According to this account, 'the second shot went through a Russian tumbril and killed two horses. These two shots were sufficient: the Russian general, seeing that he was taken completely in flank, gave orders for them to limber up their guns.' The implausibility of this explanation for the Russian retreat has led later British historians to embellish it so as to improve its credibility. A 1971 history of the war upgraded the humble tumbril, claiming that 'the first shot missed, the second hit an ammunition wagon behind the guns'. In a 1999 history the solid cannon ball seems to have turned into a shell because 'the second shot hit an ammunition wagon and the explosion had far-reaching consequences. Thinking that they were in danger of losing their own guns the Russian artillerymen began retreating.'[25] Then in the latest 2004 account of the war the shell 'blew up an ammunition wagon, which was scattered to the winds in spectacular fashion'. These modern accounts do not quote any source for the gradually evolving tale of the tumbril, and show historians competing to make their accounts more cinematic rather than more historically accurate. This competition has added credence to the basic lie that Lord Raglan's two borrowed guns turned the battle by driving away the main Russian artillery batteries, and deprives the 30th Regiment of the credit. This is known to scholars as Great Man History, and is never so plentiful as in military circles. The plain truth is that the Russian artillery was routed by a humble regiment of the line, without orders, hiding in a ditch.

The French put out their own version, claiming that there were twenty-one French guns firing from behind Raglan's two; Raglan's retinue denied this but in any case by the time this French artillery joined in the 30th Regiment had done their job.[26] The reminiscences of participants may have been corrupted by regimental and national chauvinism but it seems certain that concentrated Minié rifle fire from static regiments, a phenomenon so new and unplanned that British observers may not even have recognised its significance, defeated the Russians in front of the British sector. This does not alter the fact that the early French success (also due largely to the new infantry weapon) drew Russian reserves away from the British sector and that although neither ally could abide the thought, they won the battle of the Alma together.

General Totleben, the German engineer who worked wonders fortifying the landward side of Sebastopol for the Russians in the weeks that followed, wrote an account of the war ten years later in which he reflected on the impact of the Minié rifle on the Allied troops who used it for the first time at the Alma. 'Left to themselves to perform the function of sharpshooters, they did not hesitate under fire and did not require orders or supervision. Troops thus armed were full of confidence once they found out the accuracy and immense range of their weapon.' He went on to say how perfect the Russian infantry was at fighting *en masse* (and the British remarked that the grey Russian columns looked as if they were carved out of solid rock) but the West counted on individual instruction and marksmanship. 'Our infantry with smoothbores could not reach the enemy at greater than 300 paces, while they fired on us at 1,200. The enemy, perfectly convinced of the superiority of his small arms, avoided close combat; every time our battalions charged, he retired for some distance and began a murderous fusillade. Our columns, in pressing the attack, only succeeded in suffering terrible losses, and finding it impossible to pass through the hail of bullets which overwhelmed them, they became disorganised and were obliged to fall back before reaching the enemy.'[27] The only way that Russian artillery could combat the Minié, said Totleben, was with explosive shrapnel shells (*obus à balles*) which were limited to fifteen rounds per battery. This ammunition – also called 'spherical case' in English – overcame the short range of grapeshot by enclosing it in an exploding shell that maintained its velocity for a greater distance; other sources say these shells were not available to the Russians at all.

British historians have never written as effusively as Totleben about the way the British infantry quickly mastered its new weapon. Instead they have dwelt on the imaginary successes of the artillery, thus making the repeated artillery bombardments of Sebastopol seem more sensible and glossing over the generals' later failure to exploit the Minié in their strategic thinking.

This was the Allies' secret weapon: the combination of mass production and crash training by specialist officers that ensured that every British infantryman was quickly equipped and trained with the Minié rifle and sixty rounds of ammunition so that an entire regiment or more could fire two aimed rounds a minute at the same distant target. The tremendous advantage given to the Allies by their secret weapon helps to explain how a sickly, ill-coordinated and badly supplied army of 61,000 men invaded a country whose standing army numbered one-and-a-half million without being thrown into the sea within a matter of weeks. It was a weapon that the British generals never seem to have understood during the war, but their incomprehension didn't matter as long as they let their infantry meet the Russians in the field and do what came naturally. Unfortunately they seldom did.

THE SIEGE BEGINS

The victorious Allies stayed for two days at the battlefield of the Alma before continuing their march to Sebastopol. They arrived outside the town two days after that, on 25 September. Even after this delay, if they had entered the city then they would have captured it because there were fewer than 18,000 troops inside. The Russian Army that had lost the battle of the Alma did not try to defend the city but withdrew inland to avoid being trapped.

Instead of attacking Sebastopol, or even sending in a note asking its garrison to surrender, the Allies detoured inland around the east side of the city and took possession of the ground to the south. This ground included a number of sheltered bays that could be used for supplying the Allies by sea; the British took over the small port of Balaclava and the French took Kamiesch Bay. The two armies camped on the high ground to the south and west of Sebastopol, from where there were good views of the city. They planned to land their siege guns from the fleet and quickly bombard the defenders into surrender. At the same time, though, they had to defend their rear from the Russian army that had escaped from the city and from reinforcements that were arriving in the Crimea from other parts of Russia. The French began to make camp, dig trenches, and construct siege batteries around the south and west of the city, close to their port of Kamiesch, while the British did the same around the east, much further from their own port of Balaclava.

The Allies began their bombardment on 17 October, three weeks after arrival, the delay being caused by the difficulty of manhandling heavy artillery into positions overlooking the city. During those three weeks the Russians under Totleben had been strengthening the walls around Sebastopol and building new gun emplacements out of earth. The Russians matched the Allied artillery by landing heavy guns from their own fleet, sinking the ships in the harbour to make underwater obstructions. In the first hours of the bombardment they replied strongly and

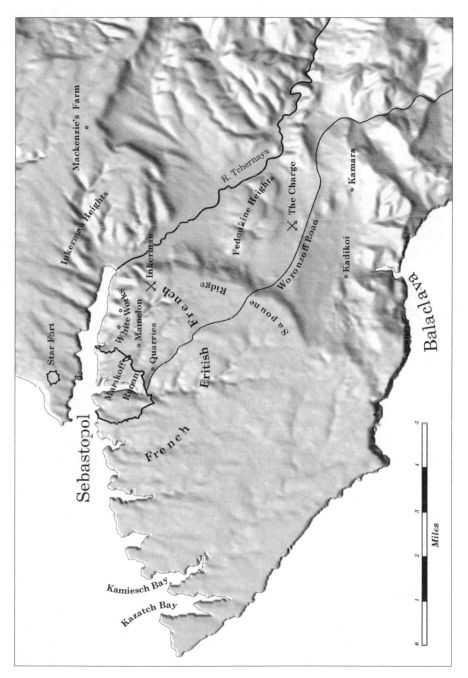

Sebastopol and surroundings after May 1855, when the French had taken over the Inkerman positions from the British.

scored a couple of direct hits on Allied powder magazines. It turned out that this was not going to be a simple Allied artillery bombardment at all: it was to be a duel.

The Turkish, French and British fleets sailed round to Sebastopol harbour and engaged the forts with broadsides during the first day of the duel. They received better than they gave, and within a couple of hours it became obvious that wooden capital ships were no match for modern fortifications. Previous naval bombardments, such as that by the Russians at Sinope or the British at Odessa, had been against civilian towns with rudimentary defences. Sebastopol, on the other hand, was custom-built for defence. The forts hurled back red-hot shot that set the Allied vessels alight before they could even get close enough to see the damage their own broadsides were causing. Although they did significant damage to the forts, the much more obvious effect on their own fleet had a demoralising effect on the Allied sailors. After three and a half hours the huge combined fleet sailed away to lick its wounds, with thirty sailors dead and hundreds wounded. Back in London and Paris, ship designers were at their drawing boards within weeks to find ways of armouring ships with iron.

On land, the Allies did not launch the infantry assault they had planned although, unknown to them, they had done enough damage for one to succeed. Again, the unexpected resistance had demoralised the over-optimistic Allied troops. The bombardment continued for a week, with the Allied troops becoming more and more dispirited as the promised early assault failed to materialise and as the Russian defences grew stronger. The Allies began to dig their trenches closer to the walls; their troops had to occupy the trenches at night to guard against sorties from the city which had begun to fill up with new troops who could still enter on the northern side. The British troops were particularly stretched because with reinforcements they only amounted to 23,000 in late October, compared to 42,000 French. Most of the Turkish troops had remained behind near the landing-place, at Eupatoria, so the total Allied land forces outside Sebastopol were fewer than 70,000. By the last week of October, they were outnumbered. There were then nearly 20,000 Russian troops in the city itself; the army defeated at the Alma, now camped a few miles to the north of the city, had been reinforced from the Balkans and now numbered 65,000. From its position on the Katcha near Bakchiserai this army under Prince Menshikov had been

sending heavy cavalry patrols into the plains in front of Balaclava to harass the British and to keep the supply lines open to the city. The British
and French infantry were camped on the uplands within a couple of
miles of the city walls; only a limited British cavalry and infantry force
was encamped on the plain.

The most vulnerable point of the Allied position was the British
supply port of Balaclava. There were fewer than 4,000 troops in and
around Balaclava to defend against an expected Russian attack on the
port. If these should prove inadequate, reinforcements would have to
march down from the heights above Sebastopol, which would take several hours. The enemy were well aware of the Allies' predicament, and
as soon as the first sizeable Russian reinforcements arrived they were
immediately sent to attack Balaclava.

5

Balaclava: They Were the Reason Why

BLUNDER OR BRILLIANCE?

The Charge of the Light Brigade, during the battle of Balaclava, is the only military event during the Crimean War that is identifiable by most British people today. The accepted wisdom is that that the Charge was a blunder: a pointless attack by cavalry at a Russian artillery position, the result of misunderstandings and antipathy between senior officers. This explanation was first popularised by Tennyson's famous poem, which was written only weeks after the event on the basis of a newspaper account:

> 'Forward, the Light Brigade!
> Charge for the guns' he said:
> Into the valley of Death
> Rode the six hundred.

> 'Forward, the Light Brigade!'
> Was there a man dismay'd ?
> Not tho' the soldier knew
> Some one had blunder'd…

Most subsequent authors have directed their research at the roles of the senior officers involved, colourful and wealthy individuals whose lifestyle and high-profile quarrels make good reading even if their relevance to the Charge is obscure. The emphasis on these great men has reinforced the view that their blunders caused the Charge, although the weakness of the explanation is highlighted by the consistent inability of historians to decide which great man was to blame – Lord Raglan, Lord Lucan, Lord Cardigan, or Captain Nolan. One recent scholarly account concludes that the only thing that is certain is that the name of the blameworthy officer ends with –an.[1]

At the time, the Commander-in-Chief of the forces at home in London came to a different conclusion about the causes of the Charge. His long-forgotten explanation seems to be increasingly borne out by eyewitness accounts from more humble participants, which are still being discovered in private archives even today. It is time to give all eyewitness accounts their due weight, and at the same time to evaluate the Charge in the context of new discoveries about the Crimean War. This approach shows that the Charge was an attack on the Russian cavalry, not on the guns, and it achieved all of the important objectives set by those responsible for it.

The basic facts of the Charge are that a large Russian army was facing the outnumbered British and French defenders of Balaclava, having cap-tured some guns from the Allies earlier in the day. Lord Raglan believed incorrectly that the Russians were retiring with the captured guns, and sent Captain Nolan with a message to the cavalry commander, Lord Lucan, to attack the Russians and prevent them from removing their trophies. The cavalry attacked, but the Russians were not retiring and were ready for them. 110 of the 660 participants of the Light Brigade were killed.

To understand why the Charge took place it is necessary to recreate the mind-set of the junior officers and other ranks of the Light Brigade, not just that of the titled generals. To take a simple example from the stanzas quoted above, it is quite clear that all the generals knew that the order was to capture some guns, and that the order was ill-considered (even Lord Raglan, who sent it, admitted in his official despatch on the battle that the Russians were not retreating after all, as he had thought). But it is almost certain that not one of the other ranks, nor even any of their officers apart from Captain Nolan and the generals, knew that the order mentioned guns or that it was obviously inappropriate. They knew that an order had arrived from on high, but the most they were told was that they were to attack the Russians in front of them. So what did they think the Charge was all about, and did their different perception influence events? If we look carefully at their reminiscences we can see that they were obeying a quite different, more sensible order that they believed had been given. Their eagerness to do so was what persuaded their generals to forget the official order and to give them their head.

The rejection of Great Man History is politically correct these days. Nevertheless, it is very productive in this case and is a good illustration of what can emerge if one starts with the assumption that great men do not always have full control of those under them. One then has to look for causes outside the hierarchical exchange of orders and protests by which great men register their supposed importance. It emerges that at Balaclava the other ranks made the decisions, as so often in this war.

INSIDE THE MINDS OF THE LIGHT BRIGADE

It was hard to get into the British cavalry. You generally had to have had some civilian work involving horses – as a groom, perhaps. The fortunate recruit was eventually matched to a horse that became his own – a horse which was often more expensive and powerful than his employer in civilian life would have owned. Trooper and mount trained together and took care of each other in luxurious conditions that would have shamed most private stables. The training in manoeuvring in formation was rigorous and scientific, the horses being submitted to sustained gunfire. Each training session culminated with a charge, the most precise and effective form of land warfare at the time – equivalent in complexity to bringing a fleet of sailing ships into battle. 'The whole system was devoted to a single end: the rapid placing of a line of cavalry in position for one swift devastating assault upon a wavering enemy.'[2] At the canter and the gallop, over several hundred yards of broken terrain, the charging squadron of British cavalrymen rode twenty-four abreast maintaining a distance of only six inches knee to knee. The line was not straight; it was trained to keep a slight arrowhead formation so as to better penetrate the enemy. The charge was not designed to kill because mass slaughter was not yet the norm in battle. It was designed rather to break the enemy's line or square with a flying wedge, and to frighten him off the battlefield.

No cinema recreation of a charge could ever capture the precision of the manoeuvre as practiced in the heyday of the cavalry; like the handling a fleet of ships of the line, it is a lost art. And now that we have come to regard cavalry as rather ornamental, and seen so many horses fall suddenly during cinematic charges, we need to be reminded of another characteristic that made the cavalry as daunting as today's armoured vehicles. Wounded horses do not fall when hit, as men tend to do out of a desire for self-preservation. Once they have been trained to ignore explosions, horses do not fear lance, sabre, bullet, shell or cannonball. Anyone who has hunted game knows that animals go on running and fighting when they are dying, because they do not know they are even wounded. This relative invulnerability helps to make a cavalry charge especially fearsome.

The 2,000 or so men of the Light and Heavy Cavalry Brigades camped on the plain outside Balaclava on 25 October 1854 did not see much hope of putting their valuable training to work. They had not seen any action worthy of the name. The Heavy Brigade had only recently arrived, and the Light Brigade had not been allowed to fight at the Alma or at the first encounter with the Russians at the Bulganak. They knew that there was no glorious role for the British cavalry in a continued siege of Sebastopol. They had been reduced to patrolling no man's land and carrying letters between one part of the camp and another. They would have agreed with the many senior strategists who wanted Raglan to change the emphasis of the campaign and attack the Russian Army in the field outside Sebastopol where he could exploit the superiority of his cavalry and infantry. The failed bombardment of the week before, which had opened with superb confidence that it would lead to immediate capitulation and then fizzled out, seemed to strengthen the argument for a new strategy. The infantry had already shown at the Alma that they were immeasurably superior to their Russian counterparts if used in the open country, but the cavalry was still untested. 'What do we want with cavalry here?' asked a staff officer who did not share the view of many regimental officers on the need to meet the Russians in the open again, as at the Alma. 'We are not going to leave this [place] till Sebastopol is taken.'[3]

The cavalry's living conditions in front of Balaclava were wretched. There had been no tents at all for the Light Brigade in their first three weeks in the Crimea, and now there were only enough for half their number. The rest, if not on duty, slept out in the cold and rain with a cape, a blanket, and an oilskin.[4] Their uniforms were filthy and threadbare, their sabres and carbines rusty, their fine horses already suffering from the effects of starvation.[5]

The relative neglect of the cavalry shows in their medical statistics. More than 150 of the Light Brigade (initially 1,477 strong) had already died of disease in four months of idleness. Hundreds were on the sick list, and in the previous month alone 4 per cent of the entire brigade had died of disease – a significantly higher proportion than in the army as a whole. The troopers did not need the hindsight of statistics – they were watching their comrades die in droves. Of those present that day, only one in six would be killed in the Charge but one in four of the survivors would die of cholera, typhoid, dysentery, frostbite, or scurvy before the war was over.[6] At the time, sickness was at its peak and the prospects of death from disease must have looked even worse than that – if the September death rate had continued nearly two thirds would have died by the end of the war.

In those days, the financial prospects for a soldier's family depended on whether he fell in action. If he was fortunate enough to receive an arm or leg wound that responded to amputation (almost the only treatment available for serious wounds) he could expect a lifetime pension, equivalent to winning the lottery. If he died in action, the regiments' and Lloyds' discretionary funds were also quite generous. But there was no provision yet for the families of soldiers who died of disease. This is understandable when soldiers were assumed to be no more susceptible than civilians of the same class to the epidemic diseases that were responsible for so much of the mortality at that time. The cholera, for example, was at the time of the Charge of the Light Brigade ravaging some districts of England as mercilessly as it was the cavalry camp. In either case the widows and children of breadwinners could expect no relief outside the workhouse.

Against this dispiriting background, it can be imagined that there was some excitement in the cavalry camp when on the morning of 25 October it was discovered that a newly arrived Russian Army under General Liprandi had the temerity to challenge the British to a field engagement in front of Balaclava. Here was an unexpected opportunity for the cavalry to show Raglan that there was a second arm that, like the infantry, could make mincemeat of their Russian counterparts in the field. An opportunity to cheat the cholera through a more glorious death, and to make use of their mounts before the dwindling forage ran out entirely.

After an exhausting forced march of 400 miles from the shores of the Danube, 16,000 Russian troops had advanced on Balaclava from the east before dawn. Between them and the port was a five-mile wide plain with a low ridge running towards them in the middle. Atop this ridge lay a handful of small fortifications manned by Turkish troops, which one after the other fell to the advancing Russians. This was the first layer of defence for Balaclava. Behind the fortifications were encamped the two brigades of cavalry under Lord Lucan. This was the second line of defence. Behind them, a regiment of 550 Highlanders, two regiments of Turks, 1,000 Royal Marines and some field artillery. The final line of defence was a British frigate moored in Balaclava Harbour with its guns facing broadside on to the gorge down which attackers would have to come.

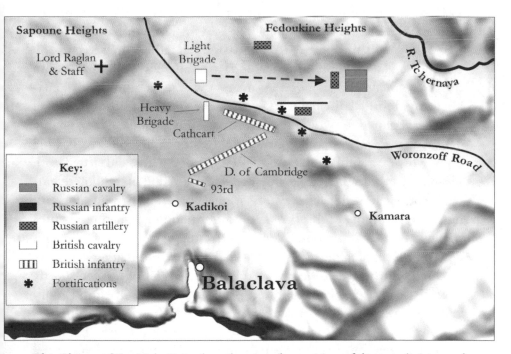

The Charge of the Light Brigade – showing the position of the two divisions of British infantry whose commander (Cathcart) disobeyed the order to attack.

As the outer fortifications fell, the Cavalry Division were ordered to mount and hurriedly put away their breakfasts and tobacco pipes. Lord Raglan arrived at the edge of the plateau, overlooking the plain, and sent an order by mounted messenger to the cavalry to draw back from their camp, towards the port. They did so, and remained facing the enemy. The Light Brigade watched from close by as their outnumbered Turkish allies, overtaken in their flight by mounted Cossacks, were mercilessly cut down even when trying to surrender. "This we had to witness close in front of our squadrons" wrote Light Brigade Sergeant-Major Loy Smith "feeling the while that had a dozen or two of us been sent out numbers of these poor fellows might have been saved".[7] Then he recounts that they watched as the same Cossacks insolently rode in among the sick horses that had been left tied up there and began to mutilate the British animals with their lances.[8] To the highly trained British cavalrymen, the sight of their sick horses being wantonly mutilated by the Cossacks would have been hard to bear. And again they were not allowed to intervene.

There could be no greater contrast than between Cossack horseman and the British cavalry trooper. A modern writer has described the Cossack in unflattering terms, 'The Cossack's father provided his son with horse, saddlery, uniform, sabre, and lance; only his carbine came from the government. He was a frontiersman – cautious, cunning, not amenable to rigid formal discipline, self-reliant and tough, all the attributes of a soldier required for scouting and to harass, hinder and delay an enemy. The Cossack wore what he pleased, seldom groomed his scruffy little pony which was broken in from the wild steppe herds, and shared with his mount an extraordinary endurance. Their method of fighting resembled that of the wolf pack, never charging home on a strong adversary but always hanging on his flanks waiting for an unguarded moment, a sign of weakness or a wound, and then dashing in for an easy kill.'[9] This description certainly fits with the Cossacks' behaviour that morning.

One Light Brigade officer who took part, in a letter written shortly afterwards to his mother, identified rivalry between the British cavalry and the Cossacks as the principle cause of the Charge. 'Now to understand why we did this rash and stupid act, you must know that lately there has been some stupid chaff about the Cavalry being afraid of the Cossacks, and Nolan made some remarks about it to Lord Lucan.'[10] This does not make it clear whether the writer thought Lucan's own reaction to the slander was the cause of the Charge, but there can be no doubt that the other ranks were irritated by the 'stupid chaff'. A month before, at the first skirmish with the Russians, the Cossacks had derided the Light Brigade when they had retreated instead of fighting (the Heavy Brigade had not yet arrived in the Crimea). Worse, *The Times* had published W. H. Russell's account of the Cossacks jeering at the British Light Brigade on that occasion, 'It was much regretted that our cavalry force was so miserably deficient, for if we had been even two to three we could have readily disposed of the vapouring Lancers [Cossacks] on the hill, who had irritated the men very much by their derisive cries when our skirmishers retired.' The footsore British infantry had evidently relished this comeuppance of the luxuriously mounted and accoutred Light Brigade, the strangely modern-sounding sneer of one infantry-man having already been quoted, 'Serve them bloody right, silly peacock bastards'.

Copies of the *Times* containing Russell's account of the humiliation of the Light Brigade would have been eagerly received in the Crimea just before the Charge, and in St Petersburg even earlier.[11] One wonders what the British cavalry thought of Russell's assessment that one trooper of the Light Brigade was only worth one-and-a-half Cossacks. Russell might not have been the most popular visitor to the cavalry camp at that time.

Now, on the morning of the charge, the British cavalry were forced to watch for nearly an hour while the Cossacks committed atrocities under their noses. It was as if the Cossacks were mocking them again, just as they had when the Light Brigade had retreated a month earlier. The men of the Light Brigade yearned to be allowed to ride out and take revenge on the marauding Cossacks, but were not allowed to.

For an hour and a quarter after they captured the fortifications, the Russians had the plain of Balaclava almost to themselves. The British cavalry were held back under the Sapoune Heights on the western edge of the plain, and a small infantry detachment of which the backbone was the 93rd regiment of Highlanders was drawn up in front of the landward entry to Balaclava Harbour. Two divisions of British infantry had been sent for, but it was to take them two hours to march down to the plain from the camps on the Sapoune Heights around Sebastopol. Balaclava seemed rather vulnerable now that the Russians were in possession of the Woronzoff Road and the fortifications that lay along it. It was up to the Russians to make the next move.

The Russian move was predictable, given the nearly open goal presented by Balaclava. Lord Raglan did predict it, and in the nick of time. He sent half of the British cavalry eastwards to strengthen the immediate defences of Balaclava just at the moment when a force of 2,000 Russian cavalry swept over the Woronzoff Road heading south towards the vulnerable port. The British cavalry detachment, consisting of most of the Heavy Brigade and outnumbered at least two to one, turned and charged from a standing start, uphill, and halted the attacking force. Meanwhile, a detachment of 400 Russian cavalry had broken off from the main raiding body and headed towards Kadikoi, apparently unaware that the 93rd Highlanders were lying prone behind a hill in their way. The 93rd's commander Sir Colin Campbell, who at the Alma had absurdly urged his troops not to fire their Minié rifles until they were within a yard of the enemy, tried to hold them in check on this occasion too. He had made them lie down because they were under artillery fire, but they stood up when the Russian cavalry charged and Campbell angrily shouted at them '93rd! 93rd! Damn all that eagerness!'[12] They ignored him and the front rank let fly with their rifles while the cavalry were still 600 yards off. Further evidence that they acted on their own initiative comes from a report that Campbell had to hastily withdraw when his men began firing, having been sitting on his horse in front of them as if in Hyde Park.[13] The rear rank then let off another volley when the Russians were 250 yards away. The Russian cavalry veered off without contact and tried another charge from the flank. At this General Campbell remarked to a junior officer that the Russian commander knew his business. His infantry, however, knew their business better; the company at the end of the line pivoted round to meet the Russian charge and sent them away with another volley of Minié 'thimbles'.

At the Alma, the Minié rifle had proved that field artillery firing grapeshot against infantry had suddenly become obsolete, and now the 93rd had shown that cavalry too was obsolete against infantry armed with the Minié. It is heretical to say that this tactical breakthrough was brought about by the other ranks in the face of a disapproving commander. The standard view is that General Campbell's 'Damn all that eagerness' was not a rebuke to his men for firing their rifles at long range, but was instead his way of preventing them from advancing against the enemy.[14] But there is not a shred of evidence that the men were contemplating a bayonet charge at a huge body of cavalry galloping towards them, and it would have been lunacy indeed. Historians are sometimes prepared to go to extreme lengths to make the actions of great men appear to be relevant to heroic events.

These particular heroic events, now known as the Charge of the Heavy Brigade and the Thin Red Line respectively, were played out in front of a glumly stationary Light Brigade which had not been properly in action in the four months since it left England. Lord Cardigan inexplicably declined to order the Light Brigade to attack the Russian cavalry when the latter's charge had been halted by the outnumbered Heavy Brigade only a few minutes ride away. It would have been the perfect use of cavalry to make 'one swift devastating assault upon a wavering enemy'. Sergeant-Major Loy Smith described how the Light Brigade were forced to watch for more than ten minutes while their comrades were struggling against fearful odds at a distance that could be covered in a fraction of that time. 'I am of the opinion,' he added, 'that nothing but the strict discipline under which we were held prevented us breaking loose to assist our comrades of the Heavies.'[15] The Russian Hussar cavalry were accompanied by Cossack outriders on their flanks, who fanned out as was their custom looking for defeated enemy stragglers.[16] These Cossacks now had to withdraw as best they could from a dangerously exposed position between the Light and Heavy Brigades. These were the same Cossacks who had previously jeered at the Light Brigade for refusing to fight. The same Cossacks who caused the British cavalry to be mocked even by their comrades; these Cossacks were temporarily at the Light Brigade's mercy. Captain Morris, commanding the 17th Lancers, rode forward and without disguising his anger repeatedly demanded that Lord Cardigan order the Light Brigade, or if not his regiment alone, to charge the defeated enemy. Cardigan refused, Morris slapped his saluting sword against his leg in a temper, and their quarrel was embarrassingly public. The Cossacks escaped.

But did the troopers of the Light Brigade really sit so placidly? In view of the tendency of historians and others to defend the chain of command and to censor the more anarchic behaviour of the common soldier, it is worth looking at all the evidence. And not all the evidence bears out Sergeant-Major Loy Smith's loyal assertion that discipline was preserved in the face of Russian provocation. A Private John Doyle of the Light Brigade wrote in his published reminiscences, 'The Light Brigade were not well pleased when they saw the Heavy Brigade charge and were not let go to their assistance. They stood up in their stirrups, and shouted "Why are we kept here?" and at the same moment broke up and dashed back through our lines, for the purpose of following the Russian retreat, but they had got too far for us to overtake them.'It has evidently been too difficult to reconcile this evidence with the accepted view of the Light Brigade's unwavering discipline, and Doyle's version has never previously been quoted.

Doyle's account of Light Brigade troopers mutinously deserting to the front is supported by other evidence. Assistant Surgeon William Cattell, attached to the Heavy Brigade wrote, 'When the regiment was rallied and reformed hurriedly, expecting to be charged again, several other troopers fell in with our ranks, amongst them two privates of the 11th Hussars [i.e. the Light Brigade] who must have been doing a bit on their own hook.' The only historian to have quoted this unpublished account gives as his opinion that the wayward troopers came from the sick tents nearby, this presumably being less subversive of military history than if they deserted the Light Brigade ranks and got away with it.[17] No courts-martial are recorded.

The fact is that if one pulls together all the evidence, instead of selecting only the official orders, junior ranks 'doing a bit on their own hook' throughout this war seem to have been widely tolerated and equally widely denied. Lord Cardigan, for example, later swore blind that Captain Morris never argued with him over the Light Brigade's failure to attack, saying that Morris did not 'commit such an irregularity'.[18] Sergeant-Major Loy Smith assured his readers that the men under his command did not 'break loose'. Such denials make the Light Brigade seem to be just an assemblage of obedient automata, ready to go or stay, live or die, at the command of the rich aristocrats who commanded it. The reality is that it was a near-mutinous fighting machine, maddened by cholera and the appalling living conditions and by the disrespect shown to it by commanders, comrades, enemies, and the newspapers at home.

The Light Brigade watched intently as the Russians rode slowly away from them, eastwards down the long sloping part of the plain of Balaclava that is called the North Valley; north of the central ridge where the Russians had captured the fortifications at dawn. The Cossacks and regular cavalry stopped over a mile away and faced about, half-beaten although not by the Light Brigade. The Light Brigade could see from the colour of the horses and of the uniforms, even at that distance and without a telescope, which regiments there were. Some of them may have been able to see the battery of eight heavy field guns that the Russian cavalry had halted behind and which provided them with an illusion of safety. For two long hours, both sides eyed each other while columns of British and French infantry wended their way down from the plateau to take up fighting positions on the plain of Balaclava.

INSIDE THE MINDS OF THE GENERALS

Not much evidence is to hand about the state of mind of the Russian generals at this stage of the Battle of Balaclava. It is odd that they stayed put for two hours, faced by a tiny force of defenders, and allowed a much larger force to be brought into position against them. That is a mystery that may yield to future research on the Russian side, but it is the British generals whose state of mind is particularly relevant to the Charge of the Light Brigade. Were they also simply obedient to the orders of greater men, i.e. Lord Raglan, the Commander-in-Chief watching them from the plateau overlooking the battlefield, or did they share their own subordinates' particularly British readiness to act independently of such orders? If we put ourselves in the position of Lucan and Cathcart (the infantry commander) that day it is not hard to see that Raglan's orders must have been a puzzle to them from the start.

At the Battle of Balaclava Raglan started to issue orders in a very uncharacteristic way. Historians have not discussed why, at the three battles of Alma, Balaclava, and Inkerman, Raglan adopted three radically different management styles which show a definite evolutionary progression. Raglan had never commanded men in the field before this war and seems to have been learning on the job. At the first battle, the Alma, he had given no orders at all except to tell the divisional generals to advance, and that only when prodded by the French and his own generals. After that he had absented himself and remained incommunicado throughout the entire battle. This behaviour led to so much criticism of 'lack of generalship' later that one can assume that his divisional commanders probably complained at the time. Now it could not be a coincidence that at the next battle, Balaclava, Raglan issued orders thick and fast from his distant vantage point on the plateau, most of them ill-considered. During the third battle, at Inkerman, Raglan reduced his orders to a minimum again but remained near the centre of the action. It would appear that because of the trouble caused by his lack of control at Alma and his disastrous attempts at control at Balaclava he decided to seek the middle ground at Inkerman.

To someone like Lord Lucan, recipient of many ill-considered orders from Lord Raglan at Balaclava, the contrast with Raglan's hands-off approach at the Alma must have been notable. If Lucan had been of a cynical turn of mind, he might have concluded that Raglan was being deliberately obtuse so as to demonstrate that criticism of his Alma performance was unjustified (especially as that battle had been a resounding success). But Lucan appears to have been a relatively straightforward thinker, not to say simple, and it is more likely he thought Raglan was making an honest effort to improve. Either way, Lucan would be motivated to take the orders with a pinch of salt as coming from someone who was overreacting to previous criticism. That is to say, he would be inclined to discount them as most of the other generals did. In fact, out of the blizzard of orders issued that day by Raglan, the one that led to the Charge of the Light Brigade was the most obviously ill-informed but was one of the few that any of Raglan's subordinates made any pretence of obeying. We should probably therefore look for reasons for that obedience other than a determination to follow orders, which has been central to the explanation of the Charge put forward by modern historians.

For a start, half of the infantry almost did not arrive at Balaclava because Sir George Cathcart at first refused to obey an order from Lord Raglan to move his Fourth Division down to the plain. Cathcart was to be killed two weeks later in a suicidal personal charge at the Russian positions and did not have a chance to react to various uncomplimentary anecdotes of his actions at Balaclava, so it would be wrong to accept them as gospel. But according to the prevailing story Lord Raglan's aide-de-camp had to deliver the summons several times and then decline to return to Lord Raglan with Cathcart's rejection of the order before Cathcart would move.

Then, when Raglan sent the order to Lucan to withdraw the cavalry from the front line and station it under the ridge of the plateau, Lucan was so bemused by the confused order that he made the messenger move the cavalry to the spot that the messenger thought it referred to. Very soon afterwards Lucan saw that Raglan, too, recognised the inappropriateness of the order because he sent another order returning most of the cavalry to where it had been before. It was in obeying this order to return that the Heavy Brigade was attacked by the Russian cavalry and performed their own now not very famous Charge.

Then at around ten o'clock Lucan received an order from Raglan and disobeyed it outright. Raglan ordered Lucan to advance the Cavalry Division and look for an opportunity to recover the fortifications which had been lost at dawn. In this order Raglan told Lucan that the British infantry was on the way. Lucan waited for the infantry to appear, and by 10.30a.m. the two infantry divisions had at last arrived from Sebastopol with Cathcart's trailing in the rear. Lord Raglan sent the other division further south towards Balaclava to join the 93rd Highlanders in the defence of the port. He sent orders to Cathcart to advance from west to east along the line of redoubts, approximately following the Woronzoff road, and to drive the Russians out of each of the redoubts as he went. Lord Lucan sent a messenger to General Cathcart to find out what the infantry's plans were. Cathcart replied untruthfully that he had received no orders to attack the fortifications. Knowing General Cathcart's aversion to Raglan, and having in his hand a written order from Raglan hinting that he had ordered the infantry divisions to advance, Lucan must have suspected that Cathcart was disobeying Lord Raglan's orders.[19] Lucan did not obey Raglan's order to advance either, and merely stationed the cavalry in an offensive position – the Light Brigade to the north of the fortifications and the Heavy Brigade to the south.

Another important order from the High Command was also disobeyed at this time, according to one account. Sir Richard Airey, the quartermaster-general who was with Raglan and writing orders for him, sent an order to an artillery commander to withdraw his battery from near the 'Thin Red Line' (the 93rd Regiment), where it was hotly defending Balaclava, and place it to the rear where the Light Brigade had been sitting out the battle for so long. This order caused consternation at the front and was quickly countermanded by Sir Colin Campbell, the commander of the 93rd.[20]

Cathcart, Lucan, and Campbell therefore all disobeyed orders, and received no known reprimand or criticism from above for this behaviour afterwards. Cathcart's disobedience may, however, have had something to do with his pointless death two weeks later. His orders were to recapture the fortifications, and his failure to do so has been widely excused on the grounds that they had proved impossible to hold for long. This excuse is flimsy and misses the point: the recapture of the fortifications, even if they were not to be held (and they had in fact served their delaying purpose), would have been the first step in the defeat of Liprandi's army which had lost the initiative and was now stalled in no man's land. The cavalry are known to have complained bitterly later about the inaction of the infantry, and despite the face-saving public excuses it is likely that criticism of Cathcart in the army was widespread.

After nearly an hour of waiting and seeing his orders ignored, Raglan thought he saw the Russians preparing to retreat and removing the captured British guns from the fortifications. He, therefore, told Airey to send the notorious 'fourth order' to Lucan telling him to attack immediately to prevent the guns being removed. This time, Raglan said nothing about the infantry helping the cavalry. The officer delivering the (partially verbal) order, Captain Nolan, changed it en route so that it became an order to charge the Russian position directly in front of the Light Brigade. Lucan knew that in that direction he would be exposed to flanking small-arms and artillery fire from both sides, and from in front.

The written part of the order read, 'Lord Raglan wishes the cavalry to advance rapidly to the front – follow the enemy and try to prevent the enemy carrying away the guns – Troop Horse Artillery may accompany – French cavalry is on your left. Immediate.' This order was ill-considered for many reasons, for example the trivial objective and the false premise that the Russians were retreating and could be 'followed'. It is not clear from Lucan's accounts afterwards which of these clues made the order's 'absurdity and uselessness' apparent to him at the time, as he claimed some months later.[21] It is not clear either whether he actually read the order to his subordinate Lord Cardigan, the so-far dilatory commander of the Light Brigade with whom he was on the worst of terms. But it is clear from both their accounts that for once in their lives, on the subject of this order they were in compete agreement: to attack was madness.

Why did they, then, act on it? The explanation accepted by historians and the general public until now is based purely on speculation. That is that Lucan and Cardigan hated each other so much that they could not bear to discuss the situation further and find a way out of it. Naturally, if this were true neither of them could be expected to admit it, and the explanations that they themselves gave – in which they were quite consistent with each other – would deserve to be ignored by historians as they have been. The speculative explanation also has a certain robustness because of the impossibility of disproving it and because of its soap-opera plot. The explanation was originally put forward by Cecil Woodham Smith who did not try to disguise its tentative nature, 'had [Lucan and Cardigan] not detested each other so bitterly, had they been able to examine the order [from Raglan] together and discuss its meaning, the Light Brigade might have been saved.' Presumably, Woodham Smith thought that if Lucan had shown the written order to Cardigan and if they had discussed it longer than they actually did something new might have emerged that made it possible for them to do what they and the other generals had been doing all day – ignore Raglan's inappropriate new-style management. That assumes that Lucan and Cardigan would have been in trouble with their superiors if they had second-guessed an order from their distant commander just because they thought they knew better. This assumption is at the root of the speculative half-explanation that the highly skilled, intelligent, and independent-minded Light Brigade behaved like the apocryphal Zulu *impi* that marched off a cliff in obedience to orders.

The controversy about why Lucan acted on such an absurd order destroyed his army career within months. The argument raged in both Houses of Parliament and in the courts, with Lucan vociferously defending his failure to exercise his discretion and disregard the order when he knew it to be wrong. Never once in his struggle to clear his name did Lucan claim that he would have been reprimanded or otherwise officially sanctioned if he hadn't obeyed the order. Instead, he said in a letter to Lord Raglan that he obeyed it because not to do so would have 'exposed me and the cavalry to aspersions against which we might have difficulty in defending ourselves'.[22] By referring to 'me and the cavalry' he was claiming to be defending the interests of the other ranks as well as his own. As to who might cast these 'aspersions', Lucan did not say. But the Commander-in-Chief of the Forces at the Horse Guards, Lord Hardinge, had his own view about whose 'aspersions' Lord Lucan personally feared. 'Surely,' said Lord Hardinge in the House of Lords, 'when the noble earl talks of possible aspersions, it shows that his decision to attack was taken … upon the fear which he entertained of aspersions from *his officers and soldiers*'.[23]

Elsewhere, Hardinge criticised Lucan's alleged failure to show the order to Cardigan, and maintained that if he had done so Cardigan would have talked him out of obeying. In this detail, Hardinge's explanation is similar to Woodham Smith's. The difference is that Woodham Smith attributed Lucan's lack of consultation to mutual detestation, while Hardinge attributed it to pressure from the troops. Hardinge's explanation is reasonable. Lucan had already reprimanded Cardigan for failing to bring the Light Brigade to the aid of the out-numbered Heavy Brigade earlier in the day. He could hardly fail to be aware of the dissatisfaction and mutinous tendency in the Light Brigade's ranks because of Cardigan's inertia. Lucan's determination to put things right fits with Sergeant-Major Loy Smith's cryptic observation that if the Light Brigade had been allowed to go to the help of the Heavies, the subsequent Charge of the Light Brigade would in all probability never have taken place.

As for Lord Cardigan's explanation of why he was not to blame for obeying Lucan, he came close to admitting that he feared the effect on his men if he did not do so. 'I hope you will not blame me,' he told Lord Raglan, 'for I received the order to attack from my superior officer [Lucan] *in front of the troops*'.[24] No doubt another sword-slapping tirade from the furious Captain Morris, more catcalls from the ranks, or other 'irregularities' were things Cardigan wanted to avoid at all costs.

These are the only explanations offered by Lucan and Cardigan for their widely criticised failure to ignore an order which they both admit-ted they knew to be wrong. Both imply that it was the attitude of the men of the Light Brigade that determined their choice. Lord Hardinge for one believed them, but historians have ignored their testimony.

WHAT WERE THEY CHARGING AT?

They allowed the Light Brigade to charge. But what did the Light Brigade charge at? This question has never been asked before.

> 'Forward, the Light Brigade!
> Charge for the guns' he said.

So spoke Tennyson, ignorant of precisely who had said what to whom about the supposed object of the Charge. The context of the verse how-ever implies that the troopers were ordered to attack the guns, and that they knew that it was a blunder. This is very far from the truth and completely misrepresents the information available to the Light Brigade. There is strong evidence that nobody told the Light Brigade what and why to attack. Lucan definitely knew, and Cardigan and Nolan may have known, that an order had been given to detain some guns but they did not bother to explain this to any of their subordinates. Cardigan did not even tell the officer whom he told to lead the second line, and asked merely for his 'best support' in whatever was going to happen. Probably the only one who may have known the terms of Raglan's order and who reached 'the guns' was Cardigan, and it may not be a coincidence that he stopped at the guns and then headed for home, clearly seen by his men who showed no inclination to follow him as they should have done. The rest of his Light Brigade continued on *their* Charge without him, the charge they had been plotting all morning, the one that they had assumed the order gave them permission to make, the order that *should* have been given a long time ago, the order to charge the living daylights out of the Russian cavalry and most of all the Cossacks, who were sheltering behind the guns. The undelivered, sensible order that the Light Brigade invented and executed with the most brilliant results imaginable. Two of the five regiments avoided the guns entirely, going straight past into the cavalry behind. It is true that some men from the other regiments stopped and tried to seize the now deserted guns as trophies, but Cardigan's second-in-command, Lt-Col. Mayow, quickly rounded them up and made them charge the Russian cavalry instead.

One can speculate on why Lucan and Cardigan did not waste time explaining Raglan's order to their subordinates. They may have decided that the mistaken order was irrelevant to the mission that they knew that their brigade wanted to accomplish, that of scaring the Russian cavalry off the battlefield. But it is not speculation to say that at least one very important witness and participant believed that they had been ordered to charge the Russian cavalry, not to recover guns. 'They sent us down to charge the Enemy's cavalry, flanked by 2 fires [artillery batteries]'.[25] These are the words of Captain Morris, the gung-ho commander of the 17th Lancers who had mutinously rattled his sabre at his dilatory superior Lord Cardigan, words written only three days after the Charge. Morris was very badly wounded in the Charge and was carried from the battlefield unconscious and sent onboard ship to recover. In this letter (which has only very recently come to light) Morris does not even mention the terms of the real order. It is likely that his relative isolation and his injuries had prevented him from finding out about it; even three days after the battle he assumes that it was an order to attack the Russian cavalry.

Although many participants describe the order which Nolan gave to Lucan, the terms of which became notorious soon after the battle, it is unlikely that any of them had any more knowledge of it at the time they charged than did Morris. It is probable that the most any of the subordinates knew for certain at the time was that a messenger had galloped from Lord Raglan with an order; that the order seemed to call for them to attack, and that their commanders had hesitated and then had acquiesced. Private Mitchell wrote, 'we now felt certain that there was something cut out for us, but Lords Lucan and Cardigan both appeared to demur at the order'. Only one or two participants make any claim to have overheard the order at the time, and their accounts do not tally with what is known about the wording of the order and its mode of delivery. It may be that they overheard Nolan delivering an earlier, purely verbal, reminder to Lucan to retake the 'heights', not the guns, and assumed afterwards that it had been the fatal fourth order.[26]

The men, after all, had been waiting for an order to charge the cavalry. The Light Brigade had been closely watching the Russian cavalry since being prevented from charging them with the Heavies. A Light Brigade dragoon confirms that the escaped Russian cavalry were in the Brigade's sights, writing that before the order to charge was given he saw 'their broken horse again gathering behind the battery'.[27] These were the Russian cavalry who had been broken by the Heavy Brigade charge while the Lights chafed at their commander's refusal to let them join in. They included the Cossacks who, *The Times* had announced two weeks before, had jeered at the Light Brigade for refusing to fight, causing one British infantryman to declare unkindly 'serve them bloody right, silly peacock bastards'. This was the Cossack cavalry who now had such contempt for the Light Brigade that they had speared defenceless Turkish soldiers, who were begging to surrender, under the brigade's noses. This was the Cossack rabble – unworthy of the name of cavalry – who had ridden into the British camp and mutilated sick horses tied up in the lines while the Light Brigade again foolishly looked on from close by. The Light Brigade believed that this half-defeated rabble were now delivered into the Light Brigade's hands by the direct order of Lord Raglan. A frightened, wavering, enemy: the perfect target for a cavalry charge.

Lucan and Cardigan knew what the men were thinking. They could be in no doubt that if they refused to allow the Light Brigade to attack after an order from Raglan, there would be at the very least a further breakdown of discipline. The cholera had got worse since a Light Brigade officer had written two months ago 'the men and officers are getting daily more disgusted with their fate. They do nothing but bury their comrades. They say loudly that they have not been brought out to fight, but to waste away and die in this country of cholera and fever.' In the interim, at the glorious (for the infantry) battle of the Alma, Lucan had wanted to charge the retreating enemy cavalry, four times as numerous as the British and in much better physical condition, but Raglan had forbidden it. The Light Brigade knew that numerical odds of four to one against were perfectly acceptable, and had blamed Lucan for the failure to engage. All they had been able to do was to capture a hundred Russian prisoners, and then they had been ordered to let these prisoners go.[28] The troopers had now been ordered, for the first time, to fight properly; Lord Raglan had, apparently, overruled the hesitancy of their commanders. Lucan listened to Cardigan's arguments against the Charge and, possibly for the only time in both their lives, meekly agreed with him. 'I know it,' said Lucan, 'but Lord Raglan will have it.' What should Lucan have done? Called all the officers forward and explained to them that the order did not actually entitle them to attack the Russian cavalry, and that it appeared to have been issued by mistake? That if they sat this one out they would probably get their chance later? Lucan was trapped, and the only way out was to give the order to attack and leave the troops to choose the target.

To judge from the behaviour of a few who seemed in danger of missing the action, it was a popular decision. The sight of the Cavalry Division preparing to move incited a number of disqualified individuals to leave the camp and join the Light Brigade's ranks after Lucan gave the fateful order. Two prisoners held on minor charges escaped from the guard tent, took horses, and joined their comrades. The butcher of the 17th Lancers who was slaughtering cattle dropped his poleaxe, stripped the body of a dead Heavy Brigade trooper of its accoutrements, jumped on the dead trooper's horse and galloped into the ranks in his bloodstained overalls carrying two purloined swords. Lord Lucan himself questioned this outlandish personage as to his intentions, and the butcher replied that he was 'going to have a slap at the Russians'. Lucan told him, 'Go in then, and fight like the devil.' Further evidence comes from the case of the man who was placed under arrest after the order was given. The sick CO of the 8th Hussars had risen from his bed at the prospect of a fight, and after joining his regiment grumpily placed under arrest a man who was illicitly smoking in the ranks. The man was deprived of his sword belt and weapons and ordered to fall out; he refused, rode in the Charge completely unarmed, and was killed.[29] The story of the trooper named Fox, however, is probably an invention. One participant says that Fox was on duty in the camp but when the order to advance was given he rushed to his horse and joined the Charge; on his return he was court-martialled for leaving his post and sentenced to fifty lashes. After the first twenty five the colonel suspended the remainder over the protests of Fox himself who said he did not want to be under any obligation to his CO.[30] This story seems unlikely to be true because the records do not show a court-martial at this time, although they do show that Fox had been court-martialled and flogged on an earlier occasion for going AWOL with a horse.

Every mount available was now taken. The Russian cavalry, thinking themselves safe in their little bolt-hole, were about to get a surprise.

A SWIFT, DEVASTATING ASSAULT

'The Light Brigade will advance – walk – trot.'

It was a downward-sloping valley made in heaven for a cavalry charge, soft underfoot and clear of any obstructions. It was about 2,000 yards to the enemy's position, and the Light Brigade would take about seven minutes to cover the distance, with artillery batteries and musket fire pounding them from both sides and from in front.

The determination of a handful of troopers of the Light Brigade not to be left out of the Charge shows without doubt that these men at least were keen to attack the Russians. But was the whole Brigade so desperate as to justify a decision by Lucan to let it go? The reminiscences in general seem to show that there was great enthusiasm, but there are contrary voices. Many reminiscences were written long after the Charge and are probably influenced by subsequent attitudes; for example, by the portrayal of the Charge as a great blunder and by some criticism of the Light Brigade itself. On the other hand there could be some for whom distance and lucky survival lent enchantment to the memory, so that they tended to make light of the fears they had at the time. How typical were the feelings of Lieutenant Jolliffe who wrote to his father only three days after taking part in the Charge, 'The Light division (sic) accordingly got orders to advance & after emerging from the valley in which we had for some time been we could perceive the enemy's Cavalry about two miles off [Jolliffe was in the second line of regiments and may not have been able to see the Russian position as well as most of the Light Brigade] drawn up on the opposite hill. Away we trotted in high glee…'

There was one man who claimed much later that the men were *not* happy to charge. This was Private Pennington, who wrote in his memoirs in 1906 of hearing Cardigan's order that began the advance, 'We heard the words with incredulous amazement, for the madness of our errand was plain to the weakest judgement among us. The awful gravity of the moment can only be realised by those who were riding, as each one of us believed, to certain destruction.' If Pennington's recollection were true, it could invalidate the theory that Lucan and Cardigan took the otherwise inexplicable decision to attack in deference to the wishes of the men. But Pennington's retrospective claim to have known the feelings of the entire Light Brigade somewhat weakens his argument even as applied to himself. The same applies to Lieutenant Hutton who wrote, 'A child might have seen the trap that was laid for us, as every private dragoon did'.[31] If this were true one would expect the Light Brigade to ride into the trap at regulation speed so that their officers could halt them if the opposition was too strong, as cavalry were obsessively trained to do and as their comrades of the Heavy Brigade right behind them did when obeying the same order to attack. Most accounts of participants in the Charge do not describe their own feelings on being ordered to attack; it is perhaps surprising that whatever the truth they do not all make a similar claim to Pennington's which would have the effect of casting them as victims and exciting public sympathy.

The account of Private Grigg is more typical than Pennington's, giving a complacent account of the attitude of the Light Brigade's other ranks to the impending attack, 'I saw Captain Nolan, of the 15th Hussars, come galloping down from Lord Raglan to where Lord Lucan and Lord Cardigan were, and we knew then that there was something for us to do. Our men of the Light Brigade were the 17th Lancers, as fine a regiment as ever carried lances; the 8th Hussars, a nice lot of fellows, always ready for anything in the fighting way; the 11th Hussars, who all did their duty well; the 13th Light Dragoons, as good as any in the fight; and our 4th Light Dragoons, who were as ready for it as the others.' No victims here.[32] Pennington, the participant who claimed that the entire Light Brigade knew the Charge was mad, had by then become a famous Shakespearean actor, and the Charge may not have been the high point in his career as it was for others like Grigg. Neither man's distant view of his comrades' – or even his own – feelings can be entirely trusted.

More reliable would be the behaviour during the Charge. The whole Brigade speeded up much more quickly than regulations allowed, and historians have explained this by saying that they were trying to get through the flanking fire as quickly as possible. But there were other causes, according to participants. Two regiments led the Charge: the 13th Light Dragoons and the 17th Lancers. An officer in the former recorded that a man near him shouted to his neighbour, 'Come on; don't let those bastards [the 17th Lancers] get ahead of us'. And another officer confirms that the acceleration was at least partly due to the men's eagerness, 'On we went at a steady pace at first, and then we saw the Russian cavalry retiring, so all the men cheered and went on at a gallop'.[33]

The troopers themselves forced the pace despite Cardigan's attempts to hold them back to the regulation trot that would allow him to redirect them or cut short an overly impetuous rush – a common problem with cavalry where the horses become as excited as their riders. As Grigg fondly reminisced, 'The horses were as anxious to go as we were; mine snorted and vibrated with excitement.' Arguments still rage about whether bugle calls were ever made to increase the pace to a canter or a gallop, but there is wide agreement that if such signals were made they were unheard by many, unnecessary, and only sanctioned what was already happening. Pennington, the trooper who denied that his comrades were eager to charge, was resentful at what he said were allegations that the Light Brigade rode with mad recklessness, or that there was wildness in the pace. 'Nothing could have been steadier' he wrote; not an inaccurate statement on its own, but if he meant that Lord Cardigan was in control and could have stopped the rush at any moment to the gratitude of his men, he is flying in the face of the evidence. 'The time had come,' said Private Wightman of the 17th Lancers, 'when neither the commands nor the example of Lord Cardigan availed to restrain the pace of the Brigade; and when to maintain his position in advance, indeed, if he were to escape being ridden down, he had to let his charger out from the gallop [the military word for 'canter'] to the charge.' The fact is that it was the men's decision, conscious or unconscious, individual or governed by the mob, that made the advance unstoppable and this may be the strongest evidence that their mood was evident to Lucan when he allowed them to go. Lucan had no trouble reining in the Heavy Brigade when the shells began to fall among them. The Heavies had already won their glory with a charge that day on unfavourable ground against a superior enemy force, and wanted to live to dine out on the story. Lucan now ordered them to retire from the Charge after they had suffered a handful of dead from the batteries on the north side of the valley. He had some difficulty in halting Brigadier-General Scarlett, the leader of the earlier victorious charge of the Heavy Brigade, who had never been in action before that day and seemed to have suddenly developed a taste for it. He galloped on for some time after Lucan had turned his brigade back. Lucan himself received a bullet in the thigh and his nephew and aide-de-camp, Captain Charteris, was killed at his side.

The Light Brigade sustained most of its casualties in riding the 2,000 yards to the battery in the middle of the valley. In the final seconds this battery was firing canister, a short-range version of grapeshot, at point-blank range. Then the Russian gunners ducked under the carriages to avoid the oncoming lances, or heroically tried to limber up the guns and take them away.

General Rijov, who had commanded the Russian cavalry in the earlier clash with the Heavy Brigade, ordered the Cossack cavalry to rally behind the guns and to prevent the Light Brigade from removing them. Russian observers criticised Rijov for choosing the Cossacks, who were totally unsuited to meeting a charge from a body of cavalry in formation. Although none of Rijov's other cavalry regiments welcomed the idea of facing the second British cavalry charge of the day, any of them would have been better than the Cossacks. It was almost as if Rijov wanted to punish them for having goaded the Light Brigade to fury and brought this new calamity upon him.

The now-silent Russian guns were arranged in line with a twenty yard gap between each. As they reluctantly went forward and some of the smoke cleared the Cossacks saw the terrifying sight of the first line of the Light Brigade flying straight at them through these gaps, a hundred men wide and two deep, at the gallop and with their sabres and lances extended. The losses from the Russian artillery were not evident because the men had continually closed ranks as each casualty occurred. Because the first line of two regiments had forced the pace, the remaining three regiments had not been able to keep their distance or alignment but were bearing down on either side of the narrow front of the Russian battery. The sight of the Light Brigade was too much for the Cossacks, who panicked and tried to flee from what must have been their worst nightmare come true. Seeing their escape down the valley blocked by other Russian cavalry regiments, the Cossacks turned and fired their carbines point-blank at their own comrades, who in turn wheeled and charged back into the regiments behind. The entire Russian cavalry, out-numbering the Light Brigade by nearly ten to one, now turned and fled in total confusion down the valley towards the Tchernaya River.[34] It was the perfect end to a near-perfect cavalry charge. Nothing could be more satisfactory to a cavalryman than seeing his enemy shooting at his own comrades in his eagerness to leave the battlefield.

The British chased the Russians for another mile until they were forced to a halt by congestion at the bridge over an aqueduct that ran beside the river; at least one of the Cossacks fell off the bridge into the aqueduct in his haste to flee.[35] If the escape of the Russians had not been cut off by the terrain, there is no knowing how far they would have run. Only when they were baulked did it become obvious to the Russians that the Light Brigade was outnumbered, cut off, and unsupported by any other cavalry or infantry. The British cavalry had to turn and make their way back up the valley to their own lines, largely unmolested by the Russian cavalry but braving more flanking artillery fire on the way. Most of them were back where they started a short twenty minutes after they began the Charge. Their psychological supremacy over the Russian cavalry was now assured. Never again would anyone dare to say that the Light Brigade was afraid of Cossacks.

The victors of the 1968 film *The Charge of the Light Brigade*, directed by Tony Richardson, were the Russian cavalry. They are shown falling on the remnants of the Light Brigade at the guns and cutting them to rib-bons, an astonishing solecism in a film that otherwise tried very hard to stick to the facts as they were then known. It seems that the angry young men of the 1960s were as keen to portray the other ranks as losers and victims as were Tennyson and other purveyors of Great Man History. It is curious that such a concerted effort has been made to deny the ordinary soldier his glorious victory.

THE REAL BLUNDER OF BALACLAVA

The Charge was not a blunder; Lord Raglan's order was a blunder, but the Light Brigade were not told of and did not obey Raglan's order. The men substituted their own order, to charge the Russian cavalry and put them to flight. They succeeded spectacularly. The surviving troopers were initially jubilant at their success[36]; and when Lord Cardigan, who had objected to the Charge from the start, told a group of them that, 'Men, it was a mad-brained trick, but no fault of mine', a voice from the ranks replied, 'Never mind, my Lord, we're ready to do it again.' The Light Brigade's main complaint was that the infantry had not supported them. The CO of the 4th Light Dragoons, Lord George Paget, rode up onto the ridge and looked at the two infantry divisions relaxing in the South Valley. 'It's a damned shame,' he said, 'There we had a lot of their guns and carriages taken, and received no support, and yet there's all this infantry about.'[37] This was the real blunder of Balaclava: that the Allied infantry did not pounce on the rest of Liprandi's army and send it packing on the heels of his cavalry.

The infantry had arrived in large numbers by the time the Charge took place. After more prodding from the ADC who had spoiled his breakfast by making him bring his division down to the plain, General Cathcart had moved his infantry division along the south side of the ridge and reoccupied some of the fortifications which had now been abandoned by their Russian captors. But when he arrived within range of the guns that had raked the Light Brigade he stopped and conferred with the Duke of Cambridge and Sir Colin Campbell, commander of the Duke's Highland Brigade. Then, as senior infantry general, Cathcart announced that they were going no further. The reason for his decision appears to be his belief that it was pointless to recapture the fortifications because they had proved to be too weak to be of use in the defence of Balaclava. If they were as weak as that, it would have cost him little to recapture them, not for the purpose of defending Balaclava but rather as a step to crushing Liprandi's army. The failure to engage this stalled army, even after its cavalry had been routed, was a terrible mistake. Cathcart might have made more effort if he knew that the British cavalry were charging down the North Valley under fire from near the redoubt that Raglan had ordered him to recapture, but unfortunately he knew nothing of the Charge and was bewildered when Lord Cardigan and the battered Light Brigade appeared on the ridge. Seen from Lord Raglan's panoramic viewpoint, it must have been difficult to imagine that because of the lie of the land the rest of the army had been completely unaware of the cavalry's advance. Perhaps he had hoped that the cavalry attack would spur the dilatory Cathcart into action; if so he failed to understand that Cathcart was unsighted.

A simultaneous advance with the cavalry would have been preferable, but an infantry attack afterwards would also have been productive. Allied eyewitnesses talk of everyone's increasing disbelief as the remaining six hours of daylight passed without any move by the Allied infantry to fall like a wolf on the fold and devour an undersized Russian Army which had failed to reach Balaclava, had lost the initiative, and was sitting there on the plain wondering what blow was going to fall on it next after its cavalry had been routed first by the Heavy Brigade and then by the Light Brigade at odds of nearly ten to one. The ground was of the Allies' own choosing and a suitable theatre in which to exploit the overwhelming superiority of the Minié rifle. A French infantry brigade and two regiments of cavalry had also arrived, probably numbering about 4,000 men in total, so that the Allied strength was at least double this. The Allies may still have been outnumbered nearly two to one, but this imbalance was irrelevant given the power of their armament and the ignorance of Liprandi and his commanders. They were a new army, arrived only hours ago from Odessa. They did not know how to defend themselves against infantry with rifles, as is shown by Lt Godfrey's feat of winning a duel that afternoon as a single rifleman against a Russian two-gun artillery battery at 600 yards.[38]

The best way to defuse possible criticism of the failure to accompany the Charge by an infantry attack was to publicly emphasise that the Charge itself was a blunder. This Raglan took care to do immediately, with great skill. The letter that he wrote to the Minister of War has never been published and is worth quoting to show how skilfully he was to portray is as a blunder while diverting any criticism from himself:

Before Sebastopol[39]
October 28 1854
Private & Confidential
My dear Duke of Newcastle
You will read with great regret my despatch of this day reporting the operations before Balaklava.

You will hardly be prepared for the bad conduct of the Turkish troops which shewed no fight whatever and abandoned works without the attempt to defend them, which, though paltry enough, I am assured were superior to Arab Tabia [a fortress in the Balkans] that a handful of men held so long against all the efforts of Gorchakoff's army and thus they lost us some Guns of position which I thought would be safe in their hands at least for some hours. To contrast their conduct with that of our people it is worthy of mention that in each of the redoubts we had one single artillery man to shew the Turks how to use our Guns. This man spiked the Guns in the several works with one exception, alone and single handed whilst the Turks abandoned their duty and left him to shift for himself.

But you will be much more shocked to see the loss sustained by our Light Cavalry. This indeed is a heavy misfortune notwithstanding the brilliancy of their conduct and I feel it most deeply.

The written order sent him by the quarter master general did not exact that Lord Lucan should attack at all hazards and contained no expression which could bear that construction but he so considered it, taunted I believe by the Officer who carried it and who appears to have conducted himself with great impropriety and assumed an authority which was wholly *deplacé* and for which he ought to have been reproved instead of being listened to.

This officer was General Airey's Aide de Camp Captain Nolan. He actually put himself before the Squadron which Lord Cardigan led and cried almost like a Maniac 'Come on Come on'. He was killed by the splinter of a shell which burst between the poor fellow and Cardigan.

This latter who is as brave as a lion absolutely thought it his duty to point out to Lord Lucan the artillery that he was about to attack and that which would oppose him on his flanks but the latter retained the idea that he had imbibed and fancied that he had no discretion to exercise. Fatal Mistake! My only consolation is the admirable conduct of the Troops which was beyond all praise.

I have heard that there was some bad feeling between Captain Nolan and Lord Lucan and that the former entertained it on account of the latter having spoken disparagingly of the horses he [Nolan] had purchased in Syria.

I have written to you thus unreservedly and in full confidence.
Believe me very faithfully yours

Raglan

The passage about Nolan's supposed quarrel over horses with Lucan makes it appear that it was a private dispute and was unrelated to Nolan's known anger at the failure to make more use of the cavalry. Even more accomplished is Raglan's statement that the order was the product of the quartermaster-general (General Airey), who only wrote it out at Raglan's command. It seems unlikely that this letter was seen by the scriptwriters of the 1968 film in which John Gielgud played Raglan, but in that case art must have followed nature in a most uncanny way. One of the most memorable scenes shows Raglan holding up the written order in apparent perplexity, having been handed it by Lucan and saying, 'Why, this is your handwriting, Airey!'

In his separate published despatches, Lord Raglan criticised openly the general (Lucan) who had obeyed his orders and omitted to mention that General Cathcart had refused point-blank to obey them. No criticism can be directed at Raglan for managing the news in this way: if *The Times* had to blazon abroad the news of a British blunder, how much better that it should be a heroic attack than a refusal to fight? No official attempt was made to counter the press exaggeration of the Light Brigade 'disaster'. The eight guns in the battery facing the cavalry quickly increased by a factor of four, and *The Illustrated London News* reported that of 650 men only about 163 were 'safe'. The number participating was nearly correct, but in fact more than 300 had returned with barely a scratch, and fifty-eight were quickly known to be prisoners of the Russians. The Paris *Moniteur* reported 400 men lost; the *Times* said, '800 cavalry were engaged of whom only 200 returned. The 17th Lancers were almost destroyed.' These reports led to the enduring belief that hundreds had perished, whereas the reality is that 110 were killed or died of their wounds. This corrected information was soon widely available but was ignored as more important blunders made the front page and Tennyson's poem (published only two months after the event) made the Charge of the Light Brigade the symbol of all of them. Even 150 years later, popular accounts are still announcing as a 'discovery' the fact that casualties were so low.

Lucan objected strenuously when Raglan told him on the evening after the Charge that he should have used his discretion and ignored Raglan's order. Raglan's reproach may seem strange to us, too, and the action of the Horse Guards (the High Command in London) in upholding it may seem even stranger. How can an army fight a war, we may ask, if officers must exercise their discretion before obeying orders? Again one has to see it from the mid-Victorian, not the twentieth century, viewpoint. Mid-Victorian British society was a harmonious mixture of orthodox and dissenters, with most of the country's unique prosperity being attributed to the latter. The British were not simply the only nation in Europe that tolerated dissent – they *treasured* it; the absence of dissent and individual initiative was one of the main things that made foreigners foreign. In clarifying the rules on obedience to orders, the Horse Guards was simply reflecting the national values of the day. Lucan was soon sacked, not for failing to exercise his discretion but for trying to expose Raglan's pretence that he had never ordered an attack.

But criticism of Lord Lucan could not detract from the success of the Charge when seen from the point of view of the Light Brigade. As well as being a tactical victory for them, the Charge met the Light Brigade's expectations in a broader strategic sense. It was a statement, which influenced the government at home in favour of an official change of military strategy. After the Charge, we find many disenchanted officers writing to influential people at home complaining that the siege and bombardment of Sebastopol was playing to the Russians strengths in fortification and heavy artillery. Much better, they said, to engage the Russians in the open field outside Sebastopol. The Alma had shown that the Allied infantry was overwhelmingly superior to that of the enemy, now Balaclava had shown that the cavalry enjoyed a similar superiority. First, the Heavy Cavalry Brigade had beaten a greatly superior Russian force, but some of that success had been owed to prompt support from field artillery. In the Charge, the Light Brigade had removed all doubt by achieving the complete rout of the Russian cavalry without any help at all. The men of the Light Brigade knew that they had no glorious role to play in a continued siege. They wanted to fight in the open, but they were not articulate staff officers able to put their case in writing to people back in England. Their action was their statement, and it was listened to. Within a short time, circumstances would arise in which a new government would be able to order that the plan to take Sebastopol by bombardment and assault should be discontinued, and a new campaign in the open field should replace it. This change of official strategy has been kept secret ever since, which is why the Light Brigade has not been given any of the credit for it. The government's orders for a change of strategy would not be obeyed, as we shall see. That was not the fault of the Light Brigade and does not diminish their victory.

6

Winter Above Sebastopol

INKERMAN: THE UNAFFORDABLE VICTORY

A few days after the Charge of the Light Brigade, Raglan decided to abandon the port at Balaclava and share the French port at Kamiesch instead. His decision must have been widely publicised, because it is reported in many different officers' journals and letters, but was then retracted. Various people have been blamed for this about-turn but evidence is lacking. Admiral Lyons, second in command of the British fleet, had originally picked the harbour of Balaclava when the French offered to let the British have first choice; he thought the town and its buildings would be useful.' The port had proved far too small, was frequently impossible to get out of when the wind was from the south, was too far from the camp and was too vulnerable to Russian attack. Nevertheless the British kept it on, and after the loss of its outer fortifications Raglan had to detach more troops from Sebastopol to strengthen Balaclava's inner line of defences.

The main worry of the Allies was that the Russians, now superior to them in overall strength, would break out of Sebastopol and overwhelm the Allied camps around it. Two days after the Charge of the Light Brigade the Russians attempted the strongest such sortie to date. They sent five thousand troops out of the north-eastern corner of the city to march east and then south to climb onto the plateau and attack the camp of de Lacy Evans's division which occupied the extreme right of the Allied position. Evans had only two and a half thousand men at his disposal, the rest of his division being elsewhere on trench duty. This was to be Evans's last battle, after nearly fifty years of service, and he excelled himself in it as did the common soldiers who formed the picket lines in front of his camp. These pickets were supposed to offer only token resistance and give the alarm, but they seemed so enamoured of their new rifles that they would not run from twenty times their number, only falling back slowly. Evans refused pleas from volunteers to go to the aid of the pickets with the words 'Not a man!' As at the Alma, he busied himself borrowing artillery from other divisions, installing it out of sight behind high ground from where the enemy would be at its mercy if they advanced far enough. When they had, he unveiled his guns and bombarded the Russians into mass retreat. With such tacit cooperation between the general and his rank and file, there was little need for middlemen in the shape of regimental officers who typically wanted nothing better than to hurl themselves at the enemy at the head of their troops and be the first into Sebastopol. The officer in charge of one of the pickets did summon them to a bayonet charge, but he candidly admitted that they ignored him and carried on firing their rifles instead.[2] He consoled himself by observing that most of the Russian casualties were from this rifle fire rather than from Evans's artillery, again showing that the soldier could be relied on to do the right thing even if he received orders to the contrary.

The total dead in this action were in the low hundreds, mostly Russian. It became known as Lesser Inkerman, because ten days later the Russians attacked again in the same position with much greater force in what became the battle of Inkerman proper. It may be that the earlier sortie was a practice run, because at the larger battle the Russians used different tactics which would have succeeded better against Evans's habitual tactic of relying on artillery. But at the main Battle of Inkerman Evans no longer commanded the Second Division and his successor responded in a completely different way to the Russian attack. Evans had been ill since the army had arrived at Sebastopol, often remaining in his tent all day huddled in blankets and giving and receiving orders through the closed doorway. After Lesser Inkerman he remained in bed for several days, and on October 30th he fell from his horse and was badly bruised. He went onboard ship in Balaclava Harbour to recuperate. Hearing the sound of gunfire at dawn on 5 November he arose and, fortified by his usual drastic stimulant of mercury, rode up to the camp to observe the battle but did not take part.

25,000 Russian reinforcements had arrived in the previous few days, finally giving the Russians a significant numerical advantage over the Allies. A total of 35,000 Russians (compared to only 5,000 in the previous battle) climbed onto the plateau at the right of the British position with a heavy force of field artillery during the night of 4—5 November. This part of the plateau is sometimes called Mount Inkerman, as distinct from the Heights of Inkerman which overlook it from the east side of the Tchernaya Valley. What the Russians had learned in their previous sortie was that the Allies had not prepared the ground here properly to aid their defence. It was still thickly covered with scrub oak trees as high as a man, offering cover right up to the muzzles of the defending artillery at the summit of Mount Inkerman, in front of the camp of Evans's Second Division.

There were two large ravines leading up to Evans's camp, and the Russian plan was to approach along these two ravines and assemble their attacking force on the ridge between them. If they could take the high point of this ridge they planned to entrench and fortify it with heavy artillery, thus extending the defence line surrounding the southern part of the city as far as the Tchernaya River. Half the attacking force, under General Soimonov, was to come from Sebastopol via the Careening Ravine, the other half under General Paulov was to come from the army camped on the Heights of Inkerman on the opposite side of the Tchernaya valley. Paulov's army had to cross the Tchernaya River before climbing up the Quarry Ravine to meet Soimonov's force in front of the British position. Before they could cross, they needed to repair the bridge across the Tchernaya that they had destroyed to make their position on the north bank more defensible. Once they had occupied and fortified the ridge on the south bank, however, this repaired bridge would link the city's defences with the north bank which was entirely in Russian hands, making it easier to get supplies and troops into the besieged southern part of the city.

General Dannenberg, who was to command the whole force once it was united, objected to the routes chosen for the Russian advance, probably because they would lead to a very large combined force being crowded together on a narrow ridge only a few hundred yards wide. He wanted Soimonov to take a more westerly route on the side of the Careening Ravine, but his orders were either not received in time or disobeyed, with the result according to Totleben that the superior Russian

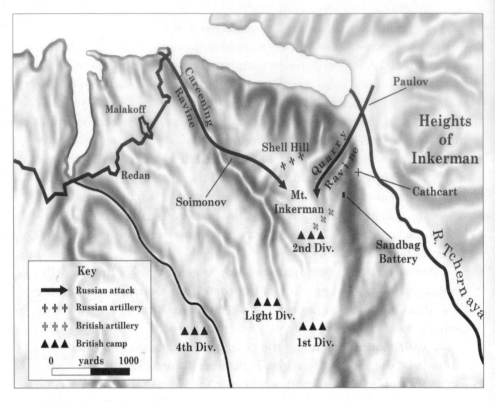

The Battle of Inkerman.

forces could not be brought into action all at once. It also took much longer than expected to repair the bridge over the Tchernaya in the early hours of the morning, so that Soimonov initially attacked alone.

In the previous battle, Evans had followed his favourite tactic of falling back to his main position when attacked and installing his main force and his guns in hidden ground on the reverse slope of a hill to await the enemy on ground of Evans's choosing. The Russians seemed to anticipate this strategy and planned to counter it by engaging the British artillery from a distance with a superior artillery force of their own. They brought up no less than ninety field guns to Shell Hill, the second-highest summit of Mount Inkerman at about 600 feet above sea level and 600 yards or so from Evans's camp. But General Pennefather, Evans's successor, reacted quite differently and sent troops forward in all directions to engage the enemy wherever they could find them. Evans,

1 Florence Nightingale.

2 Napoleon III.

3 Lord Cardigan.

4 Lord Palmerston

5 Sir John McNeill in 1866.

6 Sir George Brown.

7 Sir John Burgoyne.

8 Sir George de Lacy Evans.

9 Sir James Simpson.

10 Lord Raglan.

11 Marshal Pélissier.

12 Omar Pasha.

13 William Howard Russell.

14 Sir Charles Napier.

15 Lord Lucan.

16 General Canrobert.

17 General Totleben.

18 Interior of a Russian artillery battery. The rope shields are to protect the gunners from Minié bullets.

19 The Malakoff, with a telegraph installed by the French after its capture.

20 The British Greenhill Battery. A rare photograph in which the buildings of Sebastopol are visible in the distance.

21 Inside a British mortar battery.

22 View from the mortar battery towards the Mamelon (r) and the Malakoff (l).

23 Balaclava Harbour: the landing place for railway stores.

24 Balaclava Harbour: the landing place for war material.

25 The British cavalry camp, taken from about a mile west of Kadikoi looking north-east. The Sapoune Heights are in the background. This photo was taken in the summer of 1855, when a superior road (partly visible in the right middle distance) had been built from Balaclava to the Sapoune Heights, replacing the tracks seen in the centre.

it will be remembered, had refused to allow his men to do the same because he wanted to lure the Russians towards him. Some military historians criticise Pennefather for abdicating command and letting his men do what they wanted[3], but like Raglan's abdication at the Alma it seems to have worked because of the men's ability to act independently.

The battle began at 5.45a.m. on a rainy, misty morning with very poor visibility which caused some of the Russian troops to lose their way. With reinforcements from other divisions drawn by the sound of musketry, Pennefather's defensive force consisted early on of only 3–4,000 infantry and sixteen guns. The Russians initially drove the British back, but as reinforcements arrived the British rallied and General Soimonov and other senior Russian officers were killed, which robbed the Russian infantry of some of its momentum. By about 8a.m. the battle had become an artillery duel with the weight of artillery favouring the Russians; orders to bring up heavy British artillery from the siege reserves were misunderstood and three eighteen-pounder guns only arrived much later, dragged by 150 men. Meanwhile, British troops in groups of a few score advanced into the brushwood seeking out the Russian columns and artillery. The Russian General Totleben later wrote that the damage done by the Russian artillery 'could only partially compensate for the enormous losses which the enemy's riflemen inflicted on the Russian artillery. A veritable cloud of riflemen, hidden in thick brushwood, opened a very violent and accurate fire against our artillerymen at a distance of 800 paces. Only some of our guns from time to time rained grapeshot (*mitraille*) upon the English riflemen. But the discharge only checked the fire of the enemy's riflemen for a moment, for after they recovered from their momentary fear [the range being too great for grapeshot to have much effect] they only continued even more energetically to decimate our ranks. At the same time, the English batteries fired shrapnel at our infantry and artillery, but it was more the fire of the enemy's rifled small arms than that of his artillery which hit our artillerymen, of whom the greater part were killed or wounded.'[4]

One Russian regiment that became lost stumbled on an abandoned earthwork on the extreme right of the British line overlooking the Tchernaya and, taking it for an important position, occupied it. This was the Sandbag Battery, originally built as an artillery emplacement to reply to Russian guns shelling from the north bank. It was not built for defence by infantry, but as the battle raged on it became the focus of much fighting as first one side and then the other captured it. It changed hands at least seven times, and 500 Russian and 200 British troops perished in the struggle for this useless position. General Sir George Cathcart, who had refused to attack the Russians at Balaclava with his 4th Infantry Division in support of the Charge of the Light Brigade two weeks earlier, arrived near this position in reinforcement of the British lines and apparently thought that he could outflank the Russians by descending towards the river valley. The Russians he met gave way before him, and he and half of his division followed them too far, his men firing their rifles until their ammunition was spent. The Russians brought up more troops behind him and Cathcart, unsupported, found himself cut off. When Cathcart's body was recovered, an unposted letter to his wife was found in his pocket, pierced by a bullet, in which he told her that his infantry division had been six miles away when the infantry failed to support the Light Brigade at Balaclava ten days earlier.[5] This false alibi is evidence that he regretted his inaction that day at Balaclava, when he had let slip a chance to use his 'red infantry' against a Russian army in the field. His impetuous action at Inkerman looks like a desperate attempt to redeem himself

Early in the afternoon the Russians realised that they could not hold the ridge against the increasing reinforcements sent by the Allies. The Russians had made a diversionary attack against the French 'army of observation' stationed on the heights overlooking the valleys to the south, but it was so unconvincing that the French had no hesitation in sending troops from there to the main battle. The Russians managed a more or less orderly withdrawal back to Sebastopol. About 750 British and French combatants were killed at Inkerman, and at least four times as many Russians. Among the dead were eight generals – five British and three Russian.

Despite their victory, the British Army was filled with gloom after Inkerman. The nature of the struggle had changed. Until that point everyone expected that the next day or the day after would bring the fall of Sebastopol. The defeat of the previous Russian attack, essentially by a British picket line, had encouraged this idea. In fact, the Allied commanders had been preparing to launch the final assault on Sebastopol on 7 November[6], but now they realised that they had underestimated the Russian reinforcements. Now that the Russians were force-marching whole divisions to the Crimea from throughout Russia, the Allies would have to slaughter thousands of Russian conscripts to achieve their goal. There was suddenly no prospect of a knockout blow.

Billy Russell of *The Times* noticed that at Inkerman, for the first time, evidence of cowardice was plainly visible among the British troops, up to four or five of them hastening to the rear supporting a slightly wounded comrade.[7] While some disappeared to replenish their ammunition, others fought on with rocks, bayonets and rifle butts, and the brave perished in disproportion to the prudent.

Officers were disillusioned too – over 10 per cent of them left the Crimea forever in the two months following the battle of Inkerman, and nearly half as many again spent the winter at home.[8] One who left forever was the ailing sixty-seven-year-old General de Lacy Evans, after a row with Lord Raglan. He urged Raglan to give up the siege immediately after the battle of Inkerman, and as he was too discreet or politically astute to publicise his arguments they remain unknown. Raglan's nephew and aide-de-camp, Calthorpe, was outraged; he thought that Evans's illness must have affected his mind because he proposed the evacuation of the Crimea, or rather 'such was the meaning, if not the actual words.' One would have preferred to know Evans's actual words; whatever they were, Raglan replied that his proposal would mean leaving behind the guns and the French Allies, who had relied on British transport to get to the Crimea.[9]

Two days later at a council of war Lord Raglan had to accept a French suggestion that they would take over the ground of the Battle of Inkerman, leaving the British, now down to 16,000 effectives, to occupy only about a fifth of the trenches around Sebastopol in addition to defending their port of Balaclava. The French also insisted that no assault should now be made on Sebastopol for the foreseeable future. In view of this several generals advised Lord Raglan to raise the siege and withdraw the troops to new ground 'if the idea of the army being embarked was impractical'. The Duke of Cambridge proposed that the British troops should be withdrawn to the neighbourhood of Balaclava, a proposal which shows that not everyone was oblivious to the difficulties of supplying the army in the coming winter over the seven-mile track from the port. Raglan rejected these suggestions, and decided to keep the army where it was on the plateau. The Duke of Cambridge, like Evans, went home disillusioned on the sick list.[10]

THE LOSS OF AN ARMY

William Filder, the elderly civilian commissary-general in the Crimea, first learned on 8 November that the British Army would winter on the plateau outside Sebastopol, and immediately began to worry about how his Commissariat would supply the basic necessities of the troops at such a distance from the port of Balaclava. Commissary-General Filder wrote to his superiors in Whitehall on November 13 that the single unmade track to the British camp might become unusable when the bad weather arrived, especially if fuel had to be carried up in addition to other supplies.[11] He also warned the army officers responsible for maintaining the track, who ordered Turkish troops to improve it. They were unequal to the job, and nobody did anything else about it thereafter. If the Cabinet in London had been alerted to the gravity of the situation they could have sent experienced navvies from England with their own carts, horses, and tools, who could probably have arrived in time to improve the road by Christmas.[12] The Cabinet could alternatively have instructed Raglan to shorten his supply lines by withdrawing either from Balaclava or from the plateau. But the Cabinet was not properly alerted because the Commissariat (the source of the alarm) was at the time in political limbo.

In the summer, in response to complaints about mismanagement, the Cabinet had removed the Minister of War's responsibilities for the colonies and in exchange given him control of all military departments including the Ordnance Department, Finance, the Medical Department and the Commissariat. Some of these had been under other ministries; the Commissariat, for example, was part of the Treasury. There had been strong pressure on the Cabinet to appoint Lord Palmerston to the enlarged Ministry of War but the Duke of Newcastle, the incumbent, would not step down. Palmerston was also said to be too old, at seventy. Newcastle remained in position, but (according to his Prime Minister) refused to accept full responsibility for the Commissariat until he could move into new War Office premises and acquire more staff. The Commissariat therefore remained under divided ministerial responsibility. The Treasury civil servant in charge of the Commissariat, Sir Charles Trevelyan, and the Minister of War were old antagonists. In 1846—7 when Newcastle had Cabinet responsibility for Ireland Trevelyan had obstructed his efforts to relieve the potato famine because he thought that government should not be involved in famine relief. There was a certain *déjà vu*, therefore, about the situation of the ordinary soldier in the Crimea, many of whom were Irish. Trevelyan claimed that he passed (unofficially) the commissary-general's warning about the inadequate road to the Minister of War, but the Duke of Newcastle denied receiving it. The Duke said five months later that he only gradually became aware toward the end of November that the road was impassable and then only because the army complained that it could not get new siege guns up to the camp to replace those that had been worn out in the first bombardment. This shows that he had been focussed on the Ordnance Department's needs rather than the Commissariat's. When Newcastle found out that the guns were not getting through, he reacted by planning for a railroad that would be in place for the transport of guns and ammunition for the planned spring offensive. He testified to this effect to a Parliamentary committee of enquiry a few months later, even then he did not seem to realise that the road had been required for the supply of basic necessities to the troops throughout the winter.[13] The minister jointly responsible for the Commissariat was the Chancellor of the Exchequer, as head of the Treasury. That minister did not testify to the parliamentary committee in which the Duke of Newcastle admitted his neglect; he was W.E. Gladstone, and he was destined for high office.

Commissary General Filder's fears soon came true. The day after he first wrote to warn the Treasury about the road, a storm of hurricane force struck the Crimea with devastating results for the Allied armies. Tents and equipment were blown away and the first snow of winter began to fall on the ruined camps. Though several men died of exposure, the loss on land was nothing compared to that at sea. Because of the continued Russian threat to Balaclava, many ships had been forbidden to enter and were moored outside where they were exposed to a lee shore. The Royal Navy vessels managed to weather the storm, but the civilian supply ships were less fortunate. Eight of them were wrecked outside the harbour, with the loss of hundreds of lives. One was a fine new screw steamer, the *Prince*, which had on board 700 tons of winter clothing for the troops as well as medical stores. This and much other desperately needed cargo was lost. Two large French ships outside their harbour at Kamiesch also went down with all hands, as did a Turkish line of battle ship at Eupatoria. Dozens more ships were badly damaged.

Raglan immediately instructed the Commissariat to purchase replacement stores in Constantinople at any price. The government in London did the same and only three weeks after the storm a replacement cargo of winter clothing sailed from London. But by the time these supplies arrived the track from Balaclava to the camp had been ruined by heavy rain and traffic and the goods remained in port. The troops were put on half, quarter, or no rations for days at a time. The army horses died of starvation, although staff officers with a forage allowance and those regimental officers who could afford to maintain private horses rode into Balaclava where private merchants offered supplies at exorbitant prices. The common soldier lived on a diet of rum, meat and biscuit whenever the Commissariat could deliver it. The meat was preserved in salt and the soldier did not have cooking-pots big enough to wash or cook it so his gums were lacerated by salt and scurvy. The only industrialised country in the world was filling its merchant fleet with untold millions in supplies and depositing them with great precision in Balaclava where undeliverable clothing, vegetables, medicines and weapons piled up alongside a harbour choked with filth. The port came to resemble a post-apocalyptic wasteland of corpses and merchandise.

Up on the plateau the exhausted and starving troops were now dressed in rags unless they had been able to improvise or to steal clothing from dead Russians. They were eloquent testimony to just how long it can take for exposure, starvation, and fatigue to kill a man. Those who could walk manned the trenches to guard against Russian sorties. The trenches were not like those of the First World War, in which men lived, but rather shallow ditches where they worked in shifts. Men often marched a mile or two through mud and snow to the trenches and then spent twelve hours sitting in the ditch, or twenty-four on sentry duty out in front. Often they were found frozen to the ground at the end of their shift. The average soldier spent nearly half his time on sentry or trench duty, and the rest hunting for food and fuel and cooking facilities or sleeping in his threadbare muddy tent. There was no time even for basic hygiene; offal, inadequately buried corpses and excrement littered the camps.

In the middle of November there was at least one suicide and the first desertions of British troops occurred, typically of sentries crossing no man's land to seek sanctuary in the Russian fortifications. Sometimes his comrades fired at the fleeing man[14], but if caught his punishment was light by later standards. Of 166 men court-martialled for desertion, only one was sentenced to death and his sentence was commuted to transportation. The most common sentence was a short term of

imprisonment. Given the conditions and the mild punishment, it is surprising that desertion wasn't more common.

Although Commissary-General Filder was widely blamed during and
after the war for not delivering supplies to the camp, the fault lay much
higher in the military and political organisation for leaving the besieging
army dependent for supplies on a single unmade road that had become
a morass. Filder, it is true, behaved with Scrooge-like parsimony when
sending up supplies from Balaclava but he had to make the best use of
extremely limited carrying capacity of the track on which carts could
no longer pass and less efficient pack-animals had to be used instead.
Filder may have been used as a scapegoat; a historian sympathetic to
Lord Raglan made the unlikely claim that Raglan countermanded his
order to relocate the port because Filder told him that he could not
undertake to supply the army except through Balaclava.[15] Even if such
a threat was made (and there is no official record of it) and even if Lord
Raglan did give in to a civilian so meekly, Filder is on record as saying
a few days later that he would not be able to supply the army through
Balaclava unless the army improved the road. The person who blocked
the abandonment of Balaclava as a port has probably not, therefore, been
identified and must bear much of the blame for what contemporary
critics called 'the loss of an army'.

THE SECRET OF SCUTARI

The government had persuaded the Sultan to lend a large barracks
at Scutari, on the Asian side of the Bosphorus at Constantinople, as a
depot, hospital, and possible winter quarters for British troops. The sailing distance from the Crimea was about 300 miles, and after the battle
of the Alma in September the wounded had been evacuated to Scutari.
There was criticism from newspaper correspondents of the treatment
of the wounded before, during, and after their evacuation, and the government reacted by sending thirty-four-year-old Florence Nightingale
and a party of thirty-eight nurses to the hospital at Scutari. The Cabinet
Minister responsible for this decision was Sidney Herbert, who had
been demoted in the reorganisation of the War Office in the summer.
His responsibilities for army finance and for the Medical Department
were now subordinated to the Duke of Newcastle as Minister of War.[16]

Sidney Herbert knew Florence Nightingale as a friend of his wife; the two women shared an interest in hospitals.

A party of thirty-eight female nurses hardly seems an adequate response to a crisis in the army. But Nightingale was a different matter. She was one of Britain's leading experts in hospital administration, having studied the organisation of hospitals in many countries in Europe and having for the past year been chief executive of a hospital in London. She was better-educated than most Cabinet ministers, which isn't necessarily saying much, and if women had been admitted to universities she would probably still hold the record for the youngest-ever graduate. If women had been allowed into Parliament she would have been a very strong contender for Prime Minister. Her level of education is not immediately apparent to those who envisage her as a nurse or who have read her popular writings. Her family were successful industrialists; they owned a woollen mill in the Derwent valley, the cradle of the industrial revolution, where Nightingale spent much of her youth living within sight of the factory and in close proximity to its workers. Her near relatives included parliamentarians who had successfully championed religious freedom and it would be hard to find a family more representative of what had made Britain the world's most powerful and prosperous state. Nightingale herself was on intimate terms with key members of the parties in the government coalition – Sidney Herbert in one camp and Lord Palmerston in another.

She was of course a woman, and women were denied many rights in Britain at that time: to attend university, to vote, to sit in Parliament, to operate bank accounts, to own property when married, and so on. It would be a mistake to think that this made women powerless in Britain, any more than Jews, Catholics, and Dissenters who were also denied some rights but wielded power nonetheless. Nightingale had acquired power from her family background and her own achievements, and she acquired more when Sidney Herbert sent her to the Crimea. Her new powers did not only come from her public title as Superintendent of Nursing; she was also under private instructions from Sidney Herbert to report confidentially to him on the shortcomings of the Army Medical Department.[17]

She was not a charity worker; she was a functionary of the state, an extraordinary if not unique status for a woman at the time. In her Superintendent's role, as Sidney Herbert informed the newspapers, 'She will act in the strictest subordination to the chief medical officer of the hospital [Dr Duncan Menzies].' Menzies's rank of Deputy Inspector General of Hospitals in the Army Medical Department was officially equivalent to the combatant rank of lieutenant-colonel. Superintendent Nightingale, therefore, occupied a position in the military hierarchy equivalent to a major. Towards the end of the war Nightingale was promoted to General Superintendent of the Female Nursing Establishment of the Military Hospitals of the Army, reporting to Sir John Hall. Hall held the rank of Inspector General of Hospitals which was equivalent to brigadier-general so his subordinate, General Superintendent Nightingale, was entitled to think herself as on a par with a full colonel.[18] There is no suggestion that her rank was actually a military one, but it is important to realise that she was not just an up-market camp-follower. She was a part of the hierarchy, and the fact was not welcome to those above her.

Her status was important to her because she was trying out her plan of putting a high-ranking woman in charge of all the female nurses in a hospital. She thought this was the key to improving civilian hospitals in England, where until that time sexual harassment of nurses dissuaded middle class mothers from allowing their daughters into the profession. On the Continent, where the nurses were Catholic nuns, she had seen that parents were happy to entrust their daughters to the care of a Mother Superior who was usually from a noble family, who could maintain discipline and defend her nurses even against high-ranking men. Nightingale planned to introduce a secular version of this system in England; Scutari was to be a pilot project for her. If she could keep her nurses safe from predatory NCOs, then a teaching hospital with its dissolute medical students would no longer be a threat.

She and her nurses arrived at Scutari on 4 November 1854, the day before the Battle of Inkerman. The Army Medical Department officers resented her presence and refused to give her or her nurses any instructions. Nightingale could have gone to work immediately, if only feeding the patients – many of her nurses were nuns who had experience of nursing without medical supervision. But she refused to work or to allow her nurses to work under such conditions. Sidney Herbert had said she would act 'in the strictest subordination to the chief medical officer', and that was what she insisted on doing: she threatened her nurses with dismissal if they attended a patient without instructions from a doctor. The doctors at first refused to instruct the nurses, so Florence Nightingale and her unhappy band sat for three days and four nights in their quarters making bandages and occasionally treating a sick civilian. On the fourth day there was a surge of arrivals from the Crimea: wounded from Inkerman and sick men suffering from the onset of winter and evacuated because of the continued Russian threat to Balaclava. The doctors, overwhelmed, asked the nurses to help in the wards and Nightingale told the women to get to work.[19]

This incident has given Nightingale a reputation for 'subservience' to the medical profession. If insisting on receiving orders from doctors who refuse to give them – and winning the contest – is subservience then this reputation is deserved. It was evidently the kind of subservience that Dr Hall did not relish. One can understand why, because taking orders gave her and her nurses the right enjoyed by every British subordinate to officially question those orders. For example, Nightingale asked a male orderly to give a patient a hot water bottle because his feet were cold; the orderly, a corporal, said that he could not do so without a doctor's approval. She insisted on sending for the overworked Duty Medical Officer who made it obvious that he should not have been troubled for such a trivial matter. Most nurses would have been overawed and would have avoided causing such trouble in future, but Nightingale wrote a politely sarcastic letter to the senior surgeon in charge of the ward, ridiculing the regulations. If this was subservience, it had a sting in the tail.[20]

Despite the attentions of Nightingale and her nurses, the death rate increased dramatically. In the single month of January 10 per cent of the entire British Army in the East died of disease. In February the death rate of patients at Scutari was calculated at 42 per cent per annum of cases treated, having risen from 8 per cent since Nightingale arrived four months earlier. More than 10,000 unwounded British soldiers died in the hospitals in the five months following the great storm in November, fostering the popular notion that the army had been decimated by 'General Winter'. This popular notion had already been implanted by the story of Napoleon Bonaparte's retreat from Moscow. Who can forget the pathetic paintings of soldiers and horses of the *Grande Armée* struggling through the drifts or frozen rigid in the snow? It is an idea that lends itself to simple and effective imagery. Such picturesque ideas may be so powerful that they can never be corrected. They depict a small truth in such a forcible way that they obscure a larger truth. In

War and Peace Tolstoy tried to dispel the popular notion that the Grand Army was destroyed by the cold during the retreat from Moscow. Tolstoy's new thesis was that Bonaparte's army received its mortal wound at the battle of Borodino, in September 1812, before it even arrived at Moscow. But however true Tolstoy's thesis, it in turn hides an even greater truth. That greater truth is that Bonaparte's army was destroyed in the summer, long before the Battle of Borodino, and by disease alone. That army numbered 442,000 men when it crossed the Niemen River into Russia in June 1812. When it took the field at Borodino in September, it had already shrunk to 127,000 and it lost another 28,000 in that battle. Borodino has always been regarded as a particularly deadly battle, but what of the 300,000 men who died of disease on the march into Russia even before it took place? It was the loss of those men – two thirds of his entire invasion force – that defeated Bonaparte. The thermometer did not drop below zero until he was on the way back to France, and his total losses during the retreat were only a third of those in the advance.

Sickness had always killed far more soldiers than battles. Epidemics in armies were commonplace, and no explanation had been required for them. But the British Government now sought an explanation, and responded to the Crimean crisis by sending out two civilian-led teams of experts to examine the sanitation and supply arrangements of the army respectively. These teams began their work at Scutari, the suburb of Constantinople where Nightingale's hospital was located, at the beginning of March 1855. The Sanitary Commission consisted of two doctors (Sutherland and Gavin) and an engineer (Rawlinson). Gavin was tragically killed in an accident in camp, and Rawlinson was invalided home after miraculously surviving a glancing blow from a Russian cannonball. The Supplies Commission consisted of Sir John McNeill and an army troubleshooter, Colonel Tulloch. Each of these teams of experts had a different explanation for the deaths of nearly 12,000 soldiers in hospital, the vast majority of them unwounded. The Sanitary Commission, under Dr Sutherland, believed that the men's sickness had been caused or aggravated by poor sanitation in the camps and hospitals. The Supplies Commission under Sir John McNeill believed that inadequate rations and clothing had weakened the soldiers so that hospitalisation and medical treatment could not save them.

Nightingale and these civilian commissioners banded together as the nucleus of a reform group who would challenge the more conservative military men and their generally subservient medical subordinates. She welcomed Dr Sutherland's measures for improving ventilation, sewage, and water supply in her hospital, but she firmly believed that the Supplies Commission under McNeill had the answer to the problem. McNeill interviewed Nightingale extensively when preparing his reforms for the army, and her comments showed what she thought about his plan to feed the common soldiers better, 'Sir John McNeill is the man I like the best of all who have come out,' she wrote to her sister. 'He has dragged the commissary general out of the mud. He has done wonders. Everybody now has their fresh meat three times a week, their fresh bread from Constantinople about as often.'

McNeill had led an extraordinary life. Now aged sixty, he first qualified as a doctor and went to work as medical officer to the British Embassy in Persia. He proved so skilled at 'harem diplomacy' that he was eventually appointed Ambassador to Teheran. He accompanied the Shah's army on a military expedition to Afghanistan, helping to ensure that the Shah's attack on Herat failed despite support from the Russians who were using the Shah to expand their own empire. McNeill published an anti-Russian pamphlet that made him popular with Lord Palmerston, then Foreign Secretary; the Russians had further cause to resent him because of his rumoured involvement in an attack on their embassy in Teheran. The Russian Ambassador, Griboyedov, was trying to recover some young Russian girls who had been kidnapped for harems in Teheran; the Persians would not give them up so Griboyedov held some Persian girls hostage in the Russian Embassy. The Persian girls escaped and claimed to have been raped and a Persian mob sacked the embassy and murdered the occupants including Ambassador Griboyedov. Some Russian observers at the time alleged without justification that McNeill had instigated this massacre, further enhancing his reputation for intrigue.[21] When McNeill returned home to Scotland he was put in charge of relieving the potato famine in the Western Highlands in 1845, and was widely credited with avoiding the mass starvation of the kind that occurred in Ireland. He was therefore well-qualified to relieve hunger among the troops in the Crimea and to negotiate the tricky political obstacles in his way.

McNeill left Scutari and went on to the Crimea after only a week. A few weeks later, Florence Nightingale went on the first of three visits to the Crimea which kept her there for five months in all. This first time she was only there for a month inspecting the new hospitals that had been opened now that a sudden evacuation of Allied troops had become less likely. While there she fell ill and was delirious with fever for several days. While she was in this state she wrote a letter which has until now defied attempts to explain it. Now that it can be decoded, it sheds a new light on her emotional life; had its contents been clearer, it would have been destroyed by her family like many other too-revealing letters from her voluminous archives.

Nightingale is widely thought to have never consummated a sexual relationship in her life, and to have been emotionally repressed. For several years before the war she had planned to marry Richard Monckton Milnes, a highly sociable politician, and there did seem to be real passion in their relationship; however she broke off with him when she decided to work and never to marry. When she went to the Crimea she was aged thirty-four, not especially beautiful but with a graceful figure and pleasant features. At least one of the surgeons at Scutari dreamed of marrying her, noting with approval her '£30,000 and estates in Hampshire and Derbyshire'.[22] This surgeon's feelings were not reciprocated, but the coded letter that she wrote when she was supposedly delirious in hospital in the Crimea points to a hitherto unsuspected infatuation that was to have important consequences.

Heights of Balaclava
Castle Hospital
May 21/ 55
Dear Sir John,

I can hardly tell what brings me to you. Last week a Persian adventurer appeared to me like a phantom, showed me papers by which Mr Bracebridge seemed to have drawn upon me for £300,000. I sent for him. He said very little, neither denied nor assented but said no [one] would ever [believe] that I had [seen] the papers there for the first time. This is all, dear Sir John, that I have to say. Have you any advice to give? I come to you because you have shewn me much kindness. Dear Sir John, Yours truly, Florence Nightingale.

The three bracketed words are missing because someone has torn off a corner of the letter, perhaps to remove an indiscreet note about its contents. Inserting them makes the letter seem lucid, but still not rational. Mr.

Bracebridge (who was the husband of her best friend and who performed her financial transactions as only a man could do at the time) would never have claimed that he had authority to spend what was a preposterously large sum in those days. We know from Bracebridge that she did send for him in her delirium and accuse him of this fraud.[23] It is also known that Nightingale was not friendly to Bracebridge, and tolerated him only for the sake of his wife.

The strangest thing in the letter is the reference to a 'Persian adventurer' who unmasked Bracebridge's alleged fraud. How, we may ask, would she have recognised a person in her dream as a Persian adventurer? Would Sir John McNeill scratch his head over this part of the letter as we might? No, he would not, because it would immediately be obvious to him that 'Persian adventurer' was a coded reference to himself based on the anecdotes he had told her of his experiences in Teheran. McNeill's Persian reputation was subject of open discussion, as Bracebridge himself reveals when writing about McNeill's concern for Nightingale's illness, 'I met Sir John McNeill there. He was questioning Mrs. Roberts [who was nursing Nightingale] about her with as much interest as he ever did the Shah's ministers.' Far from being the most obscure part of Nightingale's letter, this was a clear-headed statement that she had seen McNeill in a dream or vision in which he acted as her protector. Furthermore, her use of code shows that she wanted to keep confidential the fact that she had dreamed of him.

It is pointless to speculate here whether Nightingale was having an affair with this Persian adventurer, whom she then regarded as the saviour of the army. So little is known about how the Victorians conducted their love affairs that the likelihood of a physical relationship cannot be estimated. McNeill was married, and at sixty old enough to be her father; in fact he had all the qualities that her unworldly father (to whom she was very close) lacked in her eyes. He was also very handsome, or at least a photograph taken eight years before shows that he was then very handsome indeed: slim, with long hair, aquiline features, and piercing eyes.[24] Whatever the nature of the relationship with McNeill she was sensitive enough about it to write in code about her dreams of him in what could be seen as slightly incoherent love letter. And there is some evidence that her family may have been uneasy about the relationship. After the war she decided to stay at his house in Scotland on her way to meet the Queen. In his letter to her arranging this visit,

McNeill used the highly unusual salutation 'Dear Miss Florence'. No man other than close family members ever addressed her by her first name. Like all Nightingale's letters this one was probably passed around the family and it must have raised several eyebrows. A letter went back to McNeill announcing that due to the illness of an unspecified friend in Scotland Nightingale would not be able to stay with him. Nothing else is ever heard of the alleged sick friend, but McNeill's subsequent letters to Nightingale begin with the more usual salutation 'Dear Miss Nightingale'. She did meet him in Scotland, however, and afterwards she wrote to him, 'I have so little time to write now that I cannot give myself the indulgence of telling you how much good you did me: body, soul, and mind…' Her use of the word 'body' is striking but probably quite innocent. Nevertheless, it is odd that the only time this letter has been published its editor (Zachary Cope) silently omitted that word. Such omissions, and the failure to recognise her emotional relationship with McNeill, have helped to perpetuate Nightingale's 'iron maiden' image.

This close friendship with McNeill contributed to what Nightingale later saw as a terrible mistake on her part. He convinced Nightingale that the soldiers were dying in her Scutari hospital because the army had deprived them of basic supplies, particularly food rations. According to McNeill, the Russian/Persian siege of Herat that he had witnessed had failed because of starvation among the besieging force, not the besieged as one might expect. He was one of the few observers in the Crimea who had experience of a modern siege. His fellow supplies commissioner wrote to McNeill, in a context that showed that McNeill agreed with his diagnosis of the condition of the Allied army besieging Sebastopol, that 'the real disease was starvation'.[25] This was equivalent to saying the army was sending Nightingale 'the wrong type of patient', already dying when they arrived at the hospital. Nightingale publicly endorsed McNeill's view at the time, but after the war she became convinced that he had been wrong, and that the patients had been killed by poor sanitation in the hospital itself. She decided that they could have been saved if the sewers and water supply had been improved earlier. Her infatuation, by encouraging her to believe McNeill's diagnosis, had led to a fatal missed opportunity.

During the Crimean War, as in so many others, the enemy was not General Winter but General Hospital. It was the statistics that Nightingale derived from the Crimean hospitals that first allowed civilian epidemics to be understood and controlled by improvements to building sanitation. (The information did not reach the public domain quickly enough to prevent the deaths from sickness during the American Civil War outnumbering those from wounds by two to one). The great proponent of control of epidemics – in civil life even more than military – was Florence Nightingale. Her post-war mission was to use the terrible lessons of Scutari to end the scourge of epidemic disease and premature death in the civilian population, largely caused by inadequate building sanitation. To do so she and her colleagues had to undo the damage caused by the abolition of the General Board of Health in 1854, and change the hearts and minds of the wealthy citizens who enjoyed the right to vote. Between the end of the Crimean War and her death in 1910, life expectancy in Britain climbed from thirty-nine to fifty-five years – the steepest rise in recorded history – because of the fight against epidemics which was won long before any treatment or vaccination for the diseases themselves was available. This fight was largely inspired by Nightingale's frank assessment of the failure of her hospital at Scutari.

'Let us now ask, how was it that our noble army all but perished in the East?' she wrote shortly after the Crimean War. 'And we shall at the same time learn how it has happened that so many hundreds of millions of the human race have by pestilence perished before their time.'

The figures that Nightingale presented to show how 'our noble army all but perished in the East' cover the first five months after Nightingale arrived at Scutari, during which time the death rate in her hospital rose dramatically. She did not discover these figures until one year after the war, and they convinced her how unimportant her improved standard of nursing was in saving patients lives, compared to sanitation. She was desperate to publish the figures in her officially commissioned report into the hospitals, as a wake-up call to civilian public health officials. The government would not allow publication, and Nightingale's 1857 nervous breakdown probably arose from this conflict. After her recovery, she leaked the figures to influential people to increase political pressure for public health reform. Her leaked secret report showed that the government's failure to select proper hospital buildings caused the high death rate, not medical incompetence or lack of supplies. It did this by showing just how fatal her hospitals at Scutari were compared to others, during the time she was in charge there. 'It has not been shown before,' she wrote, 'how much of that mortality was due to the frightful state of the Hospitals at Scutari; how much it depended upon the number which each Regiment was unfortunately enabled to send to those pest-houses'. This was a drastic put-down of her own reputation, forced out of her by her commitment to the Unitarian belief that mankind can only learn by confronting its own mistakes. The novelist and reformer Elizabeth Gaskell was one of those to whom Nightingale sent her secret report. Gaskell wrote back, 'You have done nobly the disagreeable work you had in your way; you have not shirked it but given it plainly and simply out... Nobody shall see those books but my own family. Nor does anyone know that I have them.'[16]

Biographers and historians claimed that her secret report contained no more than the published one. Possibly they did not read it. They say that her habit of asking the recipients to keep it confidential (a reasonable precaution to justify the sharing of an unpublished government report) was a publicity stunt to ensure that the recipients would circulate it! Nobody would have dared to say such things when she was alive, but with Nightingale safely dead in 1910 the stage was set for the *Dictionary of National Biography* to give her the credit for having immediately reduced the death rate at Scutari by her nursing activities despite a total absence of building sanitation. Only because she widely leaked her secret report, and recipients preserved copies of it, has Nightingale's version of events and what she considered to be her great lesson to mankind now been rediscovered.

Some of Nightingale's admirers today think it wrong to emphasise her belated discovery that her hospital at Scutari had been lethal, holding that it detracts from her achievements. Nightingale herself believed that her discovery was of the greatest importance, and deliberately sacrificed her reputation as an angel of mercy to publicise it. Some may think that she was merely neurotic to dwell on the topic. Those who value Nightingale's intelligence and education, rather than just her nursing, may be inclined to respect her judgement on the matter.

As a result of the early censorship of Nightingale's whistleblowing, she is less well known for her post-war political activity than she is for her wartime achievements. The latter were considerable even after the layers of propaganda and sentimentality are stripped away. She instituted several reforms including the granting to soldiers of the right to send their pay home through the Post Office, which curtailed an epidemic of drunkenness at a stroke. She successfully managed a team of female workers from several different religious groups in the face of great hostility and in so doing eliminated widespread public prejudice against women, nurses, and religious orders. Of her original group of thirty-eight nurses, eighteen were nuns (ten Roman Catholic and eight from an Anglican sect), six more were from a semi-religious High Anglican institution and fourteen were professional nurses. The spectacle of eighteen nuns being allowed by their superiors to work under the orders of a lay person was remarkable. The public hostility that nuns had to endure in Britain at that time can scarcely be imagined today; the Roman Catholic church was seen as putting Rome's authority above that of the Crown, and even Anglican sisters were assumed to be closet Roman Catholics. Anglican nuns were often spat upon or vilified in the street, which no doubt sharpened their sense of mission. All this was to change after the war, and Nightingale's success in persuading these women to work together at Scutari helped to create new public respect for working women, nurses, and religious sisterhoods.

Unfortunately the idealisation of Nightingale's hands-on wartime activities has identified her in the popular mind as a nurse. She nursed at Scutari, occasionally, but only in a similar way to high-ranking visitors who did what they could to help when surrounded by a humanitarian catastrophe. Her responsibilities and qualifications lay elsewhere. The same can be said of Mary Seacole ('the charismatic black nurse' according to the cover of a recent biography) who went to the Crimea as an entrepreneur to run a pub from which she dispensed medical treatment and supplies. Seacole stayed closer to the action than Nightingale, courageously touring the battlefields dispensing first aid to the wounded. But she was a doctor rather than a nurse. Nightingale regarded Seacole as a menace to the sobriety of her subordinates – not unreasonably, given the new image of nurses that she wanted to create – and also as a 'quack'. This last opinion may have been over-harsh, because Seacole had as much medical experience as the majority of English physicians at the time. Compulsory medical licensing only came in after the Crimean War, and even then the most usual way to qualify was to present evidence of an apprenticeship to an apothecary. Seacole had worked in Jamaica with her mother dispensing drugs for many years, and would certainly have been as knowledgeable as most English physicians. It is still fashionable for Seacole's admirers to call her, at best, a 'doctress' even though it is now politically incorrect to call a female actor an actress. In European ears the term evokes second-rate or perhaps 'indigenous' medicine. Seacole used the term of herself, it is true, but in her Creole culture the word would not denote inferiority compared to the male equivalent because female doctors were considered superior in Creole society. By continuing to use the Creole term in a European context, Seacole's admirers are avoiding comparisons with average English doctors which would not have been flattering to the latter. (The doctors in Nightingale's hospital were above average; many of them were young civilians on contract, 'tomorrow's men', newly qualified to superior standards). Imagine the reaction from today's medical community to a biography that identified Seacole as 'the charismatic black doctor'!Probably about as hostile as the military reaction to the idea of 'Colonel Nightingale'. So these two overachieving women are condemned to be safely isolated by history from comparison with males and to compete with each other as nurses, a role that does not do the remotest justice to either, for the absurd title (bestowed by a recent film documentary) of 'the Real Angel of the Crimea'.

THE FALL OF THE GOVERNMENT

In her confidential role as trouble-shooter for the Cabinet, Nightingale sent many reports home about defects in the medical and supply organisations. These reports and others from people who had visited the East convinced the Cabinet that the generals were not being honest about the situation. The worst offender was Lord Raglan, the Commander-in-Chief, who refused to admit that problems were not being solved. His relationship with the Minister of War, the Duke of Newcastle, began to deteriorate in December 1854 as Raglan began to blame the government and the latter learned what was really happening in the East. In one exchange, Newcastle asked Raglan indignantly, 'Surely you do not mean that I in England could mend the roads?'[27] His protest might have been more appropriate if he had not already contracted in England for a railway which arrived in the Crimea three months too late to save the troops. He could instead have immediately sent out shiploads of England's famous navvies, with tools and carts, who could have sorted out seven miles of road in a matter of weeks.

Newcastle complained to Raglan that many of the reinforcements were sickening and dying days after landing, in part because there were no tents for them and nobody even to guide them to the camp. Raglan in turn protested to Newcastle that the recruits coming out were mere boys of sixteen. While the Russians had their conscripted serf levies and the French their civilian reserves, Britain was finding it difficult to replace and reinforce their volunteer troops. There was never even a mention of the possibility of conscription – what was universal in other European countries was unthinkable in Britain at that time. Instead, the Cabinet decided to recruit foreign mercenaries into new Polish, Swiss, and German legions. The Cabinet needed new legislation to train these legions in England, so Parliament had to be reconvened in an unusual winter session. This created new difficulties for the government because the House of Commons became obstreperous at the interruption of the hunting season, the disturbing news from the front, and increasing evidence of government incompetence. *The Times* began to criticise Raglan and Newcastle, and at the end of January 1855 a respected maverick MP, John Roebuck, moved for a House committee to enquire into the conduct of the war. Before the debate even began the leader of the government in the Commons, Lord John Russell, resigned saying that this had all happened because in the summer his Cabinet colleagues had overruled his suggestion that Lord Palmerston should be Minister of War. The revelation that the government's leaders had been too weak even to enforce their will on their own Cabinet for the last six months was a mortal blow, and when Roebuck's measure was passed by the House Lord Aberdeen and his Cabinet resigned.

In the middle of a war, with its outnumbered army perishing beyond hope of succour under the command of generals who did not seem to care, Britain suddenly found itself without a government.

7

The Allied Change of Plan

NEW GOVERNMENT, NEW WAR

Queen Victoria and Prince Albert tried to find ways of avoiding calling on their least favourite politician, Lord Palmerston, to lead a new government but finally bowed to the inevitable and the old statesman took his place at the country's helm for the first time on 6 February 1855.

Palmerston, now aged seventy-one, had been in government since his early twenties as a Lord of the Admiralty, Secretary at War responsible for army finances, and then as Foreign Secretary for nearly a quarter-century until he fell out with Queen Victoria and her husband in 1852. Relegated to the unfamiliar and unglamorous role of Home Secretary in the departing administration he had demonstrated his versatility by enforcing strict rules on clean air and public health which were unpopular with voters (who did not at that time include working men). In his earlier long career as Foreign Secretary he had been aggressive in supporting British national and individual interests with threats of force, often cheekily insulting the more autocratic governments of Europe, and this made him a popular choice as Prime Minister. The country thought of him as a saviour capable of dealing expeditiously with foreign despots, incompetent generals, and uppity Royals alike.

John Roebuck's House of Commons committee of enquiry into the conduct of the war produced voluminous parliamentary papers but little in the way of tangible results. Lord Palmerston's first act as Prime Minister was much more productive: he sent the civilian experts including Sir John McNeill to the Crimea to correct the defects in the sanitary and supply arrangements of the army. Florence Nightingale had been sent by former cabinet ministers who were now in disgrace, but her friendship with Lord Palmerston was as close as it had been with them. Her appointment would have been more typical of Lord Palmerston, who was keen to introduce into the army the civilian expertise that had made Britain the workshop of the world and who did not mind stepping on the toes of the military hierarchy. Palmerston did not hesitate either to put his stamp on diplomatic negotiations with France, Austria, and Russia aimed at securing a satisfactory peace. His liberal aim had always been to roll back the Russian empire's recent and ongoing conquests, not just to neutralise Sebastopol and the Black Sea. Poland, the Crimea, Georgia and Circassia, all recent Russian conquests, were now seething with revolt and Palmerston had a free hand to exploit their discontent. He was therefore determined to take a much tougher stance in negotiations with Russia than the previous government.

In the dying days of the previous British administration, Russia had signalled through Austria that it was prepared to negotiate peace on the basis of the Four Points put forward by the other Great Powers. The first point was that Russia should give up all its existing rights to intervene in the semi-autonomous Turkish Balkan provinces; these rights would be taken over by the Great Powers, effectively extending the Concert of Europe to European Turkey. The second point was that the Danube (which flows into the Black Sea) should be opened up to foreign commerce; this would greatly benefit Britain which wished to import grain from the Balkans. The third point was that the Straits Convention, the treaty allowing only Russia and Turkey to maintain significant naval forces in the Black Sea, should be revised 'in the interest of the balance of power in Europe', which meant at least reducing Russia's privileges. The fourth point was that Russia would relinquish all rights to protect Christians in the Turkish Empire. These Four Points had been confirmed in notes between Britain, France and Austria in August, as a result of determined British and French efforts to bring Austria into the war against Russia. Austria was not prepared to be publicly identified with a project for the dismemberment of the Russian Empire – the goal of the more warlike members of the British and French Governments – and therefore insisted on a statement of limited objectives. But the third point was vague enough to accommodate the more bellicose views inside the

French and British Governments. The exact terms of a treaty to replace the Straits Convention were not yet defined by the three Powers, and could at the limit cost Russia some of her territory.

In a time of very sparse land communications, a dominant naval presence in the Black Sea was the key to Russian control of her conquests in the Crimea, the Ukraine, Bessarabia and the Caucasus as well as her ability to control traffic on the Danube and to continue to expand through conquest in the Balkans, the Caucasus, and Turkey. The dominance was assured by her installations at Sebastopol, considered to be the biggest military and naval arsenal in the world[1] and located in one of the finest natural harbours. A revision of the Straits Convention unfavourable to Russia could mean any of three things: allowing other foreign warships into the Black Sea (with Turkey's consent, of course, for non-Russian vessels which would have to enter through the Bosphorus); banning all warships from the Black Sea; or banning only Russian warships. These are in ascending order of severity for Russia, with all but the first promising to destabilise her control of her territories on the shores of the Black Sea as well as depriving her of her only permanently ice-free route for naval vessels into the world's oceans.

Russia had at first dismissed outright the possibility of negotiating on the basis of the Four Points. Austria applied pressure by mobilising its army and by signing a further treaty with France and Britain implying that if peace were not assured by the end of 1854 Austria would take other steps – intended to mean that she reserved the right to declare war on Russia. As a precondition of signing this treaty, Austria asked France and Britain to define the 'Third Point' (about the Straits convention) in a way not too harsh on Russia, so that the latter would accept and make an Austrian declaration of war unnecessary. France and Britain, who wanted to draw Austria into the war, struggled to find a definition of the third point that would be acceptable to Austria but could later be clarified so as to be unacceptable to Russia and so bring Austria into the war. France and Britain won this round, because the definition of how the Straits Convention should be revised was almost as vague as the original: the new definition simply said that the Russian domination of the Black Sea should cease. As before, this meant anything from admitting foreign navies to banning the Russian navy. Austria also insisted that any territorial concessions from Russia would have to be approved by Austria first, and then signed the new treaty with France and Britain which strengthened the joint commitment to the Four Points made in the diplomatic notes which they had exchanged in August.

Meanwhile, on 20 November, after losing the battles of Alma, Balaclava and Inkerman, Russia suddenly announced that it had changed its mind and was ready to negotiate on the basis of the original Four Points. Britain and France now each became nervous that the other might side with Austria in putting forward a milder interpretation of the demands on Russia, and to prevent this signed a separate bilateral agreement under which neither would agree to peace except on the most stringent possible definition of the Third Point, namely that all Russian warships must be banned from the Black Sea and her naval facilities there (including Sebastopol) must be permanently destroyed. This agreement was readily signed by both France and Britain and kept secret from Austria and Russia.

When Russia announced that it would negotiate on the basis of the very vague Four Points, Britain and France prayed that the negotiations would fail as soon as Russia found out that Austria had agreed that, 'Russia's maritime dominance in the Black Sea shall cease'. If Russia balked at this severe definition of the Third Point, it would make it unnecessary for France and Britain to admit that they had agreed an even tougher interpretation behind Austria's back. The Russian Ambassador to Vienna asked for time to consult his government, and on 6 January 1855 he announced that he had received instructions to agree to the cessation of Russian maritime dominance in the Black Sea. France and Britain therefore found themselves reluctantly obliged to agree to peace talks aimed at finding a way to implement this.

Tsar Nicholas I of Russia died on 2 March 1855; rumours circulated that he killed himself.[2] His son and heir Alexander II was less bellicose but did not want to begin his reign with a capitulation. The peace talks opened in Vienna on 15 March, with France and Britain determined not to settle for less than what they had not yet been able to obtain in the field: the destruction of Sebastopol. They knew that this would be unacceptable to Russia not just because it was a reduction in her sovereignty, but also because to yield terrain that had not been captured by the enemy was to betray those who had fought there. If the Allies had already captured Sebastopol, the Tsar could have presented its permanent destruction as *force majeur* to the Russian people. But he could not so easily hand over something that had been successfully defended with so much blood.

Even if Tsar Alexander had agreed to hand over Sebastopol, he might have been rebuffed. By now, things had changed because Palmerston was Prime Minister and the Four Points had only just satisfied his needs when first put forward at the time of the invasion of the Crimea. The demand for the destruction of Sebastopol had in fact been the lowest common denominator of opinion in the French and British Governments. Palmerston and Napoleon III, the most bellicose statesmen of the two countries, had always wanted much more. Back in November, Palmerston had alarmed his more pacific Cabinet colleagues by his remarks to the effect that after the sacrifices in the Crimea the Four Points were as obsolete as last year's diary.

The tough stance of France and Britain at the peace talks brought into the open the fact that Austria did not endorse all their war aims.[3] Russia rejected the demand for the elimination of all Russian naval power and bases in the Black Sea but indicated that it would accept a rewriting of the Straits Convention to the effect that the other Great Powers would be allowed to match its naval strength in the Black Sea. This could have met the demand agreed with Austria for a 'cessation of Russian domi-nance' but it did not satisfy the French and the British requirement that Russian warships should be banned from the area. The deciding factor in France was that Marshal Vaillant, the Minister of War, thought that the French Army would lose face if it withdrew from the fight without having secured the destruction of Sebastopol.[4] This was far more important to France than the question of Russian dominance in the Black Sea area, where France had few interests. Both Britain and France at the begin-ning of May 1855 repudiated an agreement to the Russian compromise made by their Foreign Ministers in Vienna, who both resigned. The war continued, without Austria. The British public were enraged that Austria had drawn back again, but did not of course know that their own government had tried to keep Austria in the dark about their real war aims.

Keeping the Russians out of the Black Sea, and defending Turkey against Russian aggression, fell far short of the war objectives that the new British Prime Minister had been pursuing. Lord Palmerston had written to his colleagues when he had been a subordinate member of the Cabinet ten days before Britain declared war in March 1854, 'My beau ideal of the result of the war which is about to begin with Russia is as follows: Aland (islands in the Baltic) and Finland restored to Sweden.

Some of the German provinces of Russia on the Baltic ceded to Prussia. A substantive kingdom of Poland re-established as a barrier between Germany and Russia... The Crimea, Circassia and Georgia wrested from Russia, the Crimea and Georgia given to Turkey, and Circassia either independent or given to the Sultan as Suzerain. Such results it is true could be accomplished only by a combination of Sweden, Prussia and Austria, with England, France, and Turkey, and such results presuppose great defeats of Russia. But such results are not impossible, and should not be wholly discarded from our thoughts.'[5] This had alarmed Lord Aberdeen, the Prime Minister, who was hoping that the war would soon be over so that the government could 'return zealously to the work of domestic reform, as soon as we were relieved from foreign exertions. But instead of this, we have the plan sketched out [Palmerston's 'beau ideal'] of a "thirty years war"'.[6] Now, a year later and with Lord Palmerston installed as Prime Minister the prospect of a larger war, whether or not it would last thirty years, seemed closer. The improving weather, the disentanglement of British supplies in the Crimea, and plans for the construction of a submarine telegraph line across the Black Sea and a railroad to the camp seemed to be a basis for optimism.

When the transport difficulties in the Crimea became publicly known through Billy Russell's despatches, a British railway contractor had pro-posed to build a railway from scratch within a matter of weeks linking the port of Balaclava with the camps which were spread out between four and seven miles away. At the beginning of February 1855 his civilian construction team of 530 navvies and supervisors landed with a collec-tion of equipment hastily borrowed from railway depots around Britain. Within seven weeks they had constructed seven miles of track and were hauling fifty tons of artillery ammunition from the wharf up to the camp each day using horses and stationary steam engines to pull the railway wagons. At about the same time an electric field telegraph was con-structed linking the camps of the various divisions to each other and to Balaclava. The submarine telegraph to London also came into operation on 13 April. Sebastopol would surely quickly fall when these techno-logical marvels were brought to bear, leaving the Allied armies free to pursue Palmerston's ambitious goal of rolling back Russian conquests in the region.

But Sebastopol did not fall. Using the guns and ammunition hauled up by the railway, the Allies began their new bombardment of

Sebastopol on 9 April. This was the 'Second Bombardment' – the first, in mid-October, had ended in failure because the Russians had replied so ably with artillery of their own. Now the Russians had a new advantage. They had spent the winter lull building up the fortifications around Sebastopol with the only material that could withstand the Allied shells: earth. Their chief engineer, Totleben, was trying out a proposal made by the Scottish writer on architecture, James Fergusson, who had published his 'Proposed New System of Fortification' in 1849. Fergusson argued that masonry forts such as those defending Britain ought to be replaced by constructions of earth. The Russians had already discovered the truth of his claims; their huge masonry forts on the seaward side had proved quite vulnerable as the shattering of their stones caused many injuries. On the landward side they therefore threw up enormous masses of earth and made underground chambers in it for their infantry and gunners.

The Allies' Second Bombardment lasted for seventeen days, and the plan was for the infantry to assault the fortifications when it stopped. It had so little effect, however, that the Allies hesitated – they were astonished to see every morning that the damage of the previous day had been completely repaired with earth overnight. Earlier in the year, the Russians had even expanded their fortified area by capturing and fortifying a small hill outside the eastern suburbs, known to the Allies as the Mamelon. They had also heavily fortified another new area near to it, known as the White Works. The Russian artillery in these new fortifications was causing heavy French casualties, and would be even more dangerous if the advanced trenches were filled with infantry preparing to assault. The Russians had also constructed mini-fortifications known as rifle-pits in no man's land, from which their sharpshooters kept up a harassing fire on Allied gunners. The most troublesome of these was The Quarries, in front of the British sector. Half way through the Second Bombardment, the Allies decided that they would not assault the main fortifications but would instead assault and capture these three objectives first. Plans were made but General Canrobert (who had taken over command of the French forces from St Arnaud on the latter's death from sickness) changed his mind and the Second Bombardment ended without an assault. Canrobert wrote to his Emperor that in the face of the successful Russian resistance to the bombardment, an assault would be too dangerous.

This was a defining moment in the conflict, even more crucial than the moment after Inkerman when the victorious but exhausted Allies postponed the assault on the city that they had planned for 7 November. The delays since then could be put down to the rigours of winter, but now they had failed even though they were rested and resupplied and equipped with every convenience including their marvellous railway. From the perspective of liberal politicians in the Cabinet, the moment when the assault was cancelled on 25 April 1855 was the moment when the siege really lost all meaning for the Allies. Their attack on Sebastopol could have been a demonstration that in modern Europe an aggressor state, however powerful on its own, was impotent against the united efforts of the other Great Powers who could swoop down and obliterate its most precious military asset at will. It had been supposed to demonstrate that, but in fact had demonstrated the exact opposite. The combined forces of the two greatest powers with all their wealth and superior technology were held at bay by a Russian naval base with rudimentary fortifications. This was no way to convince the Austrians and Prussians to join the Allies in a war to end the Russian threat forever.

The failure to produce the desired quick result easily persuaded the new British Government to abandon the siege which had been the brainchild of discredited former ministers. The Cabinet issued new orders to Lord Raglan which the Commander-in-Chief did not just disobey but subverted while feigning obedience, ruining any chance of a decisive result to the conflict. This is the best-kept secret of the war, and could have justified a charge of mutiny. Mutiny is defined in the British Army as an 'organised act of disobedience or defiance by two or more members of the armed services'. In mitigation it can be said that organised disobedience was common among all ranks and often produced the right result, so it may be fair to cut the generals a bit of slack. Elements of the French Army probably colluded with Lord Raglan, but as they were under separate command and not subject to the Army Act this collusion alone would probably not be sufficient to turn Lord Raglan's disobedience into mutiny. Mutiny requires two, and the second in this case was Raglan's second-in-command Sir George Brown, who admitted in an unpublished memorandum after the war that he knew of the orders that Raglan was disobeying. He seems to have been to only person with whom Raglan shared the secret.

The new Prime Minister, Lord Palmerston, had come to power through popular dissatisfaction with the progress of the war, and the ministers who had created the previous strategy were not in Palmerston's new more liberal government. Among the conservative politicians who had left was Sir James Graham, who as First Lord of the Admiralty had been the strongest proponent of an attack on the naval installations at Sebastopol, and the Duke of Newcastle, the former Minister of War, who had allowed the army to serve Graham's strategy by advancing on Sebastopol from the landward side. The Graham/Newcastle strategy had not worked. The Royal Navy's wooden capital ships had proved incapable of inflicting damage on well-built forts and had shown themselves to be extremely vulnerable to the forts' big guns. On land also the Russian artillery had proved more than a match for the Allies. Both sides had by now become expert marksmen with their artillery, trimming the fuses on shells to perfection to make them burst over a precise target and bouncing the solid cannon balls off natural features to reach hidden hollows in the ground like a golfer chipping onto a green. The Allies did possess a new rifled cannon, the Lancaster, but it had not performed as well as the rifled infantry musket. The cannon's rifling consisted of a spiral bore of oval cross-section with the intuitively predictable result that the long iron shells met with great friction and tended to take part of the barrel with them as they left. The experience of the siege seemed to validate the predictions of most military strategists in Britain that it would be impossible to subdue Sebastopol unless the whole of the Crimea was first cleared of Russian troops.

Although Lord Palmerston had supported the decision to capture Sebastopol, it was always on the assumption that the Allies would surround the city and quickly starve it into submission, rather than carry it by bombardment and assault. It was also, for him, merely the first step in a more ambitious campaign against Russia. Events seemed to be bearing out the objections raised by military strategists to the strategy of delivering a single knockout blow to Russia's main naval base in the east, and alternative strategies now began to attract more attention. In the middle of April 1855 the Foreign Office sent a diplomatic envoy to meet Schamyl and other tribal leaders in the Caucasus, to discover whether they could unite as an effective fighting force against Russia and what form of government they aspired to if they should obtain their freedom with Allied help.[7] And liberating the entire province of the Crimea – only captured by Russia from Turkey within living memory – now began to replace the goal of capturing or destroying Sebastopol. As a military strategy this would be more compatible with the long-term goal, shared by the new

Prime Minister and by Napoleon III, of downsizing the Russian Empire. It would count on the support of the native Crimean Tatar population, who had risen up against the Russian occupier in the days after the first Allied victory at the Alma and caused the Russian Governor and gendarmerie temporarily to flee the Crimean capital of Simpheropol.[8] Most important of all, driving the Russian Army before them in the field was what the Allied troops had shown themselves superbly capable of doing, at the Alma, at Inkerman and in the triumphant but unexploited Charge of the Light Brigade. The Allies' superiority over the Russians lay in the skill of their infantrymen, the range of their new rifle, and the power of the British cavalry. These advantages counted for little in an offensive siege of Sebastopol. Before the war started these strengths had been no more apparent than the weaknesses of the artillery – which was the main weapon of the siege – and of the wooden capital ships, but immediately the offensive began the Allied weakness became obvious. A few days after the failure of the first bombardment and the Charge of the Light Brigade Colonel Charles Ash Windham, aide-de-camp to General Cathcart, had written to an acquaintance in England, 'Artillery is the strong arm of the enemy, and, with a fine arsenal to back them we have attacked him in the very way, and from the very position, that he would have had us choose.'[9] The new plan to overrun the Crimea was founded not only on a change in the political climate but also on experience in the field.

Foremost among the proponents of a new strategy in the Crimea was the Emperor Napoleon III, who argued that Sebastopol could never be captured unless it was entirely surrounded and that if it was surrounded it would fall without a struggle. The Allies could not surround Sebastopol while there was a Russian Army waiting outside the city to fall on the rear of any Allied troops who tried to encircle it. Napoleon III proposed a strategy under which the Allies would give up the idea of capturing the southern part of Sebastopol by bombardment and assault. Instead they would land an army at Aloushta forty miles to the east and march towards Simpheropol, the weakly-defended capital of the Crimea and the crossroads that dominated all the province's land supply routes. The Russians would have to oppose this army in a battle in open country where the demonstrated superiority of the Allies' Minié rifle and cavalry could be used to their full advantage. The Allies' inevitable victory would give them command of the Crimean peninsula so that the whole of Sebastopol could be starved into submission and an infantry assault would not be necessary.

At the time of the failed Second Bombardment the Emperor was visiting London and Windsor, where he made a great impression on Queen Victoria with his abilities on the dance floor and found a sympathetic audience for his strategic views. The British Minister of War had heard evidence just two days before from General Sir John Burgoyne, the Inspector-General of Fortifications who had just returned from the Crimea, that further bombardment of Sebastopol was pointless[10]; Burgoyne's had been the most senior military voice raised against the planned attack on Sebastopol ever since the idea had been first discussed before the war.[11] The Prime Minister, the Queen, and Prince Albert now agreed to adopt Napoleon III's campaign strategy with some alterations. What they did not like about the strategy was that the army would have to march through a narrow mountain pass above Aloushta, of which the Emperor claimed to have special knowledge. The Allies devised a compromise under which the main offensive would be towards the Heights of Inkerman and Mackenzie's Farm, closer to Sebastopol. The Emperor's Aloushta scheme was included as one of three options for a diversionary attack, the choice among these options being left to the commanders in the Crimea. Under this compromise, the Emperor could continue to believe that if he could persuade his Commander-in-Chief, General Canrobert, to march a purely French Army from Aloushta towards the capital as a diversion, and if the advance proceeded as smoothly as he expected, then Simpheropol would fall and the ' diversion' would become the main event.

The two war ministers signed a memorandum of agreement setting out the details of the agreed campaign strategy. In British circles, this document was not 'the Emperor's plan' but was rather an Allied campaign plan. This distinction is important because Panmure made several critical references later to 'the Emperor's plan (or scheme)' which must be understood as referring simply to the Emperor's continued promotion of the Aloushta diversion over other options for the diversionary army.

On the British side, the agreement still had to be ratified by the full Cabinet. Lord Panmure wrote to Lord Raglan on 20 April unofficially outlining the details of the campaign plan and adding, 'These private communications, of course, you will keep to yourself until I am able to confirm them by a secret and confidential despatch, containing formal directions similar to those which will be communicated to the Allies.'[12] The submarine telegraph to the Crimea was coming into operation just at that time, but lengthy communications like this one still travelled by sea and took about two weeks to arrive. On 23 April Panmure sent Raglan a copy of the memorandum of agreement signed by him and Marshal Vaillant, which Raglan acknowledged on 8 May.[13] Raglan was now in possession of the details of the number of troops proposed for each component of the strategy. He also knew, because Panmure had told him, that Burgoyne had convinced the Minister of War that further bombardment was pointless. The new campaign plan was still only a proposal to the Cabinet, as far as Raglan knew, but a very well-supported one. In fact the Cabinet had by now approved the project and the 'formal directions' as Panmure had called them in an interestingly French locution, had left London by messenger on 4 May. On 8 May Raglan replied to Panmure giving his opinion on the latter's unofficial outline of the proposal and on the memorandum of agreement with Vaillant: Raglan said that the French and the Turks would agree with him that the number of troops proposed to defend the existing trenches was insufficient. He also remarked that the French were certain to overcomplicate their part of the planned field operations.[14] The following day the new telegraph brought Raglan the news from Panmure that the official instructions approved by the Cabinet were on their way, '9 may 1855 7p.m. A messenger is on his way with instructions to concert with General Canrobert active operations in the field. Make every preparation accordingly.'[15]

The official instructions for the change in strategy were quite categorical and left Raglan much less discretion than the orders which preceded his invasion of the Crimea:

SECRET AND CONFIDENTIAL

Lord Panmure to Field-Marshal Lord Raglan
War Department May 4 1855

My Lord

THE small impression which, by the latest accounts received from the Crimea, appears to have been made on Sebastopol by the heavy fire lately directed against it by the Allied armies, seems to show that the resources of the Russians are too great to warrant any expectation that the fortress can at any early time

be taken by the present system of attack. It therefore becomes absolutely necessary to consider the best course, under such circumstances, to be pursued; and I
have already apprised your Lordship, in my secret despatch of the 23rd April, that
while His Majesty the Emperor of the French was here, he fully communicated
with Her Majesty's Government on the plan of campaign which he proposed to
follow had he carried out his intention of going in person to the Crimea.

I forwarded to you the outline of the result of our deliberations, and also a
copy of the plan to which the Emperor, on the one hand, and Her Majesty's
Government, on the other, had agreed. Since then, His Imperial Majesty has
deemed it right to abandon his intention of visiting the Crimea, and has
addressed to General Canrobert a long despatch fully detailing the operations
which, if he had gone to the Crimea he had determined to undertake, so far
as his knowledge of the circumstances permitted him to form a judgement.

His Majesty, with a frankness which exhibits his anxiety to establish and
carry out the most perfect harmony of action between the two Governments,
has conveyed to Her Majesty's Government a copy of this most interesting
despatch; and though, doubtless, General Canrobert will have already made
known to you the imperative instructions of his Sovereign, I deem it to be
my duty to put your Lordship in possession of a detailed statement of His
Majesty's views, by sending you, in the strictest confidence, a copy of his letter.

It is the desire of Her Majesty's Government that, after a careful perusal
of this important document, you should enter into a cordial and deliberate
consultation with General Canrobert on all its details, and that you should,
as soon as your mutual dispositions will warrant your moving, undertake that
plan [i.e. whichever of the variations suggested for the use of the third 'diversionary' force, see below] which, in your united judgement, shall appear most
likely to be attended with success.

Her Majesty's Government agrees with the Emperor that, until fully
invested, Sebastopol cannot be taken, and that it cannot be effectually invested
until the Russian covering army is driven from the position from which it
communicates with the town.

To effect this object, we entirely concur in the proposal to divide the Allied
forces into three armies according to the agreement recorded in the document signed by Marshal Vaillant and myself, and referred to by the Emperor
in His Majesty's despatch to General Canrobert.

One of these three armies will maintain the siege [i.e. desist from the
idea of assaulting the city, but remain in position around it]. A second under
your command is intended to advance on the heights of Inkermann and

Mackenzie's Farm, so as to interpose between the town and the Russian Army in the field. The third is intended to make such a diversion as shall engage the enemy's attention, and by threatening or actually attacking his rear aid you in an attack on his front.

The main point to be decided will be the direction in which the third army will operate...

The instructions went on to define three possible directions in which the diversionary force could strike. The first option was to land it at Aloushta, nearly 100 miles away on the south coast, and strike for Simpheropol

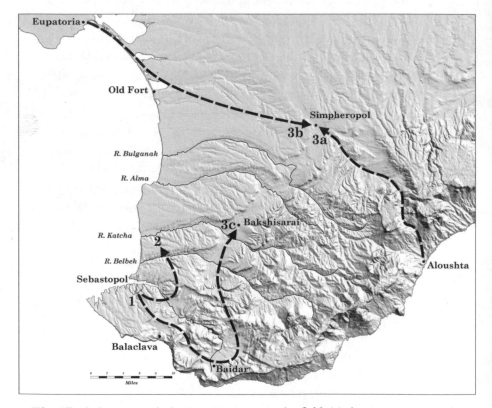

The Allied plan to attack the Russian Army in the field: (1) the siege army; (2) the main offensive; (3a, b, c) possible routes for the diversionary attack.

(the capital of the Crimea) through a mountain pass. The second was to land it at Eupatoria and strike eastwards for Simpheropol. The third was not to embark it at all, but to march it towards Simpheropol by a route that took it to the east of the Russian Army encamped to the north of Sebastopol. The Emperor Napoleon III was very attached to the first option (which the British Government thought was 'wild and impractical') and very opposed to the second, but the agreed orders left the choice of diversionary attack to the commanders on the ground who were to provide the diversionary army. Raglan was to lead the main offensive around the east flank of the Russian Army outside Sebastopol.[16]

The instructions from London required the trenches to be left in the hands of 60,000 troops (30,000 Turks and 30,000 French) who, with the help of the former siege batteries and their gunners, would guard against a Russian breakout but would not take the offensive. Before the official instructions arrived, but when he knew they were on the way, Raglan convened a Council of War in the Crimea on 12 and 14 May at which he stressed the need to secure the trenches and pointed out to Canrobert and Omar Pasha, Commander-in-Chief of the Turkish Army that it would need a very large force.[17] According to Somerset Calthorpe, Raglan's nephew and aide-de-camp, Raglan told his colleagues that the proposed campaign plan was only a 'suggestion' from London that he could follow if he thought fit.[18] But in a despatch to London a few days later Raglan admitted that, forewarned by the minister's 9 May telegram, he had known at the time of the Council of War that the official instructions had been approved by the Cabinet and were on the way.[19]

After this Council of War Raglan reported to the Minister of War that his generals agreed with him that not less than 90,000 men were needed to defend the trenches, as against 60,000 proposed by London and around 105,000 in the present offensive siege. Also he said that Omar Pasha was not prepared to let his troops take over the trenches, so that the entire British contingent would have to remain before Sebastopol (along with 55,000 French and 15,000 Sardinians) and the field campaign would initially consist only of 40,000 French and 20,000 Turkish troops. These would march inland from Sebastopol and attack the flank of the Russian Army from Baidar, in the East. The only 'diversion' would be at Eupatoria, the bridgehead that Omar Pasha held with more than 20,000 of his troops on the coast to the north, behind enemy lines. Omar would pretend to be preparing to break out of this bridgehead and cut off Sebastopol. The Russians were expecting this; they had found out that Napoleon III was amassing large reinforcements at Constantinople far beyond what were necessary for the siege and they thought he would land them at Eupatoria and march inland. Trying to forestall this they had attacked Eupatoria on 17 February but had been decisively repulsed by the Turks assisted by British and French officers and artillery and by the guns of the Allied fleets. To convince the Russians that a breakout from Eupatoria was now imminent, Omar would ship another 20,000 Turkish soldiers from Sebastopol to Eupatoria in broad daylight. The Russians would not know that the same ships would transport an even larger number of better Turkish troops – the victors of the battle of 17 February – back to Sebastopol under cover of darkness, to take part in the thrust at Baidar.[20]

Raglan told the Minister of War that when the field campaign had begun to make progress it would take the pressure off the trenches and allow him to join in with up to 20,000 more men.[21] This was seen as acceptable in London, as the Minister of War shows when forwarding Raglan's despatch to the Queen, 'Your Majesty will doubtless see with disappointment that it has not been found expedient so to carry out the plan of operations as hoped, in concert with the Emperor of the French, so as to leave your majesty's troops free to advance as instructed; but Lord Raglan still hopes, when the movement on the right and against the enemy's left is advanced, to be able to take part in the plan of operations which is now evidently about to be put into execution.' The minister warned Her Majesty that due to the extensive preparations required, the campaign was unlikely to begin before the end of June.[22] He wrote to Lord Raglan, 'Your telegraphic message expressing the difficulties of protecting the siege works is unpleasant. I confess that I thought 60,000 Turks and French could have been trusted.'

Raglan's idea of not committing British troops until an attack was already succeeding was not a bad one if he was lacking in confidence in his Allies. It had worked brilliantly, after all, at the Alma. But Raglan did not tell Canrobert that he had informed London that he would join in the offensive when it began to make progress. According to Calthorpe, who seems to have been present at some of the discussions, Raglan said that he was determined to bombard and assault Sebastopol from the south, and he told Canrobert that the greatest objection to the new strategy was that there would be no overall commander of what was sure to be a complex operation. General Canrobert immediately offered to place himself and all French troops in the Crimea entirely under his orders, which threw Raglan into some confusion. Raglan backtracked and said he would have to think about it, and then having thought about it he told General Canrobert that he would accept the command subject to certain conditions. According to French accounts[23] Raglan's conditions were that French (rather than Turkish) troops must take over the British trenches and siege batteries if British troops were to take to the field, leaving hardly any French troops to take part in the new campaign. These accounts say that Canrobert rejected this condition but do not make it clear why Canrobert, if he was so wedded to the field campaign, refused to hand it over to the British. Raglan's twenty-four year old nephew Calthorpe, who was not aware that Raglan was under direct orders to downgrade the siege and focus on field operations instead, told a rather different story. He says that Raglan's conditions for taking over command were that if the field campaign took place the French would take over the English trenches, and if an assault on Sebastopol were to take place it should include an attack on the main fortifications shortly after the outworks were taken.[24] This implies that Raglan reserved the right, if he accepted command, to launch an assault on the city (in defiance of his orders) instead of initiating the field campaign. Canrobert, however, was only offering him the command as the price of his agreement to the latter.

The following day, 16 May, an aide-de-camp delivered a laconic telegram from the Crimea to the French Minster of War sitting in his box at the *Comédie Française* in Paris at half an hour before midnight, '16 May, ten o'clock in the morning. Accept without hesitation the resignation of General Canrobert. He is very fatigued. Reply by telegraph. General Pélissier is ready to take command.' In the mails that followed Canrobert explained that he had been worn down by Lord Raglan's constant changes of position and non-cooperation in the new plan of campaign ('*du plan de campagne de Votre Majésté, devenu presque impossible par la non-coopération du chef de l'armée anglaise*'[25]). As far as Canrobert knew it was still only the Emperor's plan.

Raglan never told London of Canrobert's offer of command, the conditions he had imposed on accepting it, or the breakdown of negotiations. He said that Canrobert and he had agreed on the field campaign but that Canrobert had resigned because of his regret at having impulsively recalled a joint expedition to Kertsch, which had been agreed with the purpose of interrupting Russian coastal supply routes into Sebastopol.[26] Canrobert had received a message from the Emperor on the brand-new telegraph after the fleet had sailed for Kertsch, ordering him to assemble his forces so as to carry out the plan agreed with London for a field campaign. Canrobert insisted on recalling the French ships so that he could bring up the reinforcements from Constantinople, whereupon the British also gave up the expedition. This had caused great bitterness on the British side.

Raglan's and Canrobert's divergent explanations of the latter's resignation – despatched to London and Paris respectively on 19 May – no doubt set the telegraph wires humming between the two capitals two weeks later. It is possible that Raglan believed that by that time the assault on Sebastopol would have succeeded and the subject would be irrelevant. He may have been persuaded that it was only Canrobert's timidity that had prevented a victorious assault before. The reason why Raglan did not undertake the field campaign may have been his staff's preference for a 'quick win' that would make headlines and justify their actions to date. The dockyards of Sebastopol were of little strategic value: they were useless to Russia while the Allies were blockading them, and useless to the Allies while the Russian Army occupied the north side of the harbour unmolested. But the army had been trying to capture them for six months at enormous cost. Raglan was influenced by senior engineer officers who had promoted the plan to take the southern part of the city by bombardment and assault, rather than by surrounding and starving the whole city, and who were now promising that they could push the trenches and batteries close enough to make an infantry assault possible. The generals who might have urged a field campaign were now dead or at home, among them Cathcart, Burgoyne, Lucan, Evans, and the Duke of Cambridge. Raglan was now surrounded by those who had agreed with his strategy and who hoped to prove themselves right and Burgoyne and the others wrong. The Allied governments, on the other hand, were more concerned with the 'big picture': the overall strategy against Russia, which did not end with Sebastopol's dockyards, which included the need to conserve manpower, and which did not recognise the need to justify any General's past actions.

General Niel, the officer who was the French Emperor's informant in the Crimea, had another explanation for Raglan's reluctance to venture away from the Chersonese peninsula where Sebastopol was located: according to him Lord Raglan was 'accustomed to being at home in the Chersonese. Our Allies have railways, towns of wood, much too much of an easy life [*beaucoup trop d'aisance dans la vie*].'[27]

GENERAL PÉLISSIER TAKES OVER

General Pélissier, Canrobert's successor, had always expressed views that agreed with his Emperor's, urging only a month before that the bombardment should be scaled down and Sebastopol should be surrounded and starved into submission, not taken by assault.[28] But when he took over the command he changed his mind and aligned himself so much with Raglan's opposite view that it seems possible that the two had previously discussed a possible change of French command that would suit them both. This may explain Raglan's capricious attitude in negotiations with Canrobert. Raglan and his second-in-command Sir George Brown had already been barely on speaking terms with Canrobert because of the latter's recent recall of the Kertsch expedition commanded by Brown. Brown, as already mentioned, was the only person in the Crimea who knew that Raglan was under official orders to downgrade the siege and embark on the field campaign.[29]

When he took command General Pélissier still claimed to be an enthusiastic supporter of the new campaign plan but produced a military textbook that said that an army should not withdraw from a position facing the enemy without first hemming the enemy in as close as possible. This meant, said Pélissier, that he would have to recapture the White Works and the Mamelon, the two new fortifications on his right by means of which the Russians had pushed out their siege lines earlier in the year, before reducing the intensity of the siege and detaching a part of his army for the agreed field campaign. This subterfuge did not deceive the Emperor, who had his own informants in the Crimea and who must have guessed that Pélissier planned to assault the main defences under the guise of an assault on the outworks.

Pélissier also immediately relaunched the expedition against Kertsch which was successful. It destroyed large quantities of supplies destined for Sebastopol while incurring virtually no casualties, although the operation was marred by looting and violence against the population by Allied troops. The shallowness of the water and the lack of land transport prevented the Allies from getting close enough to the isthmus of Perekop to completely seal off the Crimean peninsula, but they now occupied many of the surrounding strategic points. The Emperor was displeased that 14,000 troops had to be left to garrison the captured points, thus depleting the forces available for the agreed field campaign in the Crimea which would have achieved the same effect and more.

At the same time another favourable event for the Allies was the arrival in the Crimea of troops from the Kingdom of Piedmont-Sardinia, at that time the only part of Italy free of foreign domination. Cavour, Prime Minister of the Kingdom, expected that his country's participation would move the Allies to support Italian liberation and unification after the war under his King's leadership. Sardinian troops, as they are usually called, were extremely well-organised and eventually numbered 20,000. Immediately on their arrival in May 1855 they helped the Allies to push forward the defences of Balaclava and occupy the whole of the lower west bank of the Tchernaya river, which shortened and strengthened the Allies' defensive lines and gave them much-needed access to fresh water. The Russians did not significantly oppose the occupation of the valleys, and the Minister of War in London complained that the Allied armies had not occupied the other bank of the Tchernaya at the same time, in accordance with the new campaign strategy which he still believed they were implementing. The minister still believed that the delay was due to the need to assemble transport.[30]

While the official instructions were still on their way to the Crimea in mid-May Lord Palmerston urged his Minister of War to send telegrams to Raglan underlining the need for immediate implementation of the field campaign, matching the telegrams that the French were sending. On 4 June, after repeated urging from the Prime Minister, the Queen and the French Ambassador, the minister sent another telegram to Raglan which has never been noticed by historians, 'We are anxious that no time should be lost in making a movement against the enemy. You will concert measures with General Pélissier and Omar Pasha as to the best means of executing it either by the Tchernaya or by cutting off the enemy's communication with Simpheropol.'[31] Queen Victoria received a copy of this telegram and wrote that 'she entirely approves the telegraphic orders which have been sent, in concert with the Emperor of the French, to the Allied generals, and trusts that they will have the desired effect'.[32] Raglan took no notice, and Paris and London's agreed military strategy fell by the wayside. The bombardments and assaults on Sebastopol continued at heavy cost.

The 4 June telegram urgently requesting Raglan to begin operations in the field disproves previous historians' view that the British Government had long before that date lost interest in the field campaign 'suggestion'. According to the British histories, the British Cabinet would not agree to the Emperor's strategy, and the Emperor spent the rest of the summer trying to persuade his generals to implement his plan without the British. The image of the young Emperor playing at being a commander with his new telegraph machine, bombarding his long-suffering generals with armchair strategies, is guaranteed to bring a smile to the lips. But the submarine portion of the telegraph line to the Crimea, it must be remembered, had been installed at vast expense by the British and not by the French. Did the British install the line just so that they could speed up requisitions for new boots? Would it not have occurred to the British Government that a telegraph line would make it practicable to dictate joint strategy from London and Paris? Before the telegraph, such control from home was impossible because they depended on sea communications which had ensured that orders arriving in the Crimea were based on information that was at least five weeks old.

The telegraph offered a possible solution to London's dissatisfaction with Lord Raglan. On 4 January 1855, shortly before becoming Prime Minister, Lord Palmerston had concluded that Raglan could not be sacked. 'It is quite clear,' Palmerston wrote to the then Minister of War, 'that in many essential points Raglan is unequal to the task that has fallen to his lot, but it is impossible to remove him...' There were now many officers in London and Paris with Crimean experience, among them General Evans whom Palmerston greatly respected though his radical party politics made it impossible to give him command of the army. It may be that politicians saw the telegraph line from London to Sebastopol as a possible solution to the shortcomings of Raglan and his staff – if they could not be removed, they could be controlled from London and made to follow policies devised by wiser and more experienced heads.

Not until 1908 was it revealed that the French and British Ministers of War had signed an agreement during the Emperor's visit in April 1855 to abandon the offensive against Sebastopol. Even then, half a century after the war, no public information was available on whether the whole British Cabinet ratified the agreement or whether orders were ever sent based on it. There was no thirty year rule, no newspapers and historians waiting to break the news of three decades-old scandals released to a Public Record Office. The complete official orders seem to have remained secret until Lord Panmure's and Lord Raglan's papers entered the public domain, well into the twentieth century. Like other 'events that never happened' the agreed field campaign has attracted only cursory attention from historians who misrepresented it as the madcap scheme, never endorsed by London, of an Emperor whose military ability was easy to ridicule because of later failures with Mexico and Prussia. Some writers have quoted a phrase used in the Minister of War's private papers – 'wild and impractical' – as a judgement on the field campaign, although a careful reading shows that this was only a judgement on the Emperor's preferred option for the diversionary force. No document, official or otherwise, has been published until now showing that Raglan received direct orders to embark on the field campaign. The only historian ever to claim that Raglan disobeyed the orders is Clive Ponting, who gave no sources or details and mistakenly claimed that Canrobert (rather than Pélissier) also disobeyed them.

Soon after the Peace was signed in 1856, a French semi-official account of the war blamed British non-cooperation for the failure of the plan to march on Simpheropol and liberate the Crimea. This was the first the public knew of such a plan, and the book touched a raw nerve in Britain especially because with hindsight the plan seemed a good one. Why didn't the government strongly urge Lord Raglan to cooperate with this plan, asked the United Service Journal. The question remained unanswered by the British Government, and the French were too polite to provide enlightenment.[33]

Would the field campaign have succeeded? The Allied forces of about 180,000 in the Crimea at that time (excluding cavalry and artillery, and excluding 33,000 on the way or waiting at Constantinople) far outnumbered the Russians (about 100,000 of which half were tied up in Sebastopol)[34], and there is no reason to think that Allied commanders were unaware of their numerical superiority. Raglan's reluctance to take the field because of fears for the safety of the reduced army before Sebastopol was not without foundation but, had he wanted to, he could have mothballed Balaclava and shared the French port of Kamiesch thus reducing significantly the defensive manpower requirements around Sebastopol.

General Rose, the senior British liaison officer with the French in the Crimea, knew that the French were discussing a field campaign, and that some of them were concerned about the lack of water on a march up country and the Allied infantry's vulnerability to superior Russian cavalry strength on the plains. He claims to have convinced French colleagues that these concerns were exaggerated. The supposed vulnerability to Russian cavalry, he told them, was based on failure to grasp that the Minié rifle now protected the infantry from that danger, and the shortage of water could be overcome by marching from Eupatoria to Simpheropol up one of the water courses, probably the Bulganak. After the war ended, it transpired that Rose's plan was what the Russians feared most. This shows that there were officers in the Crimea who had learned enough to lead the field campaign – but Rose did not know that Raglan had been ordered to commence one and had no influence at British headquarters. With all their advantages in the field, and with a local population hostile to the Russians it does seem likely that the Allies could have captured the whole of the Crimea and restored it to semi-autonomy under the Turks.[35]

It is also worth asking whether the liberation of the Crimea, Circassia, and other Russian provinces would have been acceptable to Austria, whose concurrence was required under its agreement with France and Britain if Russia were to lose territory. Austria tended to be more sympathetic to Russia than France and Britain, but recent research indicates this was purely a tactical approach to keep peace negotiations going, and that Austria wanted peace not so as to protect Russia but to protect her own fragile empire from disturbance. Austria had much more to fear from an expansionist Russia than did France and Britain, and in fact it was a Russian armed challenge to Austria in the Balkans that triggered the First World War sixty years later. Austria's reluctance to declare war on Russia in 1854/5 is understandable given that at the end of any war she would be much more exposed to Russian vengeance than France and Britain. But there was no reason whatever for Austria to object to a liberated Crimea or Circassia or Poland, which could only be to her advantage. In fact, Austria did later demand and benefit from the only minor Russian cession of territory to result from the war. This shows that Austria did not insist on preserving the integrity of the Russian Empire.

RAGLAN MEETS HIS WATERLOO

At the beginning of June, Pélissier informed his generals in a council of war that he was not going to comply with the instructions of his Emperor to take to the field against the Russian Army outside Sebastopol. Instead he was going to fall in with Raglan's plan to first assault the three Russian outworks (the White Works, the Mamelon, and the Quarries) with infantry and then storm the main fortifications of Sebastopol in the same way immediately after. The attack would begin on 7 June. His generals protested in favour of following the Emperor's instructions but Pélissier curtly silenced them.[36] Pélissier's demeanour and reputation did not encourage dissent. In physique and manner he resembled, according to some, a wild boar; his main claim to fame was having suffocated to death with smoke several hundred Algerian men, women, and children who had taken refuge in the caves of Dahra. According to Prince Albert he was so fat that he could not ride, and if true this may help to explain his aversion to field operations.[37]

Pélissier's assault on Sebastopol's outworks was preceded by a thirty-six-hour Third Bombardment which this time focussed on the strong points of the fortifications rather than being aimed at the city as a whole. Among the weapons used were twenty-seven thirteen-inch mortars which fired more than 8,000 shells weighing 200 pounds each. A mortar was fired at a high angle and therefore did not move and have to be re-aimed after each shot like a cannon; these huge mortars therefore could be fired all night although they had to be allowed to cool down between shots to stop their thick barrels melting. At night the burning fuses of their shells whirled round and round as they followed their high trajectory, making a continuous firework display.

Just as Pélissier was leaving his headquarters to watch the infantry assault on the Russian outworks on the evening of 7 June, a telegram from Paris was handed to him in which the Emperor ordered him not to make the assault. Pélissier put the telegram in his pocket and took great pleasure in later showing it to his subordinates.[38] The infantry assaults succeeded in taking all of the outworks, but attempts to follow the retreating Russians into the main fortifications were repulsed with heavy loss. Pélissier decided to delay the main assault on Sebastopol until the newly-captured outworks could be armed and turned against the Russian defenders; this change of plan may show that the Emperor's

26 The head of the harbour of Balaclava, taken from the north-west.

27 Camp of the 5th Dragoon Guards, part of the cavalry camp.

28 Ships outside Balaclava harbour in the gale of 14 November 1854. The *Prince* is about to go on the rocks, her cut-away rigging having fouled her screw. In the centre, the *Avon* is succeeding in the daring manoevre of steering directly for the land and finding the tiny entrance to the port.

29 Destruction after the fall of Sebastopol: the Public Library and the Temple of the Winds.

30 The British twenty-one-gun battery in action, just to the right of the Woronzoff Road. The fortification straight ahead is the Redan, and on the right is the Malakoff. Two ten-inch and one thirteen-inch mortars are on the left..

31 The Malakoff from the French lines.

32 Camp of the 3rd Battalion, Grenadier Guards, at Scutari on the way to the Crimea. Of those men identified, Lt Davies (leaning on muskets) and Colonel Hood (no.23) were killed in the trenches six months later. The huge barracks behind later became Florence Nightingale's hospital, where a number of the men photographed probably died.

33 The dry docks at Sebastopol.

34 The interior of the Redan after its capture.

35 Col Doherty, other officers, and men of the 13th Light Dragoons. Lt Chamberlayne (clean shaven, left front) achieved fame for nonchalantly carrying his saddle back after having his horse killed under him in the Charge of the Light Brigade, saying it was too valuable to lose

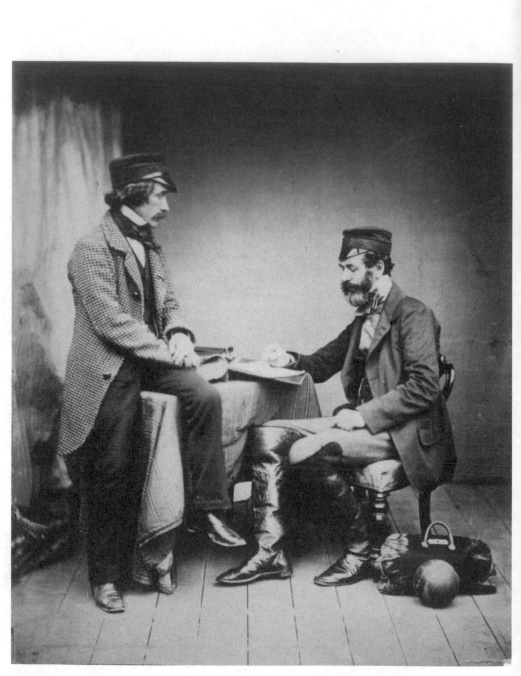

36 The original Sanitary Commission's two surviving members. Dr Sutherland is on the left; Mr Rawlinson was hit by a Russian cannon ball which he retrieved as a souvenir and has placed on the floor beside him.

37 Raglan, Omar, and Pélissier at a Council of War on 7 June 1855. In the evening of the same day Pélissier launched his successful attack on the Mamelon, having received meanwhile a telegram from Napoleon III ordering him not to attack.

38 Raglan outside his headquarters with Pélissier and their aides.

39 Men of the 68th Regiment, later known as the Durham Light Infantry.

40 A private in full marching order. The chimney shows that the floor of the tent is dug out and a stove installed.

41 Sixty-eight-pounder Lancaster gun in the Diamond Battery. The figure at top is Captain William Peel of the frigate *Diamond*, favourite son of the late Sir Robert Peel, the former Prime Minister. Captain Peel took part in several land battles including Inkerman and the Waterloo Day assault on the Redan. He won the VC, and died of smallpox in India during the Mutiny.

42 A quiet day in the mortar battery.

43 Commissariat difficulties. The port of Balaclava is in the background and the track to the camp is axle-deep in mud at Kadikoi.

44 Sebastopol and its harbour seen from the eastern end of the Allied lines. The flat-topped hill fort is the Malakoff; to the left is the gentler slope of the Mamelon.

45 Horse ambulances carrying the sick and wounded up to the hospital above Balaclava Harbour

46 The *Volcano* Steam floating factory ship. Built to support operations in the Baltic, this vessel had a foundry capable of melting two tons of iron, a half-ton steam hammer, assorted punching and shearing presses, a lathe capable of machining a piston seven feet in diameter, and many other machines.

47 Cable laying plough for field telegraph cable. Although arguably the telegraph had been used in earlier wars, the Crimea was the scene of the first field telegraph designed to connect parts of the camp and even ships offshore.

48 The new railway carrying wood for huts to the camp. This scene is close to that shown in the engraving of 'Commissariat difficulties' – the church at Kadikoi is visible in both. Initially horses pulled the trucks on flat ground and a stationary engine with winding gear hauled them up the slopes.

49 Machine for pressing bullets out of solid lead rod. This method was used for Minié bullets as it was quicker and more accurate than casting. This particular machine was made for the French, who liked grooves in their bullets on the theory that it helped stabilize them like the feathers on an arrow.

50 The Glatton, one of about forty iron-clad floating batteries constructed in 1855 after it became obvious that wooden walls were no match for Russian fire from the shore. The ship was armoured with four inches of iron and was said to be unsatisfactory at steaming, sailing, stopping and steering. Extra rudders were hung from the boat davits to remedy the latter defect.

telegram was not completely without effect. The occupation of the former Russian outworks was costly: over 6,000 Allied soldiers dead and wounded in capturing them and hundreds more falling every day in holding them, more exposed as they were to Russian guns than the previous advanced Allied positions. It was not a situation that the Allies could afford to prolong.

The Emperor refrained from telegraphing his congratulations to Pélissier for a whole week. He then frostily explained the delay, 'I wanted, before congratulating you on the brilliant success that you obtained on the 7th, to know how much sacrifice it cost. I learn the numbers from St Petersburg. I admire the courage of the troops, but I draw your attention to the fact that a pitched battle that would have decided the fate of the Crimea would not have cost you more men. I persist, therefore, in the order that I have caused to be given to you to resolutely enter into the field campaign.' Several angry exchanges between Pélissier and the Emperor followed, during which the Emperor clarified that the objective was the Crimea, not its naval base:

> If the instructions [for the field campaign] are too absolute, modify them, it is impossible to close one's eyes to the evidence and not to tell you that the key to the Crimea is Simpheropol, and that an expedition like the one to Kertch, but with twice as many men, debarking at Aloushta and finishing in Simpheropol, would be of more decisive effect than all the bloody attacks on Sebastopol.

In response, Pélissier wrote to the Emperor on 15 June blaming the British for the failure to undertake the field campaign, begging that, 'Your Majesty should recognise also that Lord Raglan has never received from his government orders as formal as those which it pleases Your Majesty to give to me. There lies the difficulty.'[39] If Raglan had shown Pélissier the official despatch dated 4 May or the telegrams of 9 May or 4 June ordering him to downgrade the siege and undertake the field campaign, Pélissier would not have been able honestly to say this. Did Pélissier really believe that Raglan had no firm orders? Considering that historians have denied for 150 years that Raglan ever received such orders, it seems quite possible that Pélissier was also in the dark. Raglan was accustomed to playing his cards close to his chest. Even his nephew and aide-de-camp, Calthorpe, believed it when he related that the plan for a field campaign was only a 'suggestion' from London.

General Pélissier decided to cross his Rubicon and undertake a full scale infantry assault on Sebastopol on the 40th anniversary of the Battle of Waterloo (18 June 1855). He hoped that the alliance would from then on have a joint victory to celebrate on the day previously associated with their last mutually hostile encounter. Like many successful generals before him, Pélissier had been made overconfident by his successes at Kertsch and the Mamelon, and seemed to believe that his leadership guaranteed success. The result was a disaster for the Allies.

The assault was preceded by the Fourth Bombardment on 17 June. Pélissier insisted that the key to capturing the city lay in taking and holding the Malakoff Tower, the strongest and highest point in the fortifications. The Malakoff was close to the French trenches on the eastern perimeter, and the French infantry was to assault it on the morning of 18 June. Most of the strong points in the Russian fortification wall were simply protruding angles from which fire could be directed sideways at other parts of the wall if they were attacked by infantry. The rear of these protruding angles was left open like any other part of the wall, so that if invaders did manage to penetrate them they could not use them as forts against the town; they could be swept by cannon fire from other forts and from ships in the harbour. The Malakoff was different; it was a stronghold fortified on all sides and if it was captured the occupants would have protection against counter-attack as well as being able to fire on any part of the city or its fortifications from this highest point. The Allies agreed that no assault could succeed unless the French captured the Malakoff.

The strongest point in front of the British lines was known as the Redan, after the technical term for a protruding angle in a fortified wall. This was open on the Russian side, as explained, and being less than 1,000 yards in front of and below the Malakoff it was at the mercy of the latter's guns. Nobody could hold the Redan if the Malakoff was in enemy hands. The Redan was opposite the small British section of the trenches, and it was agreed between the Allies that the French would first take the Malakoff, and then as soon as they had silenced the Russian guns there the British infantry would storm the Redan. This arrangement was almost certain to lead to unnecessary British losses, because the Russians could have been be relied on to evacuate the Redan as soon as the French brought artillery to bear on it from the captured Malakoff. But Lord Raglan thought it essential that the British (who were stung by French criticism of their failure to send more troops to the Crimea) should storm *something* and take it in hand-to-hand fighting against the Russians, otherwise it would not be a joint victory. Other demonstration attacks were to be made along the length of the front, but Pélissier insisted that only those on the Malakoff and Redan were to be seriously pursued. He rejected Raglan's suggestion that simultaneous assaults should be attempted elsewhere in the fortifications. According to Raglan, he was concerned that if French troops burst into the town they would run riot and become vulnerable to counter-attack when in disorder.

The plan was for the French infantry to move into their advanced trenches under cover of darkness, when the mortars would be firing to keep the Russians busy and the horizontally-firing Allied guns would be quiet as usual because of the difficulty of re-aiming them at night. At dawn (3a.m.), with the storming parties hidden in the trenches, all the Allied guns would open up again over their heads for three hours, keeping the Russians off the parapet so they could not see how close the French were nor repair the damage before the French infantry swarmed into the Malakoff at 6a.m. immediately after the bombardment stopped.

In a heated French Council of War the evening before the assault, Pélissier belatedly decided that in the three hours of daylight the Russians could not fail to see the French infantry in the trenches waiting to storm the Malakoff, and would bring up infantry reserves to defend it. He therefore decided that his infantry should attack at daybreak; there would be no time for a horizontal bombardment. Pélissier also replaced General Bosquet, who knew the trenches and Russian positions well, by another general who didn't, after a personal quarrel with Bosquet. These changes increased the chance of mistakes being made by officers who were unsettled by them. Pélissier also insulted another of his senior officers who was due to lead part of the assault, General Mayran, so severely that Mayran went to his post saying '*Il n'y a plus qu'à se faire tuer*' (There's nothing left for it but to get killed).[40]

It was General Mayran, in his eagerness, who made the principal error, mistaking a shell for the signal for the pre-dawn assault and starting off too early. He then got lost and stumbled upon an unimportant Russian sentry post. His troops fired their rifles in the dark, which prematurely betrayed their position and strength to the Russians, who turned out in great numbers before the French troops had begun their main assault and unleashed their artillery in the direction of the rifle flashes. By the time Pélissier arrived (late) at his command post a battle was already under way on the right of the French line, and he immediately sent up the signal for the general attack even though it was not yet time as dawn had not broken. The French troops assembling for the attack had not yet got into their assigned positions, so the assault which had got off to a ragged start continued in the same way all along the line.

The Russians always stood to arms in large numbers on the fortifications during the hour before dawn, because the Allies always advanced their trenches and batteries under cover of darkness. Unless it was to take advantage of some dramatic overnight progress of the trenches, therefore, dawn was not the best time to launch an assault especially as artillery (most of which required visual sighting) could not be used beforehand to soften up the defences. Regardless of the errors and confusion, therefore, the plan for the assault was flawed from the start.

When dawn broke Lord Raglan, seeing the French being shot down before the Malakoff, decided to give the rocket signal for the British to attack the Redan in order to create a diversion and draw some Russian fire.[41] Two storming parties of 400 men, with ladders to climb the rampart and sacks of wool to fill in the defensive ditch, were to go forward on either side of the blunt point (the 'salient') of the Redan. Sharpshooters were attached to each column whose task was to pick off the Russian artillerymen through their embrasures. If these storming parties were successful in getting their bags and ladders in place, then a larger column of attackers was to follow up from the centre.

The terrain in front of the Redan was very rocky and it had been impossible to dig trenches for shelter closer than 450 yards from the Redan. Even those trenches were skimpy in width and the men poised to assault were packed in them three deep. The men came out of their trenches in disorder, and then had to cross 450 yards of open ground before arriving at the various obstacles in front of the Redan including a barricade of tree trunks with the branches still on them (the '*abbatis*') the ditch with a wooden palisade of sharpened stakes on the opposite bank, and finally the rampart whose embrasures held thirty-two-pounder guns (calibre six inches) which had been loaded with musket balls almost up to the muzzle. The British riflemen could not make much impression on the artillerymen behind these guns, because shields of coiled rope several feet in diameter had been wound around the barrels as a defence against rifle bullets. The guns poured an unearthly storm of metal at the men as soon as they emerged from the trenches. Mostly newly-disembarked recruits incorporated into regiments that had lost heavily through battle and sickness, no body of men were ever more deserving of the name of cannon fodder. They and their officers could only assume that the French must have captured their objective, and went forward not knowing that they were only supposed to be a diversion and not a serious attack and that they would be slaughtered by the Malakoff's guns if they succeeded. They were swept away like leaves, the officers in advance suffering particularly badly. When the men faltered at the loss of their officers, more senior officers came from behind to rally them and the survivors again went forward headed by Colonel Yea on the right and Major-General Sir John Campbell on the left. Both the colonel and the general fell dead, and the few surviving troops never got closer than the *abbatis*, where they crouched and fired their Minié rifles at the Russians who were now lined up on the parapet shooting down at them. The Minié had no superiority at all over the Russian smoothbore musket in this situation. General Sir George Brown, overall commander of the assault decided not to commit his support troops and no more than a third of the storming parties got back to their trenches.

The Allies, repulsed, opened a vengeful bombardment on the fortifications which caused heavy losses among the Russian infantry who had assembled behind the Redan and the Malakoff in anticipation of another assault. Panic set in among the Russian troops and it is said that many tried to flee the city. Lord Raglan, who had a lot to lose by the failure, went to Pélissier and urged him to make a second attempt but Pélissier's generals told him that the men were too dispirited. One British officer who reached the *abbatis* and returned only lightly wounded wrote to his sister that afternoon proffering an opinion on strategy which would not have pleased Lord Raglan, 'I think we are all wrong sticking to this place; I say, take the open and fight round, Sebastopol then might fall.'[42] This was, of course, exactly what Raglan had been ordered to do instead of trying the assault that had now failed so miserably. It must have been an open secret in the camp that General Canrobert had wanted to give up the idea of an assault. After the previous bombardment of April he had not actually announced that he was not going to make the expected assault, but instead made a speech to the officers in every unit saying that 'if we cannot get in at the door, we must get in by the window'. This metaphor was widely understood to be a reference to a proposed march upcountry.[43]

About 250 British troops were killed in the Waterloo Day attack. The French officially lost six times as many dead, and one French general accused Pélissier of understating French losses by nearly 2,000.[44] It is hard to estimate how many of the wounded died or were invalided, but it seems likely that the Allied forces were permanently depleted by 6,000–7,000 men as a result of this failed assault. Pélissier blamed the defeat on General Mayran, who had succeeded in his ambition of getting himself killed, saying that if Mayran had survived he would have court-martialled him. It was customary in those days for generals to lead their divisions into battle, and it is noteworthy that on this occasion four out of the five Allied generals so doing were killed.

During the customary truce which was arranged so that both sides could bury their dead the Allied and Russian officers conversed and Lord Raglan's nephew noticed that the Russians were more cold, reserved, and melancholy than on previous similar occasions. He remarked to a Russian officer cadet that the Allied losses were heavy, to which the boy replied, 'Losses? You do not know what the word means! You should see our batteries; the dead lie there in heaps and heaps. Troops cannot live under such a fire of hell as you poured on us!'

The noble feelings that had led one British officer to deplore what he saw as the needless British slaughter of Russian conscripts at the Battle of the Alma were heard of no more. In the beginning, the British would not fire at a wounded Russian who was limping away. A month before Waterloo Day when a British officer saw that a wounded British soldier and his would-be rescuers were being shot at he said, 'What brutes those Russians are, to fire at wounded men and those who go out to help them!' He was taken aback when one of his men replied, 'Oh, I don't know that, they have only turned over one of our men and we killed six of theirs trying to get off a wounded man the other day.'[45] At the Waterloo Day assault, the British temporarily captured some rifle pits, but had to abandon them when the rest of the assault failed. 'We had a large number of prisoners which we took in the rifle pits,' wrote a British officer, 'they laid down their arms, but when they found we did not take the town they began to be very troublesome & we could not send them to the rear as that would have been certain death for all, therefore I am sorry to say they were killed.'[46] British chivalry, so frequently in evidence at the start, had not survived the horrors of the war.

Raglan's excuse for sending British troops to certain defeat and death at the Redan on Waterloo Day was that 'if the troops had remained in our trenches, the French would have attributed their non-success to our refusal to participate in the operation'.[47] The British Army now constituted only 30,000 of the Allied strength of over 200,000 so it is understandable that Raglan was under pressure to show the flag. What has not been understood until now, because the truth about his disobedience has been hidden, is just how much Raglan had at stake in this assault of 18 June. Success would have at least partially excused his duplicity, but failure would surely result in his being called to account. The Waterloo Day anniversary chosen for the attack now took on a macabre significance for the British commander, because it was on that anniversary of the great battle in which he had been beside the winning commander that he met his own Waterloo. One week later Raglan was dead, officially of cholera although the prevailing view in the Crimea was that he had turned his face to the wall and lost the will to live. As Florence Nightingale records, 'A private letter was read to me about his illness, from a medical man in camp. The diarrhoea was slight, but he was so depressed by our defeat of Waterloo Day ... that he sank rapidly without sufficient physical reason. It was *not* cholera.'[48] Nightingale did not of course know just how much Raglan had at stake on Waterloo Day.

Raglan's memory benefited from the peculiar Victorian institution *De mortuis nil nisi bonum*: 'Of the dead speak kindly or not at all.' Although we may still say "never speak ill of the dead", the religious rigour with which the custom was observed in Victorian times has no equivalent now. From being castigated on all sides Raglan suddenly went to being universally praised, his failings not being excused or forgiven but simply not mentioned.

I'm a General, Get Me Out of Here

THE POISONED CHALICE

The question now arose, who should replace Lord Raglan as Commander-in-Chief in the Crimea? There were no enthusiastic candidates; on the contrary, the generals who might have been candidates were suddenly anxious to leave the Crimea from sickness or other causes. The bombardment-and-assault strategy had gone so hopelessly wrong that it is not surprising if the generals failed to see the chief command in the Crimea as a sensible career move.

'We hear that all the generals and officers are knocking up [giving up and going home] – bad news indeed!'[1] wrote a young officer on his way out from England. Another officer closer to the scene had his own explanation for it, 'Our generals, I am happy to say, know whose fault it [the failure of the Waterloo Day assault] was, as it has had this effect on them[:] General Estcourt, very ill indeed, not expected to live. General Brown is very ill indeed, gone on board ship. General Pennyfather has gone home ill. General Eyre ditto, not home. General Codrington, ditto, on board ship.'[2]

Two of the original five of Raglan's divisional commanders – General Evans and HRH the Duke of Cambridge – had already left some months before with medical permission but also in a state of profound disagreement with Raglan. Long before Raglan's death, the question of replacing him had arisen because of his failure to deal with incompetence among his staff.

The obvious choice for a replacement for Raglan was between General Simpson and General Sir George Brown. One of the first things Lord Palmerston's new government had done was to send out Simpson four months before in the new post of Chief of Staff to Raglan. Simpson had been under instructions to write a report to Raglan on the perform-ance of the headquarters staff, particularly General Airey and General Estcourt, the Quartermaster General and Adjutant General respectively. These two were blamed by almost everyone except Raglan for the suf-ferings of the army in the past winter. Raglan had refused to remove them from their posts, and presumably the government hoped that Simpson's report would force him to do so. But Simpson wrote to the new Minister of War on 16 April 1855, 'Nor have I any fault to find with Airey and Estcourt. I think the line that ought to exist, distinguishing their respective departments, was not so distinct as it ought to have been; and as both come to me now, I am trying to make it so, and to keep the two branches from clashing.' Simpson reported to the Minister of War on the military prospects in a much more gloomy tone, 'The Russian earthworks, *à la Ferguson*, are too tough for us ... we are in a *regular fix*! It is impossible, my Lord, that any military man of experience could have recommended the descent of this army in the Crimea, and *whoever* has ordered this expedition has much to answer for.' It may be wondered whether Simpson's good report on Raglan and his staff was partly moti-vated by a desire not to be seen as a possible replacement for any of them in this 'regular fix'.

The first candidate for Commander-in-Chief in the Crimea, General Sir George Brown, had been officially recognised as second-in-command to Raglan at the same time that Simpson had been sent out. Brown had been Raglan's particular confidant and strongest supporter among the divisional commanders. He was sixty-five and a Peninsular War veteran, and went before a medical board himself when Raglan lay ill. According to one of the members, the board ordered Brown home but he refused to accept the ruling and said that he wanted to return to his duties. A few hours later Raglan died, and Brown then decided to go home after all, saying that if he stayed he would be given command of the army. He said he was worried that if he took command and then resigned due to ill-health later it might be misconstrued.[3]

So General Simpson was appointed as temporary and reluctant suc-cessor to Raglan. He wrote to the Minister of War on 30 June, 'I sincerely trust, my Lord, that a general of distinction will be sent immediately to command this Army… I have put myself in Orders to command until instructions from England shall come, but my health is sure to give way, as I have constant threatenings of gout in spite of all the care that I take … I … hope soon to be relieved from work that is too much for me. All our generals fall sick one after the other.'

Lord Palmerston, annoyed by the callous sacrifice of British lives in the Waterloo Day assault, told his Minister of War to send Simpson specific instructions never to agree to a British assault except at a point where a breach had already been made in the defences and enemy artillery had been prevented from covering it. Palmerston was old enough to remember the Duke of Wellington's initial mistakes at the siege of Badajoz, where the British had launched a premature assault because two French armies were on the way to relieve the city.[4]

As for Pélissier, on learning of the unauthorised assault and costly defeat the Emperor persuaded Vaillant, his Minister of War, to dismiss him. The general survived by the skin of his teeth: instead of dismissing him by telegram, the minister sent the despatch by mail. Vaillant was able to change the Emperor's mind while it was *en route,* and by telegram he recalled the letter from Marseilles where it was waiting between train and mail boat. Pélissier, who hated the telegraph and complained to the Emperor of being 'paralysed by an electric wire from Paris' could later reflect that he owed his dukedom and his annual pension of 100,000 Francs to this same electric wire after it annulled his dismissal.

Seemingly subdued by his narrow escape, Pélissier earnestly promised the Emperor that he would follow his orders for the main offensive in the field, if not the diversionary attack: he would attack the Heights of Inkerman and McKenzie's Farm. However, he found a reason to continue the bombardment of Sebastopol: he said that it would make the Russians fear another assault and lure reinforcements inside, weakening their army on the north side.

THE USELESS PRIZE

Now that they had humiliated the Allies by depriving them of the quick victory that they needed, it had become as pointless for the Russians to hold onto the southern part of the city as it was for the Allies to capture it.

The new Tsar Alexander II had been opposed to his late father's invasion of Turkish provinces that precipitated the war and had not been buoyed up, as Nicholas had been, by the initial success of the Sebastopol defences. Now he could see that continued success in holding Sebastopol would only increase the costs to Russia. It had become a murderous self-renewing open system, with new Russian conscripts being continually fed in from the north and shells being hauled up by railway from the south to kill them, while the fortifications were continuously being rebuilt to welcome yet more doomed men.

In Russia the war was generally seen as a disaster that was entirely the fault of the late Tsar because he had invaded Turkey without justification. There had been considerable pressure on him to abdicate, and if he had not died at an inopportune moment such an abdication or even a *coup d'état* might have ended the war sooner. His successor, Alexander, at first gave signs of wanting peace at any price, but as time passed and he did not take the step of agreeing to the last of the Allies demands – the permanent destruction of the Sebastopol military installations – he began to hope for some small success to save face. He was prepared to stake all on a pitched battle, and he ordered the commanders of the Russian Army outside Sebastopol to attack the besieging Allies.

On 16 August 1855 at the Battle of the Tchernaya the Russian Army outside Sebastopol attacked the French and Sardinian troops guarding the lower left bank of the river. The Russian attack was hopeless, as their generals knew it would be; it does not appear that they had any serious plan and were merely going through the motions to please the Tsar. Their troops attacked in solid columns as always, and were massacred by the Allies' efficient rifle fire. After this defeat the Russians knew that they could never dislodge the Allies from their trenches and batteries around the southern and eastern sides of Sebastopol. They were reconciled to giving up this part of the city with its naval dockyards, and had been improving the fortifications on the northern side in anticipation of holding out there. While they still occupied the northern side it would be impossible for the Allies to use the harbour or dockyards, as they would be in range of Russian guns. Soon after the Battle of the Tchernaya the Russians began to build a floating bridge so that they would be able to transfer their forces to the northern side under the protection of these guns instead of having to fight their way out of the southern part of Sebastopol by land.

The French and British Governments were also united in the view that Sebastopol had become a secondary issue. The first priority must be to keep a positive balance of territorial and other gains against Russia so that negotiations could be entered into at any time from a position of strength. If the Allies had enough gains they could demand the destruction of Sebastopol even if that city was not in their possession. It wasn't as if Sebastopol was actually worth anything to the Russians in the war – it had been neutralised by the naval blockade for nearly two years, and could be indefinitely. The Russian activity on the frontier with Turkey in the Caucasus was causing much more concern to the politicians in London and to Omar Pasha, the former Austrian soldier Michael Lattas who was Commander-in-Chief of the Turkish Army. A Russian Army of 30,000 troops, well-equipped with artillery, had been besieging the Turks' strongest frontier fortress of Kars all summer. Omar Pasha had never wanted to invade the Crimea with the Allies, and had been begging to be allowed to take his troops to the Caucasus to counter the Russian threat to the Turkish homeland. This, of course, had been originally suggested by the government in London as a possible alternative to invading the Crimea, and Raglan had ignored the suggestion. Now Simpson and Pélissier would not let Omar go and Simpson was cavalier about the possible fall of Kars and even Constantinople, 'It is true,' he wrote to the Minister of War in mid-July, 'the Russians gaining possession of Kars, which seems not improbable, will be very dangerous to Constantinople; but the Crimea seems to me of greater moment still, as the battle must be fought here in preference to Kars.'

The Cabinet were unimpressed with Simpson's opinions on geopolitical strategy, and they were further irritated by his pessimism and lack of drive on taking over from the deceased Raglan. The Minister of War told him on 4 August to let Omar go, 'It is absolutely necessary to preserve the Asiatic territories of [Turkey] from Russian hands, because their possession would give to Russia something which she had captured with her bow and spear, and which she would be able to offer as a *quid pro quo* when the period for negotiating returns.'

In defiance of his instructions from London, Simpson continued to obstruct for another six weeks Omar's departure with his Turkish troops to rescue Kars. Omar's plan was not to relieve Kars directly but instead to march on Tiflis, the weakly-defended capital of the Russian province of Georgia, and thus to cut the supply route of the Russian Army besieging

Kars. The Russians recognised the danger, and on Omar's appearance in the Caucasus they changed their plan; instead of surrounding Kars and waiting for starvation to force its surrender, they launched an all-out assault on it. The town had been extensively fortified by British engineers and was under the command of British officers, and the Russian attack was decisively defeated. The news of this caused jubilation in London. The government's policy of detaching Omar seemed to have worked in the nick of time by forcing Russia into a premature attack. But the reprieve of Kars was to prove only temporary, and the six-week delay in allowing Omar to go to its rescue had sealed its fate.

Simpson and Pélissier had staked their reputations on a victory at Sebastopol and could not be expected to pay attention to Kars and the bigger picture. The government's new priorities also explain why the Cabinet placed restrictions on Simpson's freedom to assault Sebastopol. They were not confident that Simpson could resist the overbearing Pélissier's demands for another suicidal diversionary British attack on the Redan, so had expressly forbidden it, 'I shall notice officially your abandonment of the direct attack on the Redan,' wrote the Minister of War to Simpson.[5] He also noted that the French, according to Simpson, had accepted this refusal. Assuming that the minister had also passed on the Prime Minister's insistence that a breach be first made in the defences and freed of Russian artillery fire, it was difficult to see how the British could ever participate in an assault. Although concentrated bombardment could throw down a section of rampart into the ditch, the Russians had each section of the fortifications covered by so many different batteries that it seemed impossible to neutralise all artillery fire. The ditch would be cleared and the rampart rebuilt each night by the Russians, at the cost of great losses from Allied mortar fire.

By now the British Government realised that Pélissier was calling the shots in the Crimea and that the Emperor was not going to grasp the nettle and dismiss him. It was pointless therefore to instruct Simpson to undertake a field campaign, but they were on the verge of unilaterally withdrawing from what they saw as a useless siege. Prince Albert articulated well the prevailing opinion in London in August 1855. He noted that Raglan had said that the British Army could not survive another winter above Sebastopol. Simpson agreed with Raglan's view that the railway would sink into the winter mud – it had been built rapidly without solid foundations – and the army would starve once more. They would have therefore to leave the trenches soon, and Simpson's own opinion was that once lifted the siege could never be resumed. The French had now sapped up to the *abbatis* of the Malakoff, only twenty-five yards from its ditch, and the British saps at 200 yards from the Redan were as close as they could be, so that Russian fire was killing and wounding an estimated 260 Allied soldiers a day in these exposed trenches.[6] What then could be gained by continuing to besiege the city in this way? If the Allied infantry could not assault now they never would be able to in which case the trenches were worse than useless and should be abandoned. The Prince recommended that unless an assault succeeded in a very few days the whole idea of a siege should be dropped, the trenches given up, and the army placed in safety for the winter.

This logic must have also been apparent to Pélissier and Simpson, who put in motion what would have to be the final attempt to take the town by infantry assault. There had been a Fifth Bombardment in mid-August, with the objective of disabling some Russian guns that were impeding the advance of a French sap towards the Malakoff, and on 5 September the Sixth Bombardment commenced. Pélissier had an opportunity to realise a general's dream: to fight exactly the same battle again but this time to get it right. His plan was nearly identical to that of Waterloo Day, except that he would not make the mistakes of attacking at dawn and of relying on confusing visual signals. Again, the Malakoff was the main objective; once that was taken the Allies would attack along all their lines.

On 8 September the bombardment was continued in the morning so that the Russians would have no opportunity to repair the fortifications. The Russians had been seen removing stores from the south to the north side of the harbour across their floating bridge since early in the bombardment, which filled the attackers with confidence. Early in the morning the French exploded three huge mines in front of the Malakoff without, however, weakening it significantly. At midday, the Allied bombardment slackened as it often did to lure Russian infantry out of their bunkers. The French had ensured that all senior officers had watches that were working and synchronised. At exactly midday their infantry surged out of the trenches in front of the Malakoff and threw ladders and planks across the ditch. Once across, the French found the fortification almost deserted as the guard was being changed and some of the garrison had gone to lunch thinking that the halt in the bombardment was just a trick (as indeed it was). Despite furious counter-attacks during the rest of the day, the Russians never managed to dislodge the French, and the southern half of the city found itself threatened by artillery fire from its own strongest fortress. All the other French attacks against the long line of fortifications were driven back. Pélissier had been lucky at the Malakoff.

As for the British, Simpson had disobeyed his instructions from London and ordered another direct frontal attack on the Redan. They had not been able to approach their saps closer than 200 yards, because the ground was rocky and the Malakoff artillery could fire sideways down the trenches if they dug any closer. The British storming party, initially 1,000 strong and composed of men from several different regiments, therefore had to cross 200 yards of open ground and obstructions under almost point-blank artillery fire before reaching the salient point of the wall. Enough of them managed to cross the *abbatis* to throw down ladders, rubble and gabions – the wicker earth-filled baskets that formed part of the defence – into the ditch to make it possible to cross. Many of them climbed up the parapet but there on its sloping outer face they stayed, hesitating to enter the fort and face the fire of Russian infantry massed in the open rear of the fortification. Many officers leapt into the fort to vainly urge their men to a bayonet charge, and died there. Other officers went back to ask the commander of the Light Division, General Codrington, to send forward masses of troops in solid formation so as to force the leading men into the Redan, but were apparently unable to persuade him that it was worthwhile. At the Redan, the Russian defenders then came forward to the parapet and began to fire on the hundreds of men clinging to its outer slope like bees, whereupon the men broke and ran in complete confusion back to the trenches. The trenches being crowded with wounded men as well as support troops, Codrington suspended further action. It was supposed to have been his and the Light Division's opportunity to redeem their poor performance at the Alma, where one brigade of the division had rushed at the Russian earthwork instead of advancing in line, to be driven back in a rout, while the other brigade had formed a defensive square and taken little part in the battle.

500 British troops were killed in this second attack on the Redan. It was decided to renew the assault on the next day, using more seasoned troops. Predictably, however, the Russians evacuated the Redan during the night rather than face bombardment by the French from the Malakoff. In his despatch to London, Simpson claimed that he had given

orders that the British troops were only to leave their trenches after the French were 'fairly established' in the Malakoff (thus avoiding Raglan's controversial simultaneous attack in the first assault). One published version of the orders contradicts his claim: 'The Redan will be assaulted after the French have *attacked* the Malakoff.'[7] Although Simpson's version makes the plan seem somewhat more humane, the difference may have been academic in practice because the French could be described as 'fairly established' almost immediately, and the great sacrifice was in attacking the now useless Redan at all, which is one reason why the government had forbidden it. Simpson's despatch also alluded in vague terms to a slight breach in the Redan wall and a partial neutralisation of Russian artillery fire, presumably to fob off the Prime Minister Lord Palmerston with his reminiscences of Badajoz.

The Russians had evacuated the southern part of the town across their floating bridge during the night following the loss of the Malakoff in a carefully prepared operation, during which they also sank their remaining ships. They had mined most of the military buildings they had abandoned which blew up one by one, leaving only one barracks in which 2,000 horribly wounded men and uncounted dead lay in conditions which revolted even those who thought themselves hardened to the carnage.

Lord Palmerston in London was still pondering Simpson's despatch and compiling a list of difficult questions to ask him about his forbidden assault on the Redan when the press burst out in fury at reports that the Redan had been occupied and then lost, giving the French all the glory from the capture of part of Sebastopol. The newspapers heaped blame on Simpson and Codrington for using regiments that had borne the brunt of trench work and had therefore been replenished with raw recruits, and for not sending in the support troops when the British had first driven the Russians from the parapet. To read the newspapers, it would have been quite acceptable to have sent in a first wave of veteran Highlanders, who had fared better in their less onerous duties close to Balaclava, and to have seen them sacrificed to a man rather than endure this shame. But most thought that an assault led by seasoned troops would have succeeded, and it is true that Codrington and the supports would have been less likely to hold back if it had been the Guards or Highlanders instead of the humble Light and Second Divisions who were in trouble in front of them. But since the Redan was worthless anyway, it may be that Codrington was right to avoid even more slaughter.

The government was more worried that Simpson and Pélissier had now halted all offensive operations against the Russians on the north side of the harbour and wanted to blow up the dockyards on the south side. The politicians wanted the Allied armies to occupy and use the port of Sebastopol at least temporarily, which would not be possible unless the north shore was captured. Pélissier, who had promised the Emperor that he would attack the Inkerman Heights and Mackenzies' Farm instead of assaulting the fortifications, showed no inclination to do so now that he had a victory to his name. The British Minister of War, Lord Panmure, fired off a telegram to Simpson accusing him of not moving swiftly enough to follow up the victory and gain a feat of arms for the British:

> The Public is getting impatient to know what the Russians are about. The Govt desire immedly to be informed whether either you or Pélissier have taken any steps whatever to ascertain this and further they observe that nearly three weeks have passed in absolute idleness. This cannot go on and in justice to yourself and your Army you must prevent it. Answer this on its receipt.

The Minister of War followed this blunt message with a letter enquiring coldly why Simpson had attacked the Redan again:

> You will see by this mail what a hubbub has been created in the public mind by [our failure] in the attack of the 8th inst. … Shortly after assuming the command, you wrote me that it was resolved to give up the Redan as a point of attack, and I do not comprehend how I find you repeating the tragedy of the 18th June, and with the same unhappy results. You will see how The Times falls on you…

Simpson took the opportunity to resign immediately and come home on the grounds that Panmure had harshly rebuked him for not following up the victory, thus avoiding the need to resign over his prohibited attack on the Redan. The general feeling in the army was that Simpson had ordered the Redan attack as a diversion to increase the French chances of success. An attack at a weaker point might have had more chance of succeeding but have been less effective in diverting the attention of the defenders of the Malakoff. He could not have foreseen that the French would succeed so easily and would not therefore be in debt to their Allies. Raglan had admitted that his attempt on the Redan had been such a diversion, and like Simpson's it was a diversion that was not to be announced as such to the troops involved. It was not surprising that at home John Bull was now baying for more Russian blood to avenge one of the most humiliating failures in British military history.

THE END OF THE NAVAL CAMPAIGN

John Bull was also displeased with his Royal Navy. During the eighteen months of the war Britain had been trying to engage the Russian navy and attack Russian fortresses in the Baltic, the Barents Sea, and Siberia as well as at Sebastopol. These attempts, initially accompanied by much boasting, had met with very little success. At that time Russia owned Alaska, and it might be expected that hostilities would also break out on the frontier with British Canada, but both governments agreed not to extend hostilities to that area.

When war was looming in early 1854, Britain began to fear an attack near to home from Russia's Northern Fleet. The British Isles were potentially more vulnerable to blockade than Russia, and by April the ice in the Baltic Sea would melt and allow Russian ships to enter the North Sea and prey on British merchant vessels. The Allies therefore hastily mobilised a fleet to block the narrow mouth of the Baltic.

Within the Baltic, Russia's capital of St Petersburg was also its main seaport and base of her Northern Fleet. It lay at the inner end of the Gulf of Finland, a 200-mile long branch of the Baltic Sea. The city had been founded by Peter the Great in 1703, on land recently captured from Sweden, with the idea of creating a Western Europe-facing capital and realising his obsession of building a navy. In his time Russian expansion had not yet reached the Black Sea, and Russia's only commercial port of Archangel was accessible only by a long journey above the Arctic Circle. Peter the Great wanted Russia to be a European power and he built St Petersburg in the style of a European city, with classical stone buildings instead of the wood-built onion-domed churches that dominated the former capital of Moscow. But the stone facades were mostly stucco over more humble brickwork, just as Peter the Great's own cabin there was of wood painted to look like brick. 'St Petersburg is not Russia,' as Tsar Nicholas I remarked. It was a flimsy mask from behind which the real Russia gazed on an alien Europe.

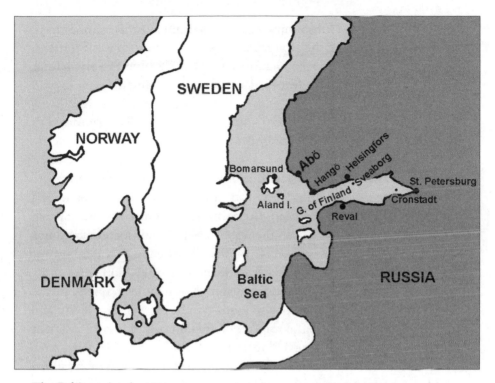

The Baltic region in 1854.

Around the Baltic approaches to St Petersburg were a number of large island fortresses designed to defend the capital, to menace Russia's neighbours, and to allow the Russian Navy to shelter under their guns in time of battle. Sveaborg, outside Helsingfors (Helsinki), Bomarsund (on the Aland Islands, like Finland recently captured from Sweden), Reval (Tallinn, in Estonia, also taken from Sweden) and, at the gates of the capital, Cronstadt. There were smaller forts at Abö (Turkü) and Hangö in Finland. The Allies' secondary objective, besides closing the exit from the Baltic, was to venture inside and try to destroy one or more of these forts, preferably Sveaborg.

Most of the Allied navies were busy in the Mediterranean or the Black Sea, escorting troopships or blockading Sebastopol, and Britain was hard put to it to assemble a fleet of a dozen steam-powered capital ships for the Baltic expedition: six line-of-battle ships (three-deckers) and six frigates (single-deckers). The British ships were undermanned by ill-trained crews, but the exit from the Baltic was relatively easy to police as it led through the narrow channels between Denmark and Sweden, which were neutral. If it met the full Russian fleet in line of battle the British force would be outnumbered: the Russians had twenty-seven ships of the line (two- or three-deckers with at least sixty guns each) in the Baltic compared to Britain's six. However the Russians had no steam-powered vessels, while the British fleet consisted almost entirely of steamships and this made it highly manoeuvrable and less constrained by ice. The Russian crews were as badly trained as the British, and had been stuck in the ice for several months so had little opportunity to practice. The Russians were placing a new weapon – sea mines – in the waters around their forts but this was before the days of high explosives and the mines, though the subject of exaggerated claims, were not capable of disabling a capital ship.

The expedition was under the command of Sir Charles Napier, a member of a distinguished military and naval family. He was an elderly and eccentric admiral who had complained vociferously when he was not given the command of the Mediterranean Fleet in 1852. He was a tireless composer of rude letters to those in authority, and it was he who had prodded the admiralty into recognising the (probably exaggerated) danger from the Baltic. At sixty-eight, he had many years of varied service behind him beginning in the Napoleonic Wars and continuing through the American war of 1812, the Portuguese Civil War, and the capture of Bierut and Acre in 1840 during the rebellion of Mehmet Ali. Many of his exploits had been both daring and lucky, although he had not had a chance to display the strategic genius in large fleet actions that was the final hallmark of the Nelson touch. He partially made up for it by being even more of a self-promoter than Nelson, and his jealousy of his colleagues and his publication of war histories which exaggerated his role made him unpopular in the service. He was a large Scot, dark-complexioned and known in his youth as 'Black Charley' and later as 'Mad Charley', when he was famous for his poor dress sense (he did not wear uniform) and personal hygiene and his slovenly way of walking. His trousers were always too short and his shoes ill-made; his copious whiskers were usually speckled with the snuff of which he was a continuous user, mixed with the remains of previous meals.

Napier boasted that he would be inside Cronstadt (St Petersburg's strongest fortress) within a month of entering the Baltic. He gave away this hostage to fortune at a dinner in the Reform Club in early March, possibly under the influence of the Scotch whisky of which he was a heavily patriotic consumer. The press admiringly reported his boasts and recapitulated his previous exploits, when Acre, Bierut, and Lisbon had yielded at his mere approach. The public were cheered by this display of energetic aggression towards the Russians after the long drawn-out appeasement process, but once through the Denmark straits the cold light of the Baltic day sobered the Admiral into a more cautious frame of mind. He refrained from engaging the fortresses or the Russian fleet, although while the ice still impeded the latter he would have had a great advantage in being able to break through it with his steamships. He went ashore in the neutral countries including Sweden, where he had an inter-view with King Oscar I in which he fancied that he was persuading his royal host to join the Anglo-French alliance against Russia. Lieutenant Theorell, a Swedish officer engaged as an interpreter, boarded what he called 'the incomparable *Duke of Wellington*' (Napier's flagship) and left a description of the Admiral:

> He was wearing a blue tunic with short trousers and big shoes, a civilian hat with gold stripes (lace), an enormously big handkerchief in all the colours of the rainbow hanging out of the tunic pocket. His movements and appearance as simple as possible. His face very badly washed, some yellow spots – prob-ably from the eggs at breakfast – round the lips and the on lower part of his face. We shook hands and he greeted me with a 'You speak English, eh?' and continued with two questions that – as he speaks Scottish in a rusty drivelling voice – I of course did not understand a word of.[8]

In reality the British Government were none too keen to encourage King Oscar at this time because they thought he was too close to the French and would reduce Britain's weight in the allowance.[9] They must have had little reason to fear that their eccentric admiral would increase Swedish enthusiasm for war; wherever Napier went the locals stared in astonishment and with apprehension, even, at this high-ranking nauti-cal bohemian who had come to smack the mighty Russian bear on the nose to awaken it from its winter hibernation.

Napier's fleet bombarded several of the smaller forts in the Baltic during the early summer of 1854. Despite his instructions not to attack undefended towns, Napier made raids on fishing villages in Finland and destroyed their non-military supplies. He wrote personal accounts of these which were published in *The Times* according to an agreement that the publicity-hungry admiral had made with its editor before leaving England. These accounts had an effect opposite to that intended, not to mention the bad impression made by the raids on the victims as well as on other countries in the region. The British Admiralty urged Napier to take more decisive action. In early June Napier was joined by a French fleet of twenty-six ships, and the combined fleet sailed to inspect the fortress of Cronstadt, protecting the approaches the St Petersburg. They found a huge complex of multiple forts, bristling with over 1000 guns, guarding a single narrow channel to the capital. They carefully sounded and charted the area for later attack but did not go on the offensive.

Meanwhile three small British ships on detachment from the fleet undertook a spirited but ineffectual bombardment of the uncompleted fortress of Bomarsund, in the Aland Islands, which was not far from Stockholm and was designed by Russia to overawe Sweden. The ships were the six-gun steam paddle sloop *Hecla* and two sixteen-gun paddle steamers. The action was memorable for the feat of Charles Lucas, a midshipman of the *Hecla*, who picked up a shell that had been fired from the fortress and landed on deck with its fuse still burning. He threw it over the side and it exploded before hitting the water, causing only minor damage and injury. When the Victoria Cross was later instituted as Britain's highest award for gallantry, Charles Lucas was its first recipient. It is remarkable that during its early years the Victoria Cross tended to be won not for killing enemy soldiers but for saving life by unselfish acts.

In July Napier received orders from home to attack and occupy Bomarsund properly. The fortress was vulnerable to attack from the landward side, and a French force of 12,000 soldiers was sent to join the Navy. This force, with its artillery, easily succeeded in capturing the fortress and its garrison of 2,000 men. The fortress could not be occupied by the Allies for long because the following winter the Russians would have been able to march an army across the ice from Finland to retake it, so the Allies destroyed it. This was the only significant result of the 1854 Baltic campaign.

With the approach of winter Napier decided to withdraw from the Baltic and defended himself against *The Times* and the admiralty – who were both pressing for more action and whom Napier believed to be in collusion – by firing off a particularly truculent despatch to his superiors at the admiralty:

Many absurd propositions have been made to me for attacking both Cronstadt and Sveaborg but I never will lend myself to any absurd projects or be driven to attempt what is not practicable, by Newspaper writers who I am sorry to say I have reason to believe are in correspondence with Officers of the Fleet who ought to know better.[10]

Coming from someone who was himself sending self-serving articles to *The Times* this might seem a little brazen, but Sir Charles Napier was an impetuous warrior with the pen. When the admiralty, offended by the tone of his despatches, brusquely ordered him to give up his command he went home and spent his twilight years in vituperative correspondence with the admiralty, politicians, and the press over his unfair dismissal and the lack of recognition of his achievements.

The following year (1855) the Allies sent to the Baltic a larger fleet including mine-sweeping equipment and a larger number of shallow-draught vessels which could operate nearer the coast. These latter vessels allowed the Allies to tighten the blockade of materials entering Russian ports, but there was only one significant action. This was the three-day bombardment of Sveaborg, the fortress defending Helsingfors (Helsinki), in August 1855. The bombardment was carried out by a large number of new small mortar and rocket-boats on the theory that large capital ships were too valuable to be exposed to fire from land installations. This strategy proved a success, although the destruction of Sveaborg was not complete and the Allies this time had no troops who could land and demolish it. Other than that, the second Baltic campaign was marred by the same exaggerated claims and attacks on civilian targets as the first.

North-east of the Baltic, in the Barents Sea, French and British warships in 1854 bombarded a couple of Russian installations which had very little military use. This caused indignation in neutral countries in the region, as with the similar attacks in the Baltic. In the short Arctic summer of the following year British and French ships again cruised the Barents Sea, and contented themselves with sinking a number of tiny Russian coastal trading vessels.

In the Pacific the action was more significant, but did not go at all the Allies' way. While the army was preparing to embark for Sebastopol in August 1854, an Allied fleet was bombarding the Russian fortress of Petropavlovsk in the Kamchatka Peninsula after having chased a Russian frigate from Peru. For reasons that are not clear, the British commander Admiral Price committed suicide in his cabin during the bombardment. The French Admiral who took over decided to assault the fortress the next day. A landing party of marines and sailors captured a gun battery but the Russians counter-attacked strongly and the Allied force had to withdraw. A few days later the Allies tried again but failed and took many casualties. They retired to North America determined to return the following year. Return they did in 1855, with a much larger fleet, but discovered that the Russians had abandoned and destroyed the settlement and withdrawn their land and sea forces to a stronger position on the border of Russia and China. The Allies could not attack them because of a lack of charts, and thus the whole Pacific campaign ended in September 1855 with Russia the overall clear winner.

THE FRENCH WITHDRAWAL

Back in the main theatre of war in the Black Sea, there was to be more bad news for the Allies. Unexpectedly, the Russians who had suffered a decisive defeat in their assault on Kars decided to renew their siege of the Turkish city. This time they planned to use the starvation method despite the advance of Omar Pasha with a sizeable force intent on cutting their supply lines from Russia and taking them in the rear. But Omar Pasha was delayed by transport difficulties after soundly defeating a Russian force opposing him at the River Ingur. Three weeks later, on 25 November, with the population of Kars starving to death and the garrison too weak even to flee, the British commander surrendered. A total of ten generals and 18,000 men were taken prisoner by the Russians who now occupied a more extensive amount of Allied territory than the Allies controlled in the Crimea. It was the success that Tsar Alexander had dreamed of, and the greatest danger to the British now was that they would be forced to the negotiating table without a clear military ascendancy. The British Government's worst fears were about to come true.

France and Britain justified the war from the start as a means to repel Russian aggression against Turkey, but the leaders were influenced by additional motives including the dream shared by Napoleon III and Lord Palmerston of dismembering the aggressive and despotic Russian Empire along ethnic lines. This dream, shared by many in Europe, could not be pursued directly by force within the framework of the 1815 Congress of Vienna which had recognised Imperial Russia as part of the balance of power. Nevertheless, it helped to mobilise sentiment in favour of France and Britain's declaration of war over the Russian incursion into Turkey.

There was one important part of the Russian Empire where Russia's rule lacked legal justification: Poland, which Russia had deprived of the freedoms it had been granted under the final act of the Treaty of Vienna. Only one week after the fall of Sebastopol the French submitted a proposal to London that Russia should be required to grant Poland's legitimate degree of autonomy as a condition for ending the Crimean War. The proposal came in a formal letter from France's Foreign Minister, Count Walewski, to Lord Clarendon, his British opposite number. Walewski reminded the British Government that both Britain and France had protested when Russia, after the Polish insurrection of 1831, had abolished the Constitution of the Kingdom of Poland in contravention of the Treaty of 1815. The fact that neither power went to war with Russia then, said Walewski, did not affect their right to take steps to remedy the injustice at a more propitious time. That time had now arrived. The Treaty of Vienna had been designed to hamper the ambitions of France, but France was entitled to demand that the other powers should honour their commitments under it. 'At the moment when the glorious successes of the Allied armies seem to warrant the hope that we may see the end of the war drawing near,' wrote Walewski, his Emperor felt that 'the moment is arrived for preparing to make the re-establishment of the Kingdom of Poland, according to the conditions stipulated by the Congress of Vienna, one of the essential objects of the negotiations for peace.'

This proposal seemed untimely to politicians in Britain, and even to Count Persigny, the French Ambassador to London. Persigny disliked his chief, Walewski, and Napoleon III thought Walewski tiresome and useless and generally tried to keep foreign affairs out of the hands of his Foreign Minister. Walewski had the job only because he was the illegitimate son of Napoleon Bonaparte by the Polish Countess Walewska, who had been one of the few admirers to visit Bonaparte in exile on Elba. Bonaparte had seduced Walewska by telling her that the consequences for her country would be favourable – always a powerful chat-up line – and now half a century later the product of the liaison was trying to fulfil the premise behind his conception.

The pompous Walewski was not admired in England either, where he had been Ambassador. He did not bear much physical resemblance to his father, being altogether more corpulent, but there was some likeness in his brow and eyes. Walewski knew this and was inclined to affect a haughty Bonaparte glare at people who had offended him, which made him appear ludicrous in London society. Napoleon III tolerated him out of a wish to recreate the famous dynasty to which they both belonged; putatively belonged, one might say, because there were rumours that Napoleon III was the son of one of his mother's lovers rather than of Bonaparte's brother. On this subject also, Napoleon III's wife the Empress Eugénie was widely rumoured to be the natural daughter of the British Foreign Secretary Lord Clarendon. It was said that the Empress' mother, on being questioned directly on this subject, replied not entirely convincingly that it was not possible because '*Les dates ne correspondent pas*'. Whether the dates fitted or not, the family friendship of earlier days partly explained the good relations that existed between Napoleon III and the British Government at the time of the Crimean War.

Lord Clarendon was unenthusiastic about Walewski's proposal that England and France agree to demand Polish constitutional rights (but not independence) as a precondition of peace with Russia. Like his colleagues, Clarendon assumed that this was only the thin end of the wedge for France because he knew that Napoleon III, like Palmerston, really wanted Poland to be completely independent. It was an emotive issue for France, because Poland had sided with Bonaparte against Russia and Russia had been punishing Poland ever since. Clarendon thought that Russia too would see a minor restoration of Polish autonomy as the thin end of the wedge. He wrote to Lord Cowley, his Ambassador in Paris, that Russia would fight for another two years against it. Like his Prime Minister Lord Palmerston, Clarendon was not worried about fighting another two campaigns against Russia, but he did not see the point of committing to Poland as a war objective at this stage. Such a commitment, even if secret, would leak out within a few weeks, he told Cowley, and Austria and Prussia would think it unreasonable grounds for prolonging the war in the current state of affairs. But if Britain and France defeated Russia so decisively that they could demand full Polish independence, 'something far better and more permanently useful to Poland than the poor measure of re-establishment that the Emperor proposes', then timid Austria and Prussia would support them.[11]

Clarendon made the revealing remark to Cowley that Count Persigny, the French Ambassador in London, agreed with the British that demanding a Polish constitution from Russia was a bad idea. Persigny, being hostile to his Foreign Minister, would have been of little use in explaining in London any nuances that there might have been behind his chief's proposal. Palmerston told Persigny that the demand proposed by Walewski would 'worry Europe and the other Allied powers without offering any advantage'. He did not think the British public would relish fighting for Polish rights.[12]

Clarendon wrote an official reply to Walewski, via Cowley, saying that Her Majesty's Government agreed with the Emperor's view that Russia should be compelled sooner or later to restore Poland's rights, but that the British public would be unlikely to accept an indefinite prolongation of the war to achieve it. He instructed Cowley to read this reply to Walewski, but Cowley read it to the Emperor at the Palace of St Cloud instead. The Emperor replied to Cowley that Her Majesty's Government had misunderstood him: it was not to be the thin end of the wedge and France had not requested any 'engagement' from Britain. He had merely wished to know whether Her Majesty's Government agreed with him that when the moment was right Britain and France could demand that Russia restore Poland's rights under the Treaty of Vienna. From Clarendon's reply, said the Emperor, this was evidently the case and he was therefore satisfied. This must have been the Emperor's polite way of accepting Britain's rejection of Walewski's proposal. Curiously, Cowley reported to Clarendon that after seeing the Emperor, 'I endeavoured to see Count Walewski, to read him the despatch, but I was unable to find him.' Cowley's mention of the Foreign Minister's elusiveness in a dry official report leaves the distinct impression that he thought Walewski was avoiding him.

If Her Majesty's Government misunderstood the proposal, it was probably by failing to see that it made a lot more sense as a sign that France was now making peace than as evidence that France was still promoting Palmerston's long-dreamed-of 'beau ideal' of a war to dismantle the Russian Empire. As a war aim it had all the disadvantages that Palmerston and Clarendon pointed out, but as an agreed negotiating position at an imminent peace conference it *did* offer some advantages to both France and Russia. Although a Kingdom of Poland under the control of Russia was not as good as a free Poland, it was better than no

Polish constitution at all. It was also better for France than anything else that might be available from Russia at the peace table at this moment. An independent Circassia, Crimea returned to Turkey, a new British Gibraltar at Sebastopol, the mouths of the Danube freed from Russian control, a demilitarised Baltic and Black Sea: what would any of these do for France? But forcing Russia to kowtow to its own Treaty of Vienna and restore the constitution of Bonaparte's old ally would be a great political success for France, and for Walewski personally. Presumably, Walewski might even think of returning to his native land in triumph as Prime Minister.

It would also cost Russia little, if anything, to restore to Poland the very limited rights bestowed by the 1825 Treaty of Vienna. Distasteful as the Polish constitution might be to Russia, it would be preferable to them that France and Britain should put it ahead of any cession of territory in peace negotiations. After all, granting the demand would not entail any new promises on Russia's part over and above those that she had already broken with impunity after the Polish insurrection of 1831. She could break them again if the Poles became unruly, and confiscate their constitution once more. Europe would no doubt protest feebly as it had done in 1831, unless it happened to be at war with Russia over something else at the time. It does not appear that Walewski knew in advance whether Russia would accept the demand – but it would be easy to drop it if it proved to be an obstacle to peace.

The Cabinet in London apparently never saw Walewski's Polish proposal as a sign that the French were determined on peace, probably because they were thinking only of continued war in the aftermath of their failure at the Redan. The Cabinet may also have been badly informed because Cowley and Persigny, the Ambassadors, were having personal communications difficulties with the French Foreign Minister that prevented them from seeing that he and others had already pushed Napoleon III in the direction of serious peace negotiations. One of the main reasons that had prevented France from making peace in the spring – the unconquered state of Sebastopol which would leave the French Army without glory – had now been removed. Immediately after hearing of Pélissier's success at the Malakoff, Walewski had begun to urge Napoleon III to withdraw France from the war, even using the ignoble argument that it was better to do so *before* Britain had a chance to recover prestige through further victories, 'Who can deny that France comes out of all this enhanced and Russia diminished? France *alone* has grown in this struggle. Today she holds first place in Europe.'[13]

A careful reading of the French proposal on Poland shows that Walewski now foresaw a quick end to the war without any cession of territory from Russia – a complete change from the Emperor's previous attitude. During the abortive peace negotiations six months earlier, the Emperor had also tried to introduce the Polish question, but at that time he had been determined to continue the war and saw the Polish cause as a way to make the war more popular in France.[14] It may seem presumptuous to claim to understand Walewski's new proposal better than two ministers as experienced in Anglo-French affairs as Palmerston and Clarendon; the only justification can be that they did not have the insight that we do into Walewski's new influence, and that they were misled by their knowledge of the Emperor's former principles and blinded by their conviction that the war was now about to be won. They may have thought that in describing it as a peacemaking proposal Walweski was misrepresenting his Emperor's motives over Poland. Earlier historians, while accepting the Emperor's verdict that his new Polish initiative had been 'misunderstood', have not put this particular interpretation on the misunderstanding. The diagnosis must therefore remain tentative. If it is true that Napoleon III had no intention of fighting for Poland at that point, the British should certainly not have accepted the proposal as it stood. That would have been equivalent to making the restoration of a few Polish constitutional rights the only other non-negotiable condition of peace apart from the previously agreed Four Points, one which would weigh lightly on Russia in the long term and do little for Britain. Britain should rather have thrown in a matching demand to balance France's Polish constitution – the freedom of the Caucasus, say, or a Turkish Crimea. Rejecting it out of hand as a badly conceived idea, and remarking gratuitously that the British public would not fight for Poland, was not the way to take part in the coming end game. And thus it was that Britain was left out of the peace discussions that began between Austria and France in the autumn of 1855. It was several months before the British Cabinet absorbed the fact that Napoleon III was determined on peace, and during that time they failed to take the necessary steps to prepare a negotiating strategy.

What was pushing France urgently towards peace was not just Walewski's desire to come out ahead of Britain. The more important reasons were that French public opinion was against a continuation of the war and the French economy would no longer support it – the war and poor harvests had caused a national financial crisis and the army in the Crimea was now suffering shortages (particularly of accommodation) to the extent that deaths from sickness there were soon to exceed the horrific British rates during the preceding winter. French public opinion was quite satisfied by their victory at the Malakoff, especially brilliant by comparison with British failure at the Redan. It is also possible that France was now eyeing Russia as a potential ally in a future struggle with the Germanic powers over the Rhine and Italy. General Pélissier, who had become even more insufferable and was threatening to resign if ordered to march against Russia in the Crimea, was rewarded by promotion to Marshal of France, by a pension of 100,000 francs, and by a triumphal title that recalled the rubble and dirt fort that had cost so much blood: the Dukedom of Malakoff. His gamble in going for a short-term gain that public opinion would acclaim, and to ignore his government's strategic objectives had maximised his personal return.

Pélissier's stubbornness was a part of the other factor that weighed heavily with the Emperor in his decision to make peace now. This was the slow progress of the war to date, due to the difficulties of fighting with a coalition force which should in theory have quickly scored decisive victories over industrially backward Russia. Although Pélissier was the main problem now, he would never have been elevated to his current position if it had not been for Raglan's disobedience. Raglan and Pélissier between them had made it impossible for the two strongest powers in the world to impose a joint military strategy. With no solution for these problems of command in sight, the idea of marching with Britain against Russia on a broad front for several more campaigns aimed at revising the map of Europe was no longer attractive to Napoleon III. In December 1855 the Emperor told his Council of Ministers, 'The Crimean War would have been the revolution that everyone expects, and that's why I undertook it. Great territorial changes would have resulted from it if Austrian indecision and the slowness of military operations hadn't reduced a great political revolution to a simple tournament.'[15] The 'slowness of military operations' was at least partly due to his Allies' inability to force their Commander-in-Chief to implement the agreed campaign plan; regardless of the merits of the field campaign itself, the failure to try it was fatal to the alliance.

9

Europe Loses the War

For two months after the fall of Sebastopol Palmerston and the Queen and most of the country looked forward to a continuation of the war until at least part of the Russian Empire had been liberated – the Crimea and Circassia to start with. In Parliament, opinion was more divided. The conservative opposition (always less hostile to autocratic Russia) favoured peace, especially the voices in the previous coalition government who had identified the destruction of Sebastopol as the solution to the 'Eastern Problem'. The latter group included Sir James Graham, the former First Lord of the Admiralty, who had done most to direct the war effort towards the destruction of this key Russian naval base. There had always been a peace party, but their opinions did not really sway the Cabinet as long as the Cabinet believed that they had the support of their French ally for a continuation of the war.

The reality was that after the storming of the Malakoff France was determined to end the war, while Russia was determined to continue it. 'Do not lose heart,' Tsar Alexander II wrote a week after the defeat to Michael Gorchakov, who had replaced Menshikov as the Commander-in-chief of the Russian armies in the Crimea, 'remember 1812 and trust in Providence. Sebastopol is not Moscow, the Crimea is not Russia. Two years after the burning of Moscow, our victorious armies stood in Paris. We are still the same Russians and God is with us.' It was an inspiring vision. A month later the Tsar wrote to Gorchakov that Russia would never meet the peace terms demanded by France and England; but peace would eventually come through a revolution in France caused by bad harvests and popular discontent.' He was right about the weakness of France, although he may have over-dramatised it; there was still much opposition in France to what many saw as Napoleon III's illegal regime.

On 17 October Napoleon III instructed the French Minister in Vienna to respond positively to an Austrian suggestion of talks between the two countries (thus excluding Britain) on possible peace terms with Russia. By 14 November they had drawn up an ultimatum from Austria to Russia, the same procedure used in late 1854 to demand peace negotiations on Allied terms. This ultimatum stated that Austria would break off diplomatic relations with Russia if the latter did not accept without reservation the non-negotiable Four Points including the demilitarisation of the Black Sea and the permanent destruction of Sebastopol. Austria had refused to support this Anglo-French demand at the last round of peace negotiations in the spring; the fact that they accepted it now shows that they were ready to endorse Allied gains on the battlefield. The threatened rupture between Austria and Russia was understood to lead to a declaration of war as soon as Austria could arrange it with the German states with which she had mutual obligations.

Austria had embellished one of the non-negotiable Four Points in a way that suited her own interests: the opening up of the mouth of the Danube to international trade was to be achieved by Russia giving up all its territory in the Danube delta. It would hand over this part of its Bessarabian province to Moldavia, Turkey's semi-autonomous province, which was committed to free trade. In addition to the non-negotiable Four Points, the draft Austrian ultimatum also said that Russia would have to allow the Allies to raise any other demands for negotiation at the resulting peace conference.

Napoleon III wrote a long letter to Queen Victoria on 15 November in which he hinted that the new ultimatum was a device to bring Austria and Prussia onto the Allied side and thus force Russia to accept more stringent terms that could be obtained at present. The Duke of Argyll, one of Palmerston's Ministers, dismissed this as 'the old wild goose chase over again' because Austria had always showed itself too cautious to enter the war. The Cabinet was further converted to the view that peace was imminent by a speech that Napoleon III made at about the same time in Paris in which he said, 'France has no hatreds, but she must have a peace which will decisively solve the objects for which this war has been undertaken.' The first part was seen as a jibe at the British popular hatred of the Tsar, supposedly shared by Palmerston. The second seems to show a reluctance to enlarge the objectives of the war. Taken together with the letter to Queen Victoria, the speech seems to have been one of the first signals understood in England of the Emperor's desire for peace. In reality, Napoleon III's desire for peace now made him likely to back down if Russia objected to some of the proposed terms, and this possibility began to worry the British Cabinet.

The Cabinet was offended when the French presented them with a document (the Austrian ultimatum) that had been drawn up without them. Britain demanded a number of amendments including the demilitarisation of the Sea of Azov and the Aland Islands in the Baltic. It also demanded that specific mention be made of Britain's right to raise the question of the independence of the Russian provinces in the Caucasus. This was included as a gesture to the hawks in the Cabinet, including Palmerston; most of the rest were by now convinced that Britain would have to accept France's terms for peace. Napoleon III rejected Britain's proposed inclusion of the demilitarisation of the Sea of Azov and the Aland Islands, and Britain withdrew them intending to raise them again as negotiable demands at the conference. On 5 December France accepted the remainder of Britain's amendments; Austria accepted them ten days later, and the following day the ultimatum was on its way to St Petersburg with the message that if the Russians did not accept the terms without reservation immediately then Austria would join the Allies. At the same time, Britain heard the first fragmentary news that the Russians had captured the Turkish fortress of Kars and the entire army besieged within and thus controlled large swathes of Turkish territory. Not anticipating this, the Allies had not included in the Austrian ultimatum any obligation on Russia to return territory captured from Turkey.

Russia at first replied that it could not accept the cessation of part of Bessarabia or the so-called 'Fifth Point' – the article under which the Allies would have the right to raise other demands during the conference. Austria responded that no discussion was possible and that it would break diplomatic relations on 18 January if unconditional acceptance had not been received. Russia finally signalled acceptance two days before the deadline, after much soul searching by Alexander II and the senior diplomats in St Petersburg. The Tsar was influenced by the news that Sweden had signed a new anti-Russian treaty with the Allies, and by a letter from his uncle the King of Prussia imploring him to make peace. Even Prussia, which was the most Russophile of all the German states, now seemed likely to join the anti-Russian coalition if the war went on. The Kars card, which Russia had unexpectedly picked up, also looked likely to win a few tricks if the peace talks were to begin now.

The peace conference began in Paris on 25 February 1856. Not surprisingly Russia immediately made the point that Kars and the north of Turkey were now hers, and that she was not obliged under the terms she had accepted to even consider handing them back. However, she might do so if the Allies dropped the so-called non-negotiable demand for Russia to give up territory in Bessarabia. Russia brushed aside the argument that Turkish territory was assumed to be inviolate because a violation of it had started the war. The British Cabinet became much more hawkish as a consequence of Russia's triumphal use of Kars and began to seriously consider continuing the war without France. Sweden was ready to provide troops, and Spain also wished to join Britain although its proposals had so far been rejected for fear of antagonising the United States which was in dispute with Spain over the latter's colonies in the Americas. Iron gunboats were coming out of British shipyards in great numbers, suitable for bombarding the Russian fortresses defending St Petersburg; a primitive version had been tried with great success by the French in an attack on the Russian fortress at Kinburn west of the Crimea. British troops in the Crimea were amazingly healthy, thanks to the efforts of the civilian railway contractors, nurses, Sanitary and Supply Commissioners, and educators who had discovered a thirst for knowledge among the troops that would keep them out of the drinking dens if supplied with books and lectures. A new, improved version of the Minié rifle was being issued to the troops; the Russians still had nothing comparable. Foreign legions had been raised, and expatriates and thwarted revolutionaries from Russia's subject countries were flocking to provide their services against their oppressor. Lord Clarendon's demand that Russia set free the province of Circassia in the Caucasus was making no headway at the negotiating table, France and Austria seeing it as a selfish British demand aimed at protecting overland routes to India. But an attack on the Caucasus would not need help from France or Austria – with a Russian Army marooned in Kars it did not seem unrealistic to plan a deep incursion into the Caucasus on the pretext of cutting off this invading army's supply lines.

Britain and Turkey could have continued the war without the French and Austrians, but at the cost of sacrificing the agreement to destroy Sebastopol and demilitarise the Black Sea, which seemed to be within reach in Paris. The French Emperor was showing more and more signs of retreating on this key demand, seeming now to want peace at almost any price. Palmerston therefore telegraphed Clarendon to meet the Emperor alone and tell him that if he let Britain down on the Black Sea issue, and accepted terms that the Allies had agreed to reject in the spring, Palmerston would have to reveal in England that France had broken their agreement and he might have to continue the war. Clarendon was to tell the Emperor that provided the Black Sea issue went in Britain's favour, Clarendon could negotiate on the other issues.

In the end Russia succeeded in bartering Kars for a reduction in the amount of territory it was required to cede in Bessarabia. Russia did agree to the permanent demilitarisation of the Black Sea and the Aland Islands, but did not concede any of Britain's additional demands. Britain finally signed the Treaty of Paris, ending the war, at the end of March 1856.

It is tempting to accuse the French of double-dealing for having quit while they were ahead, but it is not hard to see the justice of the French decision to pull out of the war. All the British wounds were self-inflicted. The French had objected to Lord Raglan's decision to attack Sebastopol, but they were prepared to follow their ally anywhere and they did so uncomplainingly once Marshal St Arnaud had stated his objections and his preference for Circassia. When British troops and recruitment proved hopelessly inadequate the French had drained their country of manpower so that at the fall of Sebastopol they had 126,000 troops there compared with Britain's 47,000, and their dead eventually numbered 95,000 compared to Britain's 22,000 (recent research has increased the estimate of Russian dead to nearly half a million).[2] It was Raglan who had provoked Canrobert's resignation and thwarted the plan of the Allied governments to seize the Crimea and avoid costly assaults on Sebastopol. The French considered that they had pulled Lord Raglan's chestnut out of the fire, and it was not their fault that it had turned to ashes in the British mouth. The south side of Sebastopol when captured had proved a useless prize: not even having a harbour but, in the words of General Codrington, successor to the disgraced Simpson, simply 'a large mutual wet ditch under fire from both sides'.[3]

At the same time as the Treaty of Paris, France, Britain, and Austria signed a different Triple Treaty under which these three powers would guarantee the independence and integrity of the Turkish Empire and would recognise as a cause for war any future threatening behaviour by Russia against Turkey. This was supposed to remedy defects in the Treaty of Paris which did not, for example, prevent Russia from massing troops on the Turkish frontier. The Triple Treaty was originally the idea of Austria, which feared that once France and Britain had taken their troops home Austria might be left to cope with any Russian infringements of the agreed Four Points. France was a reluctant signatory, as it now had no further interest in the region and was mending fences with Russia. France's reluctance was an early sign that the Triple Treaty might be hard to enforce when the signatories' goals diverged. The defects of the treaties were legion: they had not created any self-defending new buffer states, had not taken away any of the territories from which Russia was accustomed to attack Turkey, had not secured any financial reparations from Russia for the cost of repelling her initial invasion, had not strengthened Turkey's ability to defend itself, and had left the friendly Crimean Tatar population exposed to ferocious Russian reprisals. The Treaty of Paris was almost unique up to that time in requiring that a strong power desist from molesting a weaker third party. Basically, it was a Russian promise not to do it again. Russia could tear it up at any time it wanted, and who could or would begin the war all over again to restore it, if their own territory was not affected? The Triple Treaty seemed to say that the three signatories would, but if it was not convenient at the time there was no way any of the signatories could force the others to fight.

Another flaw in the Triple Treaty was that by guaranteeing the integrity of the Turkish Empire it did not allow for any legitimate separatist movements within. This was also a defect of the Treaty of Paris, which specified that the original First Point should be implemented by the Great Powers taking over from Russia as protectors of the semi-independent provinces of Moldavia and Wallachia. As soon as democratic separatist forces started to make headway in these states, the Powers found themselves obliged to yield to them. From then on Russia could claim that the Allies themselves had violated the Treaty of Paris.

Despite these obvious defects, Lord Palmerston publicly proclaimed himself very satisfied with the conclusion of the war and with the two treaties. He was putting a brave face on it; in private he admitted that the settlement would not last much beyond his lifetime. He was seventy-two.

The principal Allied war objective – the demilitarisation of the Black Sea including the promise never to rebuild the fortress and arsenal at Sebastopol – was granted by the Russians in the Treaty of Paris but honoured only for fourteen years. In 1870 Russia unilaterally repudiated this part of the treaty, and France and Britain did not contest the move. Russia rectified her other significant loss a few years later – after another war with Turkey in 1877–8 she demanded and obtained the return of that part of Bessarabia bordering the mouth of the Danube that she had ceded to Turkey in 1856.

The relative failure of the European collective security system to end the Crimean War in a decisive way was obvious to all at the time. A huge effort in a just cause with wide international backing had yielded a minimal and fragile result. The Concert of Europe, the principle of multilateral solidarity between powers in dealing with aggression, fell into disrepute largely as a result of this and was abandoned for over a century. This principle had ensured that other states acted as a check on the selfish power politics of each one; after the Crimean War these safeguards went by the board and as one historian has put it, the age of *realpolitik* began.[4] The arms race began as states tried to adapt to a new more hostile world, and a new generation of statesmen unwilling to rely on multilateral solidarity built a network of selfish bilateral treaties that encouraged states to go to war before (so they thought) their enemies could catch up in terms of arms and alliances. France, in trying to forestall the phenomenal industrial growth of Bismarck's new Germany, lost its two most important industrial provinces in the 1870 Franco-Prussian War. From then on France's determination to recapture Alsace and Lorraine was added to the explosive mix, so that when Russia's interference in the Balkans threatened a local war with Austria in 1914 the whole continent, booby-trapped by military alliances, erupted. This was the real cost of the failure of the Concert of Europe during the Crimean War.

Britain, mortified by its experience of military cooperation in the European sphere, turned its back on the Continent and concentrated on reforming the national institutions that had performed badly during the Crimean War. An era of unparalleled social reform followed. Florence Nightingale's friend McNeill – her Persian Adventurer – played an important role because his report on army supply failures triggered a constitutional crisis when Palmerston submitted it to Parliament without the consent of the Queen; the report implicitly criticised the arrangement under which the army was not under parliamentary control. Lord Palmerston won his ensuing battle against the Queen, Prince Albert, the Horse Guards and the shade of the Duke of Wellington, reducing the power of the monarchy considerably. Florence Nightingale herself devoted the rest of her long life to ensuring that the lessons of Crimean War mortality from preventable disease would be applied by ordinary people in their own homes, dramatically reducing premature death especially among infants.

The ignominious military result of the war for Britain influenced the writing of its history. Apparently unwilling to face up to how much had been at stake and how disappointing had been the result, British historians portrayed the outbreak of the Crimean War as the unnecessary consequence of duplicity, blunder, and inefficiency on the part of the vacillating and incompetent Aberdeen government and its dishonest foreign Allies. The idea that statesmen of countries with such widely differing ideologies as Britain, France, Austria, Italy, Sweden, Spain and Turkey would cooperate in the cause of peace became deeply unfashionable in the era of *realpolitik*, and their actions were to be explained as motivated purely by selfish national concerns. It is tempting to suggest that if Britain had discontinued its war with Germany in the early 1940s, history might now be portraying Britain's 1939 declaration of war as a similar blunder.

The dwelling on innumerable alleged blunders in the political history of the Crimean War has obscured the most important military mistake. This was the neglect by the Allied generals of repeated opportunities and orders to move the focus of the fighting away from Sebastopol to battlegrounds which told to their strengths: the range and accuracy of the Minié rifle, the initiative of the infantryman, and the discipline and skill of the cavalry. The lives of 117,000 skilled well-armed French and British soldiers were lost in besieging an objective – the southern sector of Sebastopol – that was of no value to either side and had been entirely neutralised by blockade. Once these lives had been wasted, France, which had supplied 80 per cent of them, simply could not afford to provide a replacement force of the same quality to start all over again. If the limited attention span of France had been properly exploited the results could have been a spectacular triumph for international cooperation. 'Cowardly' Austria and Prussia, whose doubts about whether Britain and France really were committed to throwing their menacing Russian neighbour off their backs turned out to be well-founded, would have been happy to endorse the liberation of Russia's captive dominions if they had seen a successful land-based military campaign. The blame for the Allies' missed opportunity must be attributed to the generals who refused to obey direct orders from their political masters to downgrade the siege and open a new front inland, and the politicians who did not have the courage to dismiss them. Lord Raglan's claim that he was forced to obey the conditional orders of the minister to attack Sebastopol is shown to be insincere by his disregard of later direct orders to the contrary. This is not to acquit his first Minister of War of stupidity and worse. That minister's statement to the Ambassador to Turkey after he discovered that Raglan had decided to attack Sebastopol with insufficient forces shows a failure to understand that at the very least a just war requires an assurance of success: 'failure [to take Sebastopol] could not produce a worse effect than refusal to attempt it'.[5]

For a century after the Crimean War the Russian Empire not only survived but expanded by taking control of the former Eastern European and Balkan dominions of the collapsed Austrian Empire. It is commonly stated as an insight that Stalin inherited the 'mechanisms of repression' of the Tsar; a less commented fact is that he also inherited the Russian Empire almost intact at a time when the other European Empires – Turkish and Austrian – were disintegrating. Russia lost Finland permanently, it is true, and the Baltic States and Poland during their short twenty years of freedom, but overall the 'prison of nations' (as Marxists had called Russia under the Tsars) continued to grow under Marxism. A new 'balance of power' came into being; not a multilateral arrangement of three empires and a few powerful independent states as it had been until 1914, but an opposition between East and West. The bi-polar world of two opposing blocs restored some kind of stability after the near-century of anarchy in international relations that followed the Crimean War, and it seemed for a while as if the bi-polar model was a higher stage of evolution after the 'Concert of Europe' and then the *realpolitik* models. If the bi-polar model was a natural and inevitable evolutionary development, then Palmerston's dream of dismembering the Russian empire was incompatible with progress. Typical of this view is the comment by one of the most respected political historians of the Crimean War, writing in 1981 that, 'If Palmerston had attained his goal of reducing the power of the tsarist empire to its level before Peter the Great, the European balance would have course have been completely unhinged.'[6]

Only after the recent unexpected collapse of the Soviet Union and its satellites has it become apparent that the bi-polar model was an evolutionary dead end, and that the European balance does not hinge on the existence of a Russian Empire after all. This makes Palmerston's and Napoleon III's vision seem rather less eccentric than it did when the Russian Empire seemed to be a part of the natural order of things. It has been argued that a despotic Russian Empire was necessary to defeat Nazi Germany, but that argument relies on a number of questionable assumptions.

Could the Allies have stopped the despotic expansion of the Russian empire a hundred years earlier? Would a broadening of the war, whether or not it lasted thirty years as Lord Aberdeen feared, have more quickly brought about a stable collection of independent democratic states like the Europe that we know today, avoiding some of the wars and mass murders of the twentieth century? It is possible to imagine a scenario in which a successful field campaign in the Crimea could have saved Europe from its frenzy of destruction, but it would be an exercise of little value. A more efficient field campaign would have had its chaotic failures too, no doubt.

So what is the lesson to be learned from the Crimean War, now that we know how much was at stake and the reason it was lost? This was a just war: Britain and her allies had the moral support of all Europe in going to war in defence of principles that we now value. It was a winnable war: Britain, as the world's only superpower, together with her powerful ally France, had a mighty ascendancy over unindustrialised Russia. The Allies' goals were limited (the liberation of Russia's peripheral vassal states) and achievable. And yet they failed disastrously, and by bringing into disrepute the Concert of Europe they probably put back by a century the vision that inspired them. This must be the lesson: even a just war can be counter-productive.

A Note on Sources

Unpublished Sources

It is a remarkable fact that new unused contemporary sources on the Crimean War are now becoming available in quantity. These sources are particularly those which have been buried in numerous city, county, and other minor records offices with only limited local cataloguing and research facilities. Through the internet portal known as Access to Archives, with its remarkably researcher-friendly search engine, it is now possible to find relevant records from these minor archives. They include an enormous quantity of unpublished letters and diaries in the papers deposited by less celebrated families who do not meet the criteria for entry to the national collections. This new accessibility of these records is likely to accelerate the trend away from 'Great Man History' and towards 'history from below'.

Another hitherto unused source is *Correspondence Relative to the Military Expedition to the East*. Only a small part of that document (covering 1854 only) is available in the Public Record Office. No Cabinet Office existed for the archiving of documents at the time, and it was normal for Cabinet ministers to take home their official papers when they retired. This is why both the *Correspondence*, the only complete integrated record of the official correspondence between the army and the government in 1855, and the book of Panmure's secret cipher telegrams are both in Lord Panmure's family papers in the National Archives of Scotland. Although the documents may be nearly all available in manuscript form in other widely dispersed archives, the *Correspondence* was printed and bound by the government at the time for ministers' reference, and is much easier to use.

Published Sources

A list of the main published sources consulted is included below, followed by endnotes which allow the text to be cross-referenced to them. In addition it should

be noted that the narrative leans heavily on the following published sources:
The Crimea from First to Last (Lysons) is a collection of contemporary letters from a field officer who was present throughout the Crimean campaign. Although published in 1895 the letters do not seem to have been altered to take advantage of hindsight.

Letters from Headquarters (Calthorpe) is also a collection of letters, this time from Raglan's nephew and ADC who was in a good position to report on the dissension in the High Command and on the overall military strategy. They were published too quickly (1856) to have been influenced by others' interpretations. He is often helpfully indiscreet, and his bias in favour of his uncle adds weight to his accidental revelations of Raglan's failings.

The Panmure Papers (Douglas and Ramsay) is a selection of letters between the Cabinet, the Court, and the High Command which documents the conflict between politicians and generals especially in the later stages of the siege. In it, the editors made clear that they could not yet (1908) publish the most secret despatches which were in the unpublished document *Correspondence Relative to the Military Expedition to the East* (see unpublished sources, above).

The Treaty of Paris and *The Crimean War* (Baumgart) are two works by a Continental historian, the first a detailed account of the peace negotiations in 1856 and the second a very comprehensive account of the campaign and the aims of the belligerents. These works are notable for their detailed discussion of the role of Austria and the German states.

Défense de Sébastopol (Totleben) is the account of the war published in 1863 by General Totleben, who as a relatively junior engineer officer was responsible for the remarkable fortifications of Sebastopol. His account of the battles of the Alma and Inkerman may be relatively objective as he was not personally engaged. He was wounded in June 1855 and took no further part in the war. He did perhaps exaggerate the strength of the Allies to please his Emperor, being a fervent admirer of the new Minié rifle and its user. He also relied more on French accounts of the war than on British. William Howard Russell favourably reviewed his accounts of the early battles.

The Invasion of the Crimea (Kinglake) is an eight-volume history of the war based on extensive and exclusive use of Lord Raglan's documents (including secret despatches that could not be independently verified), at the request of Raglan's family. His bias in favour of Lord Raglan and his friends, and his distaste for the all things French, were well-known and caused widespread condemnation of his history when it was published between 1863 and 1878. *The Times*, in a savage review on 23 February 1863, described his work as 'a historical romance'. Nevertheless, the fact that he was present at the battle of the Alma and knew many of the generals has led later historians (perhaps ignorant of the poor reception of

Kinglake's work by participants in the war) into the fallacy that the wealth of detail he provides may be taken at face value. It is worth bearing in mind that Kinglake was a barrister and his objective was to be an advocate for Lord Raglan rather than a historian. His multiple distortions and omissions unintentionally provide some useful pointers to skeletons in the cupboard. Those in the know (ex-ministers and the like) evidently declined to unmask Kinglake's fraud, presumably because they were as interested in hiding the truth as he was.

The War, the British Expedition to Russia, and *The Great War with Russia* (Russell). William Howard Russell, *The Times* correspondent in the Crimea, published three books of his personal experiences and reminiscences of the war at widely separate dates: 1855, 1877, and 1895. It is interesting to compare his three versions of the same event (for example, the Alma). In his first despatches to *The Times*, (1855) he seems to have repeated what he was told by other alleged witnesses. In 1877 he removed some details that were uncorroborated. In 1895 he denounced some of the earlier exaggerations that he may have unwittingly helped to promulgate, calling Kinglake's version of events a 'fairy tale'.

Illustrations

The early photographic portraits and Crimean scenes from the Library of Congress are, with the exception of Florence Nightingale and General Totleben, by Roger Fenton. The engravings from the Library of Congress are by William Simpson. The portraits of Napier, Canrobert, Cardigan and Lucan are from Nolan's *Illustrated History*. The photograph of Lord Palmerston is by Mayer and Pierson; those of the Grenadiers at Scutari and the Greenhill Battery are by James Robertson; that of McNeill comes from the *Memoir* by Florence MacAlister. The four scenes of Sebastopol after the capture of the southern part of the city are from Delafield's *Art of War in Europe* and are based on photographs by James Robertson.

Bibliography

BOOKS AND JOURNALS

Adkin, Mark, *The Charge: Why the Light Brigade was Lost* (Leo Cooper, London 1996)

Airlie, Mabell Frances Elizabeth, Countess of, *Lady Palmerston and her Times* (Hodder & Stoughton: London, 1922).

Balfour, Lady Frances, *The Life of George, Fourth Earl of Aberdeen, K.G.* (Hodder & Stoughton, London 1923).

Bannatyne, Neil, *History of the Thirtieth Regiment, now the First Battalion East Lancashire Regiment, 1689–1881* (Littlebury Bros., Liverpool, 1923)

Bapst, G., *Le Maréchal Canrobert* (Plon, Paris, 1898–1902).

Baumgart, W., *The Peace of Paris 1856* (ABC-Clio, Oxford 1981).

Baumgart, W., *The Crimean War* (Arnold, London 1999).

Bazancourt, Baron C. de, *L'Expédition de Crimée jusqu'á la prise de Sébastopol. Chroniques de la guerre d'Orient* (Paris, 1856).

Blanch, Lesley, *The Sabres of Paradise* (John Murray, London 1960).

Brown, Sir George, *Memoranda and Observations on the Crimean War, 1854–5, and Notes on Mr. Kinglake's second volume* (printed for private Circulation by Moray Weekly News, Elgin 1879).

Calthorpe, S., *Letters from Head-Quarters* (John Murray, London, 1856).

Calthorpe, S., *Affidavits filed by … the Hon. S. J. G. Calthorpe … the respondent* (John Murray, London, 1863).

Cameron, Donald, *Diary* (Crimean War Research Society Journal v4 No.3)

Carew, Peter, *Combat and Carnival* (Constable, London, 1954).

Champion, J. G., *A Sketch of the Life of a Lieutenant-Colonel of the 95th Regimen.* (Printed For Private Circulation, London, 1855).

Clifford, H., *Henry Clifford, V.C., his letters and sketches from the Crimea* (Michael Joseph, London, 1956).

Conrad, Mark, *Memoirs of a Don Cossack Artilleryman* (Crimean War Research Society Journal, vol.17 No.1, April 1999).

Cope, Zachary, *Florence Nightingale and the Doctors* (Museum, London 1958).

Delafield, Richard, *Report on the Art of War in Europe* (Washington, 1860).

Douglas, Sir George, and Ramsay, Sir George Dalhousie, *The Panmure Papers* (Hodder & Stoughton, London, 1908).

Du Casse, Baron Pierre, *Précis Historique des Opérations Militaires en Orient* (Paris, 1856)

Echard, W., *Napoleon III and the Concert of Europe* (Louisiana State University Press, Baton Rouge, 1983).

Falls, C. (Ed.), *A Diary of the Crimea* (Duckworth, London, 1954)

French-Blake, *The Crimean War* (Leo Cooper, London, 1974)

Fletcher, I. and Ishchenko, N., *The Crimean War, A Clash of Empires* (Spellmount, Staplehurst, 2004).

Fortescue, Hon. Sir J., *A History of the British Army* (Macmillan Co., London, 1899–1930).

Gallagher, J. and Robinson, R., *The Imperialism of Free Trade* (Economic History Review, 2nd Series, vol.Vi, No.1, 1953).

Gibbs, P., *The Battle of Alma* (Weidenfeld & Nicholson, London, 1963)

Goldie, S., *Florence Nightingale in the Crimean War* (Manchester University Press, Manchester, 1987).

Gooch, G. P. (Ed.), *The Later Correspondence of Lord John Russell, 1840–1878* (Longmans & Co., London, 1925).

Greenhill, Basil and Giffard, Ann, *The British assault on Finland, 1854–1855: a forgotten naval war* (Conway Maritime Press, London, 1988).

Greville, C., *The Greville Memoirs* (Longmans, London, 1874).

Griffith, Boscawen Trevor, *Letters* (Transcript by Major E. L. Kirby, n.p., n.d.)

Harris, J., *The Gallant Six Hundred* (Hutchinson, London, 1973).

Henderson, W. (Ed.), *Crimean War Diplomacy* (Jackson, Glasgow, 1947).

Hibbert, C., *The Destruction of Lord Raglan* (Longmans Green, London, 1961).

Higginson, Sir G., *Seventy Years of a Guardsman's Life* (John Murray, London, 1916)

Hume, J. R., *Reminiscences of the Crimean Campaign with the 55th Regiment* (Unwin Bros. London, 1894).

IV Hussar Journal October 1933 (account of Lieutenant Hutton).

Jocelyn, J. R. J., *The History of the Royal Artillery, Crimean Period* (Murray, London 1911).

Journal of the Crimean War Research Society.

Kelly, L., *Diplomacy and Murder in Teheran* (I.B. Tauris, London, 2002).

Kinglake, A. W., *The Invasion of the Crimea* (Blackwood, London 1863–7).

Lambert, Andrew, *The Crimean War, British Grand Strategy 1853–56* (Manchester University Press, 1990).

Longmore, T., *The Sanitary Contrasts of the British and French Armies During the Crimean War* (Griffin, London, 1883).

Loy Smith, G., *A Victorian RSM* (Royal Hussars' Museum, Winchester, 1987).

Lysons, Sir D., *The Crimean War From First to Last* (John Murray, London).

MacAlister, Florence, *Memoir of the Right Hon. Sir John McNeill, G.C.B.* (John

Murray, London, 1910).

Maurice, Sir F., *The History of the Scots Guards from the Creation of the Regiment to the Eve of the Great War* (Chatto & Windus, London, 1934).

Martin, K., *The Triumph of Lord Palmerston* (Hutchinson, London, 1963).

McNeill, Sir John, *Progress and Present Position of Russia in the East* (London, 1854).

Nolan, E. H., *The Illustrated History of the War against Russia* (London 1855–7).

Medical and Surgical History of the British Army which Served in Turkey and the Crimea (Parliamentary Paper, London, 1858).

Mosse, W., *The Rise and Fall of the Crimean System, 1855–71* (Macmillan, London, 1963).

Moyse-Bartlett, H., *Louis Edward Nolan and his influence on the British Cavalry* (Leo Cooper, London, 1971).

Munsell, F. D., *The Unfortunate Duke* (University of Missouri Press, Columbia, 1985)

Nightingale, F., *Notes on Matters Affecting the Health of the British Army* (Privately printed, London, 1858).

Our Veterans of 1854: in camp, and before the enemy (London, 1859).

Paget, Lord G., *The Light Cavalry Brigade in the Crimea* (John Murray, London, 1881).

Pearse, H. (Ed.), *The Crimean Diary and Letters of Lieut.-General Sir C. A. Windham* (K.C.B. Kegan Paul, London, 1897).

Portal, R., *Letters from the Crimea* (Printed for private circulation only, Warren, Winchester, 1900).

Ponting, C., *The Crimean War – The Truth Behind The Myth* (Chatto & Wyndus, London, 2004)

Report of the Commissioners Appointed to Report into the Sanitary Condition of the Army (Parliamentary Paper, London, 1858).

Report of the Select Committee on the Army Before Sebastopol (Parliamentary Paper, London, 1855).

Return of the names etc. of all officers in the army who remained in the Crimea etc. (Parliamentary Paper, War Office March, 1856).

Revol, J. F., *Le Vice des coalitions. Études sur le haut commandement en Crime e, 1854–1855* (Paris, 1923).

Richardson, R., (Ed.), *Nurse Sarah Anne* (John Murray, London, 1977).

Ridley, J., *Lord Palmerston* (Constable, London, 1970).

Ross-of-Bladensburg, Sir John, *The Coldstream Guards in the Crimea* (A. D. Innes & Co., London, 1897)

Rousset, C., *Histoire de la Guerre de Crimée* (Paris, 1877).

Royal Magazine, vol. 13, 1904–5 (account of Private H. Herbert, 4th Lt Dragoons).

Royle, T., *The Great Crimean War* (Abacus, London, 2000).

Russell, William Howard, *The War* (Routledge, London, 1855).

Russell, William Howard, *The British Expedition to the Crimea* (Routledge, London, 1877).

Russell, William Howard, *The Great War with Russia* (Routledge, London, 1895).

Russell, William Howard, *General Todleben's History of the Defence of Sebastopol. A Review* (Tinsley, London, 1865).

Sayer, E., *Despatches and Papers relative to the campaign in Turkey, Asia Minor and the Crimea, during the War with Russia in 1854, 1855, 1856* (Harrison, London, 1857).

Seaton, A., *The Crimean War – a Russian Chronicle* (Batsford, London, 1977).

Shirreff, A.G. (Ed.), *Crimean Letters of J. B. Patullo* (Queen's Lancashire Regiment Museum, Preston, typescript).

Small, E. M., *Told from the Ranks* (A. Melrose, London, 1897).

Small, H., *Florence Nightingale, Avenging Angel* (Constable, London, 1988).

Springman, Michael, *Sharpshooter in the Crimea: The Letters of Captain Gerald Goodlake, V.C.* (Pen & Sword, Barnsley, 2005).

Sterling, A., *The Highland Brigade in the Crimea* (Absinthe Press, Minneapolis, 1995).

Stern, A., *Geschichte Europas seit den Verträgen von 1815 bis zum Frankfurter Frieden von 1871* (Stuttgart & Berlin, 1894–1924).

Strachan, Hew, *Soldiers, Strategy, and Sebastopol* (Historical Journal 1978 p.312).

Totleben, E. *Défense de Sébastopol* (Saint-Pétersbourg, 1863–74).

Trow, M. J. *The Pocket Hercules – Captain Morris and the Charge of the Light Brigade* (Pen & Sword, Barnsley, 2006).

United Services Journal.

Walker, Sir C., *Days of a Soldier's Life* (Chapman and Hall, London, 1894).

Warner, P., *The Fields of War* (John Murray, London, 1977).

Wellesley, Sir V. and Sencourt, R., *Conversations with Napoleon III* (Ernest Benn, London, 1934).

Whinyates, E., *From Coruna to Sebastopol* (W. H. Allen, London, 1884).

Wiseman, Cardinal, *The future Historian's view of the present war* (London, 1855).

Wolseley, Viscount, *The Story of a Soldier's Life* (Constable, London, 1903).

Wood, G. N., *Evans in the Crimea* (Army Quarterly Vol. 102 p.344).

Woodham Smith, C., *Florence Nightingale* (Constable, London, 1950).

Woods, N. A., *The Past Campaign* (Longman, London, 1855).

Wrottesley, G. (Ed.), *The Military Opinions of General Sir John Fox Burgoyne* (Bentley, London, 1859).

Wykeham Martin, Mrs, *Letters written from the Crimea to several members of his family, by the late Major Fiennes Cornwallis [Fiennes Martin]. Collected and edited by Mrs. Wykeham Martin* (Privately printed, 1868).

KEY TO ARCHIVES

BL –   British Library.

CUL –   Cambridge University Library.

NAM –   National Army Museum.

NAS –   National Archives of Scotland.

Newcastle – Newcastle Collection, Manuscripts and Special Collections, University of Nottingham.

PRO –   Public Record Office, Kew.

RA –   Royal Archives, Windsor.

Endnotes

CHAPTER 1: Truth: The First Casualty of War

1 *Illustrated London News*, 10 May 1856, p.798.
2 Russell, *The Great War with Russia*, p.291.
3 Clifford, *Letters and Sketches from the Crimea*, p.282.
4 Information on Poole primarily from Lysons, *The Crimean War from First to Last*, and Griffith, *Letters*.

CHAPTER 2: Britain's Anti-Crusade Against Russia

1 See Gallagher and Robinson, *Imperialism and Free Trade*.
2 *Ibid*.
3 Baumgart, *The Crimean War*, p.14.
4 Martin, *The Triumph of Lord Palmerston*, p.155.
5 Ridley, *Lord Palmerston*, p.414.
6 Court and conservative pacifist attitude to Russia: Ridley, pp.413–4, 418; Martin, pp.103–4, 124, 149–152.
7 Ridley, p.355; Martin, p.50.
8 Liberal view that Turkey could reform: Martin, p.123.
9 Ridley, p.415.
10 Baumgart, *The Crimean War*, p.94. The ultimatum was sent 6 October and the Cabinet decided to send the fleet to Constantinople on 7/8 October.
11 The account of Sinope and Palmerston's resignation is taken from Martin, pp.149–162, and Greville, vol.7, p.108 *et seq*.

CHAPTER 3: From Phoney War to Invasion

1 Baumgart, *The Crimean War*, pp.101, 109; Kinglake, *Invasion of the Crimea*, vol.2 p.96.
2 See Wiseman, *The Future Historian's View of the Present War* for a comparison of British and French Armies.
3 Russell, *The War*, p.95.
4 *Ibid.*, pp.93–4.
5 Seaton, *The Crimean War, A Russian Chronicle*, p.180.
6 Royle, *The Great Crimean War*, pp.115–6.
7 Baumgart, *The Crimean War*, p.94.
8 This was Kinglake's claim (vol.1, p.429). He was influenced by his distaste for Napoleon III's regime, and saw ignominy in any British partnership with the French. See Baumgart, *The Crimean War*, for the latest research which invalidates the argument that waiting would have brought Austria in.
9 The incomplete and misleading version of the instructions to invade the Crimea were printed by Kinglake, (First Edition, 1863) vol.2, p.106 *et seq*. In Kinglake's third edition of the same year the omitted passages are reinstated, but without comment.
10 Fletcher, and Ishchenko, *The Crimean War, A Clash of Empires*, p.49.
11 Brown, *Memoranda and Observations on the Crimean War*, p.15.
12 PRO FO881/550 Raglan to Newcastle 19/7/54. Raglan said later (NAS, GD45/8/128/B p.476 2/3/55) that he also 'communicated' the instructions to three other admirals including Lyons, and that there was 'no dissentient voice', a claim that conflicts directly with Brown's evidence.
13 Wellesley and Sencourt, *Conversations with Napoleon III*, p.59.
14 Kinglake 2 p.98. The actual number was about 56,000 near Sebastopol and 12,000 elsewhere (Baumgart, *The Crimean War*, p.116).
15 Baumgart, *The Crimean War*, p.113.
16 PRO FO881/550, Raglan to Newcastle 19/7/54.
17 Clarendon to Aberdeen 18/12/53 quoted in Martin, p.152.
18 Graham, through Admiral Lyons, influenced Raglan against attacking Circassia: Lambert, *The Crimean War, British Grand Strategy 1853–56*, p.112.
19 Strachan, *Soldiers, Strategy, and Sebastopol*.
20 Fortescue, who mentions Shaw Kennedy's advice in his *History of the British Army*, says the Cabinet never dreamed of following it. It can only be assumed that Fortescue had not read the full text of the Cabinet's instructions to Raglan, which more than dreams of it. Although a bitter critic of Kinglake, Fortescue therefore allowed Kinglake to dupe him.
21 Blanch, *The Sabres of Paradise*.
22 See for example Surgeon Cooper's recommendations to Dr Linton in Nightingale, *Notes on Matters affecting the Health of the British Army*.
23 Newcastle Ne C 10040/2.
24 Longmore, *The Sanitary Contrasts of the British and French Armies*, quoting Chenu.

25 Portal, *Letters from the Crimea*, pp.17, 25.
26 Sterling, *The Highland Brigade in the Crimea*, p.35.

CHAPTER 4: From Success to Stagnation

1 Falls, *A Diary of the Crimea*, pp.88, 121.
2 Hibbert, *The Destruction of Lord Raglan*, p.51.
3 Gibbs, *The Battle of Alma*.
4 Fletcher and Ishchenko, p.96.
5 Totleben, *Défense de Sébastopol*, vol.1, pp.184–5.
6 Totleben, p.188.
7 Evans, letter in *The Times*, 2 July 1855.
8 Maurice, *History of the Scots Guards*, p.68.
9 Maurice claims that only one company remained at the river; Kinglake claims that nine did. Brown also claims they 'could not be induced to leave' (Brown, p.109).
10 Brown claims that the laggards of the Scots Guards were firing from the river. Kinglake's later edition says the Grenadiers were joined by 140 others including Dalrymple's Scots Guards company. See Maurice for letter from Gipps describing how the Grenadiers waited for the gap to be filled.
11 Gibbs, p.153.
12 Ross-of-Bladensburg, *The Coldstream Guards*, p.83.
13 Wolseley, *The Story of a Soldier's Life*, p.80.
14 Russell, *General Todleben's History*, p.65
15 Walker, *Days of a Soldier's Life*, p.110.
16 Higginson, *Seventy Years of a Guardsman's Life*, pp.153–4.
17 Wood, *Evans in the Crimea*, p.344.
18 Shirreff, *Crimean Letters of J. B. Patullo*, p.55.
19 Kinglake's estimate plus eight guns of Don no.3 – see Conrad, *Memoirs of a Don Cossack Artilleryman*.
20 Jocelyn, *History of the Royal Artillery*, p.149, says that the Second Division only fired 15,000 rounds, making possible only ten to fifteen minutes of fire equivalent to two hypothetical machine guns. Jocelyn's low figure is questionable in view of his claim that the Light Division fired 39,000 – more even than the First. Half the Lights were routed, the other half under Buller formed square which was not a good configuration for offensive musketry. I believe that Jocelyn must have transposed some of the figures, most likely those of the Second and Light Divisions. Bannatyne, in *History of the Thirtieth Regiment*, diplomatically gives credit to Lord Raglan's guns as well as to his regiment's rifle fire. According to Hume, *Reminiscences of the Crimean Campaign*, the 55th arrived alongside only after the Causeway battery had retired, which supports the view that the 30th should get the credit.
21 See Conrad, *op. cit.*
22 Russell, *The War*, p.182.

23 Kinglake, vol.2 p.563, for estimates of casualties. Russian dead from Totleben quoted in Baumgart, *The Crimean War*, p.120. French dead from Du Casse, *Précis Historique.*

24 Russell in *The British Expedition to the Crimea* says both of the guns with Raglan fired nine-pounder ammunition, though one gun was of the wrong calibre.

25 The effect of Raglan's two guns at the Alma: Calthorpe, *Letters from Headquarters*, vol.1, p.178; Kinglake vol.2, pp.405–7; Russell, *The British Expedition to the Crimea*, pp.303–4; Ffrench Blake, *The Crimean War*, p.59; Royle, pp.229–30; Fletcher and Ischenko, p.108

26 See Russell, *General Todleben's History*, p.58n for the British denial of the twenty-one French guns.

27 Totleben, vol.1 pp.203–205.

CHAPTER 5: They Were the Reason Why

1 Fletcher and Ishchenko, p.183.
2 Moyse-Bartlett, *Louis Edward Nolan*, p.90.
3 Russell, *The Great War With Russia*, p.128.
4 *Medical and Surgical History*, vol.1.
5 Dorset D/LEG/Z24, letter from Ellis; Pearse, *Crimean Diary*, p.47.
6 Light Brigade deaths from sickness: *Medical and Surgical History*, vol.1 excludes deaths at Scutari, which if added in would push the total up to about 150 by the time of the Charge (about fifty-nine in September alone, or 4 per cent of a strength of about 1,300); a further 132 died October–April (Nightingale), say from the same population, and there were 200 deaths after that (*Medical and Surgical History*), say half of these from the originally embarked troops, makes 232 after the Charge from the under 1,000 who were on the strength at the Charge.
7 Loy Smith, *A Victorian RSM*, p.126.
8 *Ibid.*, pp.127,144.
9 Adkin, *The Charge,* p.100.
10 Letter dated 27 October 1854 in Wykeham Martin, *Letters written from the Crimea.*
11 Evelyn got news on 19 October of the receipt in England of an 'account of the Battle of the Alma' (Falls pp.93, 98). On 26 October (the day after the Charge) he rode to Balaclava and there read Russell's despatch in *The Times* describing the Alma and the 'affair on the Bulganak' (published on 10 October but the dateline says that portions were published in later editions of the 9th). Two weeks was sufficient for a copy of *The Times* to arrive in Balaclava. Warner, *The Fields of War*, p.68 says Temple Godman received newspapers of 2 October on the 17th.
12 Hibbert, p.136.

13 See Cameron.

14 Fletcher and Ishchenko, p.169.

15 Loy Smith, p.130.

16 Seaton, p.145.

17 Brighton, *Hell Riders*, p.96.

18 Calthorpe, *Affidavits*, pp.9, 21. For corroboration of Morris's version see Carew, p.210.

19 House of Lords debate, reported in *The Times*, 20 March 1855. In fact, Raglan *had* ordered the infantry to attack, but General Cathcart had refused. (Kinglake 1877 vol.5, pp.184, 223; Adkin pp.120, 223). Lucan must have known of Cathcart's disobedience by the time of the Lords debate, but gallantly chose not to mention it.

20 Woods, *The Past Campaign*, vol.2, p.74.

21 *The Times*, 10/3/1855, p.5, reporting on the Lords' debate.

22 Letter Lucan to Raglan 30/11/1854 see *The Times*, 2/3/1855.

23 *The Times* 20/3/1855, p.5.

24 Kinglake, vol.4, p.402.

25 Trow, p.120.

26 For a discussion of Nolan's possible delivery of an earlier order, see Douglas Austin in the *Journal of the Crimean War Research Society*, January 2007, p.15.

27 *United Services Journal*, April 1856, p.545.

28 Calthorpe, *Affidavits*, p.8; and *Letters from Headquarters*, vol.1, p.184.

29 *United Services Journal,* April 1856, p.550, and Doyle, p.20.

30 Royal Magazine (account of Private H. Herbert).

31 IV Hussar Journal, p.32.

32 Small, *Told from the Ranks*, p.64.

33 Portal, p.50.

34 Adkin, p.179; Seaton p.150 (also for the 5:1 estimate).

35 Loy Smith, p.136.

36 Adkin, p.215.

37 Whinyates, *Corunna to Sebastopol*, p.168.

38 *United Services Journal*, July 1856, no.2, p.458.

39 Raglan to Newcastle, letter 28/10/54: Newcastle NeC 9893.

CHAPTER 6: Winter Above Sebastopol

1 Airlie, *Lady Palmerston and Her Times,* p.166.

2 See Champion, *A Sketch of the Life.*

3 Wood, p.344.

4 Totleben, *Défense de Sébastopol,* vol.1, pp.463–4.

5 *The Times*, 20/3/1855, p.5.

6 Calthorpe, vol.1, p.343.

7 Russell, *The Great War With Russia*, p.183.

8 *Return of the names etc. of all officers...* About 1,540 officers were in the Crimea in November 1854; about 131 left that month (ninety-five failing to return) and ninety-four left in December (seventy failing to return)

9 Greville, *The Greville Memoirs,* ii p.37. Calthorpe, *Letters from Headquarters,* vol.1, p.385 for his account of Evans and for number of effectives.

10 Calthorpe, *Letters from Headquarters,* vol.1, p.399.

11 *Report of the Select Committee on the Army Before Sebastopol,* 3rd Report pp.40, 47.

12 Burgoyne's remark that navvies could have built a road, *Ibid.,* 3rd Report p.330.

13 *Ibid.* 3rd Report pp.130, 160; 4th Report pp.296–7.

14 Calthorpe, *Letters from Headquarters,* vol.1, p.424.

15 Kinglake was the Raglan sympathiser who claimed that Filder refused to abandon Balaclava.

16 Munsell, *The Unfortunate Duke,* p.152.

17 Nightingale's private instructions to report to Herbert are referred to in her private letter to him of 25/11/1854 (BL Add.MSS.43393.f.5).

18 Morning Chronicle, 24/10/54; *Report of the Select Committee on the Army Before Sebastopol,* 1855 (Menzies's equivalent rank); *Report of the Commissioners Appointed to Report into the Sanitary Condition of the Army,* 1857 (Medical and combatant rank equivalents).

19 Woodham-Smith p.162 claims that Mr. MacDonald reported the doctors' non-cooperation to the Hospital Commission. Verification has not been found although *Report of the Select Committee,* Q 7022 may be the source. See also Richardson, *Nurse Sarah Anne,* in which Terrot alludes to the dispute.

20 Letter sold at Bonham's, 11 March 2003, Lot 512.

21 Kelly, *Murder and Diplomacy in Teheran.*

22 McGrigor file in BL Add. MSS 61192.

23 Bracebridge to Herbert RAVIC/F 2/81.

24 See National Portrait Gallery website for the portrait of the younger McNeill.

25 'The real disease was starvation': Small, *Florence Nightingale,* p.76.

26 Letter from Gaskell to Nightingale 31/12/1858, Brotherton Collection, Leeds University.

27 Newcastle NE C 9938; NE C 10011; NE C 9960.

CHAPTER 7: The Allied Change of Plan

1 Wrottesley, *The Military Opinions of General Sir John Fox Burgoyne,* p.197.

2 Mosse, *Rise and Fall of the Crimean System,* p.12. For the events leading up to the Peace Conference of March 1855 see Henderson, *Crimean War Diplomacy,* pp.98–112.

3 The account of events leading up to the Vienna talks of 1855 is taken from Henderson.

4 Henderson p.61.

5 Gooch, *Later Correspondence of Lord John Russell*, vol.2, pp.160–1.

6 Balfour, vol.2, p.206.

7 NAS, GD45/8/128/B pp.629–30.

8 Seaton, p.117.

9 Charles Ash Windham's criticism of the siege: Pearse, p.53.

10 Douglas and Ramsay, *The Panmure Papers*, vol.1, p.154.

11 Strachan, p.317.

12 Douglas and Ramsay, vol.1, p.159.

13 NAM 6807–285–1 no.95, enclosure in letter Panmure to Raglan, 23/4/55.

14 PRO WO 1/373 War Department In-letters, fol.891.

15 NAS, GD45/8/130.

16 The official orders are in NAM 6807–285–1. Royle's and Hibbert's statements that Lord Panmure thought the plan 'wild and impracticable' are incorrect: that was only Panmure's judgement of Napoleon's proposed use of the third (diversionary) force. In their instructions to Raglan (NAS, GD45/8/128/B pp.700–1, also in PRO WO 6/74) the government left it to Raglan and Canrobert to decide how to use this diversionary force. Raglan's acknowledgement of receipt of these instructions is in GD45/8/128/B p.825. Baumgart's statement that Raglan never received official orders is shown to be mistaken by these last two documents. Kinglake (vol.7, pp.236–248, 283–290) is wrong to say on p.240 that the government did not send orders before consulting Lord Raglan (implying that his criticism was enough to stop them doing so). They sent them on 4 May before receiving his response to their unofficial briefings of 20 and 23 April.

17 NAS, GD45/8/128, v, 811.

18 Calthorpe, *Letters from Headquarters*, vol.2, pp.234–5.

19 PRO WO 1/374 f137–149.

20 PRO FO/78/1128 Rose to Clarendon, 14 May 1855.

21 Raglan said that he hoped to join in the field campaign with the First Division and a part of the Sardinian contingent: NAS, GD45/8/128/B, p.811, Raglan to Panmure 15 May 1855.

22 Douglas and Ramsay, vol.1, pp.208, 216.

23 French accounts of Raglan's conditions of accepting command: Bapst, *Le Maréchal Canrobert*; Bazancourt, *Expédition de Crimée*.

24 Calthorpe, *Letters from Headquarters*, vol.2, p.239.

25 Bazancourt, Letter Canrobert to Napoleon III, 19 May 1855.

26 PRO WO 1/374 fol.249.

27 Niel to Vaillant 18/5/55, quoted in Revol, *Le Vice des Coalitions*.

28 Rousset, *Histoire de la Guerre de Crimée*, vol.2, p.209.

29 Brown, p.74.

30 Douglas and Ramsay, vol.1, p.226.

31 *Ibid.*, pp.198, 201, 210–11. The telegram: NAS, GD45/8/130.

32 Douglas and Ramsay, vol.1, p.223.

33 *United Services Journal*, June 1856, vol.2, p.159.

210

34 See Douglas and Ramsay and also Seaton, pp.188–9.

35 The merits of the field campaign plan: see Bazancourt for the Emperor's objection to the attack from Eupatoria; see *The Times*, 14 June 1856, p.5, for British objections to the Aloushta attack; see Rose to Clarendon, no.55, 11/5/55 PRO FO 78/1128, countering both sets of objections and for a compromise plan to folow a watercourse. *The Times* reference quoted makes it clear that Rose's plan was what the Russians later admitted that they feared most.

36 Calthorpe, *Letters from Headquarters*.

37 Douglas and Ramsay, vol.1, p.391 (Letter Prince Albert to Clarendon).

38 Calthorpe, *Letters from Headquarters,* vol.2, p.307.

39 Rousset, vol.2, p.250.

40 Calthorpe, *Letters from Headquarters*, vol.2 p.321. Rousset vol.2, p.263. Rousset vol.2, pp.274, 281.

41 Calthorpe *op. cit.* vol.2, p.331.

42 Lysons, p.194.

43 Rose to Clarendon, 1/5/55 PRO FO 78/1128.

44 Rousset, vol.2, p.306.

45 Clifford, p.210.

46 Letter to Rev. F.W. Meadows, Plymouth and West Devon archives ref 475/4.

47 Douglas and Ramsay, vol.1, p.246, Letter Raglan to Panmure, 19/6/185

48 Goldie, *Florence Nightingale in the Crimean War*, p.132.

CHAPTER 8: I'm a General, Get Me Out of Here

1 Griffith, p.3.

2 Springman, *Sharpshooter in the Crimea*, p.137.

3 Letter in *The Times*, 5/9/1855, from surgeon E.T. Watkins.

4 Douglas and Ramsay, vol.1, pp.248, 285.

5 *Ibid.,* vol.1, p.337.

6 *Ibid.,* vol.1, p.391 (Prince Albert to Clarendon).

7 See Sayer, *Despatches and Papers*, p.288 and Calthorpe, *Letters from Headquarters,* Appendix D

8 Greenhill, *The British Assault on Finland*, pp.145–6.

9 Baumgart, *The Crimean War*, p.43.

10 PRO ADM 1/5625/725.

11 PRO FO 519/172 f261–3.

12 Stern, *Geschichte Europas seit den Verträgen von 1815*, vol.8, pp.555–6, letter from Persigny to Walewski, 18/9/55.

13 Baumgart, *The Treaty of Paris*, p.29.

14 Wellesley and Sencourt, *Conversations with Napoleon III*, p.78.

15 Echard, *Napoleon III and the Concert of Europe*, p.51

CHAPTER 9: Europe Loses the War

1 Mosse, pp. 15–16, 20.
2 French effectives from Rousset, vol.2, p.412. Russian dead from Fletcher,
   pp. 531–2.
3 Douglas and Ramsay, vol.2, p.13.
4 See Baumgart, *The Crimean War*, for the breakdown of the Concert of
   Europe and its replacement by *realpolitik*, which somewhat revises his earlier
   conclusion in *The Peace of Paris* that the Concert survived another sixty years
   because Palmerston was prevented from continuing the war.
5 Newcastle Ne C 10437.
6 Baumgart, *The Treaty of Paris*, p.17.

List of Maps

List of Illustrations

40 A private in full marching order. The chimney shows that the floor of the tent is dug out and a stove installed (Library of Congress).

41 Sixty-eight-pounder Lancaster gun in the Diamond Battery. The figure at top is Captain William Peel of the frigate *Diamond*, favourite son of the late Sir Robert Peel, the former Prime Minister. Captain Peel took part in several land battles including Inkerman and the Waterloo Day assault on the Redan. He won the VC, and died of smallpox in India during the Mutiny (Library of Congress).

42 A quiet day in the mortar battery (Library of Congress).

43 Commissariat difficulties. The port of Balaclava is in the background and the track to the camp is axle-deep in mud at Kadikoi (Library of Congress).

44 Sebastopol and its harbour seen from the eastern end of the Allied lines. The flat-topped hill fort is the Malakoff; to the left is the gentler slope of the Mamelon. (Library of Congress)

45 Horse ambulances carrying the sick and wounded up to the hospital above Balaclava harbour (Author's collection).

46 The *Volcano* Steam floating factory ship. Built to support operations in the Baltic, this vessel had a foundry capable of melting two tons of iron, a half-ton steam hammer, assorted punching and shearing presses, a lathe capable of machining a piston seven feet in diameter, and many other machines (Author's collection).

47 Cable laying plough for field telegraph cable. Although arguably the telegraph had been used in earlier wars, the Crimea was the scene of the first field telegraph designed to connect parts of the camp and even ships offshore (Author's collection).

48 The new railway carrying wood for huts to the camp. This scene is close to that shown in the engraving of 'Commissariat difficulties' – the church at Kadikoi is visible in both. Initially horses pulled the trucks on flat ground and a stationary engine with winding gear hauled them up the slopes (Author's collection).

49 Machine for pressing bullets out of solid lead rod. This method was used for Minié bullets as it was quicker and more accurate than casting. This particular machine was made for the French, who liked grooves in their bullets on the theory that it helped stabilize them like the feathers on an arrow (Author's collection).

50 The *Glatton*, one of about forty iron-clad floating batteries constructed in 1855 after it became obvious that wooden walls were no match for Russian fire from the shore. The ship was armoured with four inches of iron and was said to be unsatisfactory at steaming, sailing, stopping and steering. Extra rudders were hung from the boat davits to remedy the latter defect (Author's collection).

Index

TEMPUS – REVEALING HISTORY

R.J.Mitchell
Schooldays to Spitfire
GORDON MITCHELL
'[A] readable and poignant story'
The Sunday Telegraph

£12.99   0 7524 3727 5

Forgotten Soldiers of the First World War
Lost Voices from the Middle Eastern Front
DAVID WOODWARD
'A brilliant new book of hitherto unheard voices from a haunting theatre of the First World War' *Malcolm Brown*

£12.99   978 07524 4307 2

1690 Battle of the Boyne
PÁDRAIG LENIHAN
'An almost impeccably impartial account of the most controversial military engagement in British history' *The Daily Mail*

£12.99   0 7524 3304 0

Hell at the Front
Combat Voices from the First World War
TOM DONOVAN
'Fifty powerful personal accounts, each vividly portraying the brutalising reality of the Great War... a remarkable book' *Max Arthur*

£12.99   0 7524 3940 5

Amiens 1918
JAMES MCWILLIAMS & R. JAMES STEEL
'A masterly portrayal of this pivotal battle'
Soldier: The Magazine of the British Army

£25   0 7524 2860 8

Before Stalingrad
Hitler's Invasion of Russia 1941
DAVID GLANTZ
'Another fine addition to Hew Strachan's excellent *Battles and Campaigns* series'
BBC History Magazine

£9.99   0 7524 2692 3

The SS
A History 1919-45
ROBERT LEWIS KOEHL
'Reveals the role of the SS in the mass murder of the Jews, homosexuals and gypsies and its organisation of death squads throughout occupied Europe' *The Sunday Telegraph*

£9.99   0 7524 2559 5

Arnhem 1944
WILLIAM BUCKINGHAM
'Reveals the real reason why the daring attack failed' *The Daily Express*

£10.99   0 7524 3187 0

If you are interested in purchasing other books published by Tempus, or in case you have difficulty finding any Tempus books in your local bookshop, you can also place orders directly through our website

www.tempus-publishing.com

TEMPUS – REVEALING HISTORY

The Wars of the Roses
The Soldiers' Experience
ANTHONY GOODMAN
'Sheds light on the lot of the common soldier as never before' *Alison Weir*
'A meticulous work'
The Times Literary Supplement

£12.99   0 7524 3731 3

D-Day
The First 72 Hours
WILLIAM F. BUCKINGHAM
'A compelling narrative' *The Observer*
A *BBC History Magazine* Book of the Year 2004

£9.99   0 7524 2842 2

English Battlefields
500 Battlefields that Shaped English History
MICHAEL RAYNER
'A painstaking survey of English battlefields... a first-rate book' *Richard Holmes*
'A fascinating and, for all its factual tone, an atmospheric volume' *The Sunday Telegraph*

£18.99   978 07524 4307 2

Trafalgar Captain Durham of the Defiance: The
Man who refused to Miss Trafalgar
HILARY RUBINSTEIN
'A sparkling biography of Nelson's luckiest captain' *Andrew Lambert*

£17.99   0 7524 3435 7

Battle of the Atlantic
MARC MILNER
'The most comprehensive short survey of the U-boat battles' *Sir John Keegan*
'Some events are fortunate in their historian, none more so than the Battle of the Atlantic. Marc Milner is *the* historian of the Atlantic Campaign... a compelling narrative'
Andrew Lambert

£12.99   0 7524 3332 6

Okinawa 1945 The Stalingrad of the Pacific
GEORGE FEIFER
'A great book... Feifer's account of the three sides and their experiences far surpasses most books about war' *Stephen Ambrose*

£17.99   0 7524 3324 5

Gallipoli 1915
TIM TRAVERS
'The most important new history of Gallipoli for forty years... groundbreaking' *Hew Strachan*
'A book of the highest importance to all who would seek to understand the tragedy of the Gallipoli campaign' *The Journal of Military History*

£13.99   0 7524 2972 8

Tommy Goes To War
MALCOLM BROWN
'A remarkably vivid and frank account of the British soldier in the trenches' *Max Arthur*
'The fury, fear, mud, blood, boredom and bravery that made up life on the Western Front are vividly presented and illustrated' *The Sunday Telegraph*

£12.99   0 7524 2980 9

If you are interested in purchasing other books published by Tempus, or in case you have difficulty finding any Tempus books in your local bookshop, you can also place orders directly through our website

www.tempus-publishing.com

Private 12768 Memoir of a Tommy
JOHN JACKSON

'Unique... a beautifully written, strikingly honest account of a young man's experience of combat' *Saul David*
'At last we have John Jackson's intensely personal and heartfelt little book to remind us there was a view of the Great War other than Wilfred Owen's' *The Daily Mail*

£9.99   0 7524 3531 0

The German Offensives of 1918
MARTIN KITCHEN

'A lucid, powerfully driven narrative' *Malcolm Brown*
'Comprehensive and authoritative... first class' *Holger H. Herwig*

£13.99   0 7524 3527 2

Verdun 1916
MALCOLM BROWN

'A haunting book which gets closer than any other to that wasteland marked by death' *Richard Holmes*

£9.99   0 7524 2599 4

The Forgotten Front
The East African Campaign 1914–1918
ROSS ANDERSON

'Excellent... fills a yawning gap in the historical record'
The Times Literary Supplement
'Compelling and authoritative'
Hew Strachan

£12.99   978 07524 4126 9

Agincourt
A New History
ANNE CURRY

'A highly distinguished and convincing account' *Christopher Hibbert*
'A *tour de force*' *Alison Weir*
'*The* book on the battle' *Richard Holmes*
A *BBC History Magazine* Book of the Year 2005

£12.99   0 7524 3813 1

The Welsh Wars of Independence
DAVID MOORE

'Beautifully written, subtle and remarkably perceptive' *John Davies*

£12.99   978 07524 4128 3

Bosworth 1485 Psychology of a Battle
MICHAEL K. JONES

'Most exciting... a remarkable tale' *The Guardian*
'Insightful and rich study of the Battle of Bosworth... no longer need Richard play the villain' *The Times Literary Supplement*

£12.99   0 7524 2594 3

The Battle of Hastings 1066
M.K. LAWSON

'Blows away many fundamental assumptions about the battle of Hastings... an exciting and indispensable read' *David Bates*
A *BBC History Magazine* Book of the Year 2003

£12.99   978 07524 4177 1

If you are interested in purchasing other books published by Tempus, or in case you have difficulty finding any Tempus books in your local bookshop, you can also place orders directly through our website

www.tempus-publishing.com